JOYFUL WITNESS *IN THE* MUSLIM WORLD

MISSION
in Global Community

Scott W. Sunquist
and Amos Yong,
series editors

The Mission in Global Community series is designed to reach college students and those interested in learning more about responsible mission involvement. Written by faculty and graduates from Fuller Theological Seminary, the series is designed as a global conversation with stories and perspectives from around the world.

JOYFUL WITNESS *IN THE* MUSLIM WORLD

Sharing the Gospel in Everyday Encounters

EVELYNE A. REISACHER

[handwritten note: ·fruit ·salty snacks ·red wine ·cheese ·baby wipes ·bread]

Baker Academic

a division of Baker Publishing Group
Grand Rapids, Michigan

© 2016 by Evelyne A. Reisacher

Published by Baker Academic
a division of Baker Publishing Group
P.O. Box 6287, Grand Rapids, MI 49516–6287
www.bakeracademic.com

Printed in the United States of America

Library of Congress Cataloging-in-Publication Data
Names: Reisacher, Evelyne A., author.
Title: Joyful witness in the Muslim world : sharing the gospel in everyday encounters / Evelyne A. Reisacher.
Description: Grand Rapids, MI : Baker Academic, 2016. | Includes bibliographical references and index.
Identifiers: LCCN 2016022012 | ISBN 9780801030840 (pbk.)
Subjects: LCSH: Missions to Muslims. | Witness bearing (Christianity) | Christianity and culture.
Classification: LCC BV2625 .R45 2016 | DDC 266.0088/297—dc23
LC record available at https://lccn.loc.gov/2016022012

16   17   18   19   20   21   22   7   6   5   4   3   2   1

To my family, friends, colleagues, and students
throughout the Muslim world
with whom I have experienced countless moments of joy

Contents

Series Preface

A mission leader in 1965, not too long ago, could not have foreseen what mission looks like today. In 1965 nations in the non-Western world were gaining their independence after centuries of Western colonialism. Mission societies from Europe and North America were trying to adjust to the new global realities where Muslim nations, once dominated by the West, no longer granted "missionary visas." The largest mission field, China, was "closed." Decolonization, it seemed, was bringing a decline to missionary work in Africa and Asia.

On the home front, Western churches were in decline, and the traditional missionary factories—mainline churches in the West—were struggling with their own identity. Membership was then—and remains—in decline, and missionary vocations were following the same pattern. Evangelical and Pentecostal churches began to surpass mainline churches in mission, and then, just when we thought we understood the new missionary patterns, Brazilians began to go to Pakistan and Malaysians began to evangelize Vietnam and Cambodia. Africans (highly educated and strongly Christian) began to move in great numbers to Europe and North America. Countries that had been "closed" began to have large movements to Christ, without the aid of traditional mission societies. And in the midst of this rapid transformation of missionary work, the alarm came out that most of the Christians in the world were now in Asia, Latin America, and Africa rather than in the West.

What does it mean to be involved in mission in this new world where Christianity has been turned upside down in less than a century?

This series is directed at this new global context for mission. Fuller Theological Seminary, particularly through its School of Intercultural Studies (formerly School of World Mission), has been attentive to trends in global mission for over half a century. In fact, much innovation in mission thinking and practice has emanated from Fuller since Donald McGavran moved from Oregon to California—as the first and founding dean of the then–School of World Mission—to apply lessons about church growth learned in India to other areas of the world. Since that time many creative mission professors have provided global leadership in mission thinking: Ralph Winter (unreached people groups), Paul Hiebert (anthropology for mission), Charles Kraft (mission and spiritual dynamics), and Dudley Woodberry (Islamics), among others.

This series provides the most recent global scholarship on key themes in mission, written for a general audience of Christians committed to God's mission. Designed to be student, user, and textbook friendly, each volume contains voices from around the world speaking about the theme, and each chapter concludes with discussion questions so the books can be used for group studies. As the "fields" of mission are changing, shifting, and "shrinking," the discussions connect the church and the world, East and West, North and South, the developed and developing worlds, each crossing cultural, political, social, and religious boundaries in its own ways and knitting together people living and serving in various communities, both of faith and of other commitments—this is the contemporary landscape of the mission of God. Enjoy the challenges of each volume and find ways to live into God's mission.

Scott W. Sunquist

Amos Yong

Acknowledgments

The idea for this book sprang from over a decade of teaching and research on Islam and Muslim societies at Fuller Theological Seminary and several decades of interactions and witness among Muslims in Europe and around the world. I am especially thankful for L'Ami, a Paris-based network of Muslim-born followers of Christ, where I experienced countless moments of joy and also developed exquisite friendships with Muslims. I owe a debt of gratitude to its founder, Dr. Farida Saidi, who has given me valuable advice for this book.

The series editors, Dean Scott Sunquist and Professor Amós Yong, invited me to contribute this volume. I am very grateful to them for their support along the way. Dr. Sunquist's close and cheerful reading of the manuscript has been a tremendous help. I am also thankful to one of my students, Gwen, who reviewed several chapters of this book.

During the months I was writing this book, my colleagues from the School of Intercultural Studies at Fuller Theological Seminary continuously cheered and prayed for me. They always greeted me with "Hi, How are you?" immediately followed by "And how is your book on joy coming along?" I have been enriched by many conversations with them around the themes included in this book.

Without Evelyne Richir and Clair and David Fung's generous offer of a pleasant place to write for a few weeks, I would not have completed the manuscript in time. They provided a calm oasis in the midst of hectic teaching terms.

Finally, this project could not have been completed without the help of the wonderful editorial team at Baker Academic, first by James Ernest and then by Brian Bolger. It was a true joy to work with them.

Introduction

Did you say "joy"? You must be out of your mind! Surely you are not writing a book about the joy of witnessing in the Muslim world? Not now. Have you heard about the gruesome beheading of Coptic Christians in Libya? Have you seen images of bombs falling on Muslim civilians in Iraq? Are you blind to current events? Is it not insensitive in the face of the ongoing violence Muslims and Christians are suffering? How insensitive it is of you to talk about joy when Christian refugees by the millions have fled their home countries in the Middle East. And have you not heard about the burning of churches and mosques in Nigeria? What are you thinking? Could you not choose a better title, one more appropriate for a book about Christian witness to Muslims? This, in a nutshell, is what some friends said to me when I told them I was writing this book.

However, I have not undertaken this task lightly. I have pondered these questions for a long time. I have spent this past decade screaming to God, praying, fasting, and lamenting about the situation in parts of the Muslim world. I don't know how many tears I have shed. I have cried my heart out concerning the Muslim world. Each time I turn on the news I am afraid I will see more social or political unrest ruining Muslim-Christian encounters. Thus I can say, like Jeremiah, "My eyes fail from weeping, I am in torment within; my heart is poured out on the ground" as I see the destruction of people, children fainting in streets of cities, and entire countries in turmoil (Lam. 2:11 NIV).

On the other hand, how can a missiologist like me not mention joy, when joy is so deeply embedded in the biblical narrative and is so clearly at the heart of God and his love for the world? And having discovered this joy, how does one relate it to challenging, and even hopeless, contexts? This is exactly the goal of this book. I tie the missiology of joy to ordinary relations with

Muslims in order to help Christians witness for Christ in the Muslim world. I show that joy is an important and neglected aspect of God's mission. Current research on the nature of human attachment also reveals the importance of joy in the formation of healthy bonds. These two separate fields of study seem at first very far apart. They are not. Both mission and human attachment research deal with the joyful aspect of personal relations. When integrated, they strengthen each other. They also open new ways for witnessing in the Muslim world. After many years of teaching and visiting churches and Christian organizations, I have noticed that Christians dehumanize Muslims in certain ways. We see Muslims as targets of mission instead of accepting them as human beings with whom we interact in everyday life. Walls have been erected between Muslims and Christians by social and political conflicts and by theological debates that have given the impression that Christians are always meeting with Muslims in extraordinary contexts. This should not be so, since today, in our global village, Muslims and Christians are likely to meet each other in any place in the world, even the virtual one. Joy can be a catalyst to relationship and witness anywhere.

I wrote this book for those who are looking for mission motivations that do not involve fear, belligerence, or despair in interactions with Muslims. I refuse to add to the long list of essays on fear- or hate-mongering. Without neglecting to address these emotions,[1] I find it more important to focus on what might be called joy-centric mission. I hope that those who want to join me on the journey of sharing the gospel with Muslim friends, colleagues, or neighbors will read this book. No prior knowledge of Islam is needed. However, this book is not only for novices. It is also for experts who are looking for new models of witness that address twenty-first-century situations.

Readers will notice that I have included sidebars with reflections by scholars and practitioners from around the world. These are Christians who are willing to share their experiences and reflections on joy-centric mission. We need voices from all parts of the world in order to understand the current nature of Christian witness. People interpret issues related to Islam differently depending on where they live. I have noticed, for example, that Christians who live as a minority in Muslim countries sometimes disagree with ways churches in Muslim-minority contexts approach theological conversations with Muslims. Diverse voices do not need to be divisive. Global conversations can and should be joyful.

1. Evelyne A. Reisacher, "Fear and Muslim-Christian Conflict Transformation: Resources from Attachment Theory and Affect Regulation," in *Peace-Building by, between, and beyond Muslims and Evangelical Christians*, ed. Mohammed Abu-Nimer and David Augsburger (Lanham, MD: Lexington Books, 2010), 157–70.

This book is not about current hot-button issues, such as jihad, polygamy, veiling, terrorism, and so on. Although these topics appear here, they are treated as concerns of Muslims in their everyday lives. I discuss six contexts in which I have observed that joyful witness to Muslims takes place: social media, art, caring for the earth, caring for the needy, urban life, and theologizing together. The outline of the book reflects the way I integrated these issues with various topics related to joy. Chapter 1 discusses joyful witness from a missiological perspective. Chapter 2 looks at joyful relations from a human attachment perspective. Chapters 3 through 8 describe how joyful witness occurs in the six types of encounters mentioned above.

Joyful Witness

I have met many Muslims since my first conversation at age thirteen with a neighbor who wanted to know more about Jesus. When I attended college, I joined a Christian student group. On campus, I used to host an exhibition table every week, presenting Bibles in many languages. I held countless conversations about my faith with Muslim students, who were often surprised to see an Arabic Bible for the first time. After college I worked for twenty years with Christian fellowships of Muslim-born followers of Christ in France. These connections led me to North Africa and the Middle East, where many of my Muslim friends had been raised. Later, when I started teaching at Fuller Theological Seminary, my Muslim networks expanded even further. I arranged for my students and myself to meet Muslim scholars and practitioners. Even now, I continue to visit Muslim-majority contexts worldwide to teach and visit churches. Many stories in this book come from the happy times that I have spent with Muslims throughout these years.

I was first attracted to the theme of joyful witness when I wrote my doctoral dissertation on the nature of the relationships between North African and French believers in evangelical churches in France.[2] While Muslims were turning to Jesus in increasing numbers, their relationships with local churches were often less than joyous and natural. In that research, I drew heavily on the findings of neuroscientist Allan Schore, who described the neurobiological mechanisms of human attachment.[3] Human attachment is one way of measuring human love and commitment. Joy plays a central

2. Evelyne A. Reisacher, "The Processes of Attachment between the Algerians and French within the Christian Community in France" (PhD diss., Fuller Theological Seminary, 2001).
3. Allan N. Schore, *Affect Regulation and the Origin of the Self: The Neurobiology of Emotional Development* (Mahwah, NJ: Erlbaum, 1994).

role in Schore's theory of human bonding. Chapter 2 will explain this in more detail.

As I immersed myself in neuroscientific literature on joy, I was curious to explore that theme in the Bible as well. Did joy play any significant role in the earliest Christian mission? How has it applied to Muslim-Christian relations in the past? I felt encouraged when I met several theologians who were interested in joy. Recently this theme has gained even more attention from Christian scholars and missiologists, as evidenced by the recent research project on the "theology of joy" at Yale Divinity School[4] and the apostolic exhortation of Pope Francis concerning the joy of the gospel.[5] This trend toward more joyful witness will be discussed in chapter 1, where I design a conceptual framework to explore joy in witness among Muslims.

This trend toward more joy in witness has often been absent from missiological literature. I remember that the first books I read about mission used phrases like "hard"[6] or "impossible" to describe this pursuit.[7] Christians have often been fearful and unwilling to reach out to Muslims because they didn't see many Muslims being converted through the ministry of others, and if some were converted, they would most probably suffer as apostates. Recently, the discourse has changed. More evangelical authors stress the importance of love and empathy. Instead of favoring confrontation and fearmongering, they highlight positive aspects of mission among Muslims and explain how those who reach out to Muslims are blessed by their encounters and positively transformed as they proclaim the gospel.[8] These authors prefer mission practices such as dialogue, friendship, and peacemaking. Sometimes, reacting against a strictly polemical approach, they feel compelled to remind their brothers and sisters in Christ of the importance of love and care for Muslim people. Recently, for example, Fuller Theological Seminary has been involved in a three-year project on peace building between Muslims and evangelicals,

4. Yale Center for Faith and Culture, "Theology of Joy & the Good Life," http://faith.yale.edu/joy/about.

5. Pope Francis, *Evangelii gaudium* [The joy of the gospel], November 24, 2013, http://w2.vatican.va/content/francesco/en/apost_exhortations/documents/papa-francesco_esortazione-ap_20131124_evangelii-gaudium.html.

6. Charles Marsh, *Too Hard for God?* (Milton Keynes, UK: Authentic Media, 2000).

7. Miriam Huffman Rockness, *A Passion for the Impossible: The Life of Lilias Trotter* (Grand Rapids: Discovery House, 2003).

8. See, e.g., Shirin Taber, *Muslims Next Door: Uncovering Myths and Creating Friendships* (Grand Rapids: Zondervan, 2004), or Carl Medearis, *Muslims, Christians, and Jesus: Gaining Understanding and Building Relationships* (Bloomington, MN: Bethany House, 2008). Also read Benjamin L. Corey, "The Call for Christians to Radically Love Our Muslim Neighbors," *Patheos: Hosting the Conversation on Faith* (blog), February 17, 2015, http://www.patheos.com/blogs/formerlyfundie/the-call-for-christians-to-radically-love-our-muslim-neighbors/.

which resulted in a multiauthored book[9] by Muslim and Christian scholars and in several peace-building workshops held in churches and mosques across the United States.

But despite these encouraging approaches, I found that the theme of "joy" rarely appears in mission discourse on Muslim-Christian relations. While anecdotal research shows joyful witness among Muslims, it is often not systematically reported. I write this book to begin to change this trend and make room for joy in our encounters with Muslims—a theme that is much more true to the biblical witness and to our theological commitments.

Joyful Encounters

Missiologists have long been interested in the impact of relationships on sharing the gospel. They have noted that generally, when relations are bad, either witness turns clumsy, ineffective, or insensitive, or no witness is borne. Obviously, when Muslims and Christians are estranged, afraid of each other, or at war with each other, the proclamation of the gospel suffers. Conversely, good relationships can advance the gospel. J. Dudley Woodberry, who researched over 720 former Muslims, found that most of them who became followers of Christ said it was because of the lifestyle manifested in those who shared the gospel.[10]

Unfortunately, today, Muslim-Christian relationships are often weak. In 2010 a survey of 2,700 Christian leaders at the Lausanne Congress on World Evangelization in Cape Town revealed that 67 percent of them viewed Muslims, as a religious group, unfavorably.[11] Although the word "unfavorable" was not clearly defined, these findings seem to corroborate other accounts that show that Christians often find it difficult to engage with Muslims. Given the poor quality of many relations and given that the theme of this book is joyful witness, we must explore how Muslims and Christians can develop healthier bonds. After a brief historical review of Muslim-Christian relations, chapter 2 explores healthy relations with a special emphasis on joy.

By looking carefully at everyday encounters, one can find examples of joy. In my classes and church meetings, I often show a YouTube video in which

9. Mohammed Abu-Nimer and David Augsburger, eds., *Peace-Building by, between, and beyond Muslims and Evangelical Christians* (Lanham, MD: Lexington Books, 2010).

10. J. Dudley Woodberry, Russell G. Shubin, and G. Marks, "Why Muslims Follow Jesus," *Christianity Today*, October 24, 2007, http://www.christianitytoday.com/ct/2007/october/42 .80.html.

11. Global Survey of Evangelical Protestant Leaders, Pew Research Center, June 22, 2011, http://www.pewforum.org/2011/06/22/global-survey-of-evangelical-protestant-leaders/.

British Muslims sing and dance along to Pharrell Williams's hit tune "Happy."[12] The "Happy" video surprises many Christians. It is almost as if many could not imagine that Muslims could be happy! Furthermore, it is hard for them to conceive that witness in the Muslim world can be pleasurable. Therefore, in chapters 3 through 8, I review ordinary encounters between Muslims and Christians. I hope this section will help Christians discover the joy of sharing the gospel with Muslims.

In the past, those who witnessed among Muslims were often experts on Islam or members of specialized mission organizations. Those with little or no knowledge felt they were not ready. But, despite the timidity of grassroots Christians, God has often used them. I can think of scores of testimonies that describe how Muslims met Jesus in everyday encounters. One woman became a follower of Christ because her colleague at work had left a Bible on her desk. Another, a friend of mine, heard the gospel through a nurse visiting her home. Through many other similar, ordinary encounters Muslims have been led to Christ. As readers look at the various types of encounters in this book, they may discover that they have connections with Muslims that they have not even considered.

Furthermore, today, occasions for meeting with Muslims are almost limitless. Contemporary societal changes in the Muslim world make new kinds of mission practices possible, many of which are presented in this book. What guided my choice of areas to address was a class that I teach at Fuller called Muslim Societies. Students in this class study Islam through social sciences rather than by a more traditional approach through theology or history. They learn a lot about Islam by studying people. After teaching this class for several years, I have identified certain areas that have been deeply neglected in missiological writings on Muslim societies. Though not comprehensive, my list is nonetheless useful. I hope that future research will broaden the scope of this study and that Christians will continue to explore new avenues for sharing the gospel in a world that continues to be transformed.

Mission among Muslims is not "extraordinary" or an "impossible challenge," though too often Christians have seen it as such. I have attended too many meetings where, when I have announced that I am sharing the gospel with Muslims, I have been treated like a rock star. It is perceived as a miracle, a unique experience! This trend has to change. We must produce mission practices that are connected with the everyday realities of people, where people actually live and hurt and hope in local communities. Witness

12. Pharrell Williams–Happy British Muslims!, https://www.youtube.com/watch?v=gVDIX qILqSM.

among Muslims happens in the most ordinary places and in contexts that mission has not yet imagined.

Perhaps one reason why Christians have not engaged with Muslims in ordinary encounters is that many have been exposed to the study of Islam from a classical approach.[13] In his chapter titled "Considering 'Ordinariness' in Studying Muslim Cultures and Discipleship,"[14] missiologist and Islamicist C. S. Caleb Kim explains that "conventional approaches do not seem to help outsiders to grasp what ordinary Muslims experience socially and psychologically, how they experience their religion in daily life, and whether and how they struggle to implement their religious ideologies practically." Other authors, outside the circle of missiology, have also underlined this scarcity of resources on "ordinary" Muslims.[15] The lack of focus in mission on the study of Muslims' ordinary life experiences, as described by Gallup researcher Dalia Mogahed,[16] may explain why Christians have not engaged with Muslims and have let "experts" reach out to them.

Yet Christian encounters with Muslims would grow exponentially if Christians recognized how many opportunities are available for such encounters. Many meetings that are already happening are not so unfamiliar and foreign as they have been made out to be in the past. As I present new and innovative models of engagement for the twenty-first century, I trust that my readers will find resources for making their journeys in the Muslim world more pleasurable. Please enter this journey with great hope and with the joy of the kingdom.

13. C. S. Caleb Kim uses the phrase "classical approach" to refer to an approach whose "focus lies mainly on historical events, theological issues, political relations, and sociological implications, thus scarcely presenting cultural experiences actually lived by ordinary Muslims." C. S. Caleb Kim, "Considering 'Ordinariness' in Studying Muslim Cultures and Discipleship," in *Discipleship in the 21st Century Mission*, ed. Timothy K. Park and Steve K. Eom (Euiwang, South Korea: East-West Center for MRD, 2014), 177n27.

14. Ibid.

15. See, e.g., John R. Bowen, *A New Anthropology of Islam* (Cambridge: Cambridge University Press, 2012), 2, 5.

16. Dalia Mogahed, "Ordinary Muslims," Gallup World Poll Special Report: Muslim World, 2006, http://media.gallup.com/MuslimWestFacts/PDF/GALLUPMUSLIMSTUDIESOrdinary Muslims030607rev.pdf.

1

Toward Joyful Witness

The first book I read on mission in the Muslim world was sad and depressing. It told the story of a country without an evangelical church. The handful of followers of Christ from Muslim families ended up arrested or dying in a car accident. When I reached the last page of that book, joy was the least of my emotions. A similar mood prevailed in my own Christian circles. When I shared my desire to witness to Muslims, my friends would usually give me a strange look as if I had told them I was sent to the galleys (or to the gallows!). And what about you? Have you heard stories of joyful witness in the Muslim world? Or, like me, have you only read the stories of suffering, pain, and loss?

Christian witness among Muslims is usually characterized as difficult and fear triggering. I often wondered why joy was missing in mission discourses related to the Muslim world. Intrigued by the lack of references, I investigated biblical texts and writings by theologians and missiologists that relate joy to the witness of the Christian community in general.[1] I found more resources than I anticipated. This should not surprise us, though it did astonish Swiss theologian Karl Barth in the mid-twentieth century, prompting him to observe "how many references there are in the Old and New Testaments to delight, joy, bliss, exultation, merry-making and rejoicing, and how emphatically these

---

1. At first, seeking a theoretical framework for joy in Christian witness among Muslims, I wanted to title this chapter "Toward a Missiology of Joy." Although what I have achieved here cannot be called a missiology of joy, the chapter offers enough evidence that future research likely will make my framework more robust.

...nded from the Book of Psalms to the Epistle to the Philippians."[2] A brief review of such references naturally supports missiological concepts that lead to joyful witness among Muslims, by both full-time missionaries and ordinary Christians.

Joy-Centric Worship

Does God dance? I raise that question in my class titled World Religions: Art and Symbols. Hindu traditions, for example, do not shy away from representing their gods dancing, playing an instrument, and radiating joyful energy.[3] But Christian students are often speechless about the idea of a dancing God. It is hard for them to imagine God in the same postures as Shiva in its cosmic dance or Krishna in its dance of divine love. To draw them further out of their comfort zone, I usually show paintings by Christian artists from a Hindu background, such as contemporary Balinese artist Nyoman Darsane's representation of Jesus dancing.[4] After that, the class usually takes up an animated discussion of divine joy and bliss.

I must confess that, like many of my students, I have long resisted the idea of portraying God dancing. Early in my Christian life, I imagined him sitting on a throne, like some emotionless icons I had seen in churches or museums. Undoubtedly, church controversies about divine emotions and the impassibility of God had affected me. Centuries after his death, church father Origen was still whispering in my ear, "The divine nature is far removed from every feeling of emotion and alteration; it always remains motionless and unperturbed on the summit of blessedness."[5] The iconoclastic period, with its prohibition of representations of God, also left an imprint in my mind. Later I discovered theologians who were not afraid of representing God and describing divine emotions. They challenged apathetic theology and dared to talk of "divine enjoyment." With Jürgen Moltmann I discovered that God has feelings,[6] and with William A. Dyrness that the church has

2. Karl Barth, *Church Dogmatics*, III/4, *The Doctrine of Creation, Part 4* (Edinburgh: T&T Clark, 1961), 375.

3. See, e.g., the section on "Dance in Hindu Mythology" in *The Oxford Handbook of Religion and the Arts*, ed. Frank Burch Brown (New York: Oxford University Press, 2014), 192–96.

4. See Victoria Emily Jones, "Jesus the Dancer, Part 7: The Art of Nyoman Darsane," *The Jesus Question*, March 25, 2012, http://thejesusquestion.org/2012/03/25/jesus-the-dancer-part -7-the-art-of-nyoman-darsane/.

5. Origen, *Sermons of Numbers* 23.2, quoted in William E. Phipps, *Wisdom and Wit of Rabbi Jesus* (Louisville: Westminster John Knox, 1993), 84.

6. Jürgen Moltmann, *The Crucified God: The Cross of Christ as the Foundation and Criticism of Christian Theology*, trans. R. A. Wilson and John Bowden (Minneapolis: Fortress, 1993).

often represented God artistically.[7] While theological controversies continue to linger, I have slowly learned to appreciate Indian paintings of a dancing Jesus. They highlight joyful aspects of God that I had not noticed before.

Are these characteristics of God found in the Bible? Several references suggest pleasant relationships between Father, Son, and Holy Spirit. For example, when the Holy Spirit descended upon Jesus at his baptism, a voice from heaven declared, "Thou art my beloved Son; with thee I am well pleased" (Luke 3:22 RSV). Later, Jesus is depicted as full of joy in the Holy Spirit and praising God (Luke 10:21). Theologian John Jefferson Davis, of Gordon-Conwell Theological Seminary, captures this reality: "Joy is a fundamental characteristic of the inner being of the Trinity; the Father rejoices in the Son, and the Son rejoices in the Father, in the communion of the Holy Spirit, now and forever. We as the redeemed people of God are on a journey into the joy-filled heart of the Triune God."[8] Raniero Cantalamessa, a Catholic priest, echoes Davis: "The Latin tradition has always left wide room for the theme of *gaudium Trinitatis* ('trinitarian joy'), with the Holy Spirit as the personification of that joy."[9] He further describes an "intratrinitarian life with fervent images of intimacy and of kisses, images that most powerfully evoke communion, enjoyment and joy."[10] Richard Burnett, quoting Karl Barth, reports that "when the doctrine of the Trinity is denied, the result is 'a God without radiance and without joy.'"[11]

And as if he wanted to confirm my earlier observation, Davis notes that "the joyfulness of the inner life of the Trinity" is missing from some of the symbols and artistic representations of the Trinity displayed on buildings where Christians worship.[12] Could this be another reason why my students and I hesitated to picture God dancing? We ought to heed these authors' observations and attend to the joyful nature of the Triune God.

Trinitarian joy is further evidenced by the way it irradiates creation,[13] including humankind. The Old Testament depicts God rejoicing over his people

7. William A. Dyrness, *Visual Faith: Art, Theology, and Worship in Dialogue* (Grand Rapids: Baker Academic, 2001).

8. John Jefferson Davis, *Worship and the Reality of God: An Evangelical Theology of Real Presence* (Downers Grove, IL: InterVarsity, 2010), 58.

9. Raniero Cantalamessa, *Contemplating the Trinity: The Path to the Abundant Christian Life*, trans. Marsha Daigle-Williamson (Frederick, MD: The Word Among Us Press, 2007), Kindle edition, location 419.

10. Ibid., location 429.

11. Richard E. Burnett, ed., *The Westminster Handbook to Karl Barth* (Louisville: Westminster John Knox), 125.

12. Davis, *Worship and the Reality of God*, 58.

13. In Isaiah 44:23, the entire creation is called to rejoice: "Sing for joy, you heavens, for the LORD has done this; shout aloud, you earth beneath. Burst into song, you mountains, you forests and all your trees, for the LORD has redeemed Jacob, he displays his glory in Israel" (NIV).

(Deut. 30:9; Isa. 62:5; 65:19) and commissioning his servant to pour oil of gladness over them (Isa. 61:3). Zephaniah assures Zion, "The LORD . . . will rejoice over you with singing" (3:16 NIV). God delights in his people (Ps. 149:4). The Aaronic blessing manifests God's shining (or radiating) face turned toward people and offering his grace and shalom to them (Num. 6:22–27). I devoted significant time during my doctoral research to this priestly benediction and proposed that God's shining face serves as a metaphor for mission.[14] It invites believers to look into God's face turned toward them to receive his blessings, and consequently adopt that same attitude of turning their face toward others, wishing them grace and peace in God. The same image is given us in Psalm 67:1–2 (NRSV): "May God be gracious to us and bless us and make his face to shine upon us, that your way may be known upon earth, your saving power among all nations."

Another sign of trinitarian joy is its repercussion or reflection on people it irradiates. God's joy resonates in us. According to Richard Burnett, Karl Barth believes that "there is both an indwelling joy of God and a joy that God's glory awakens in us."[15] God's presence becomes a source of joy for those who follow him (Eccles. 2:26). They are filled with joy in his presence, with eternal pleasures at his right hand (Ps. 16:11); their heart is filled with "gladness," "more than when their [i.e., others'] grain and wine abound" (Ps. 4:7 NRSV); they delight in him and their soul rejoices in him (Isa. 61:10). This joy becomes one of the hallmarks of the journey with God. Neuroscientists have discovered that mutual joy is one of the necessary features of healthy human bonds; so also with the relationship between God and the worshiper. Angella Son discusses this type of bond in her *Spirituality of Joy*,[16] and elsewhere defines joy as "that which is experienced when we are relationally connected to God."[17] Biblical texts are familiar with her argument, or, to put this in the correct order, her arguments flow out of Scripture. For example, the psalmist shouts, "Then I will go to the altar of God, to God my exceeding joy" (Ps. 43:4 NRSV). He is attracted by this joy that pulls him toward the altar of God. John Piper calls this form of pleasure experienced in relationship with God "Christian hedonism."[18] Those who "attach to God"

14. Evelyne A. Reisacher, "The Processes of Attachment between the Algerians and French within the Christian Community in France" (PhD diss., Fuller Theological Seminary, 2001).

15. Burnett, *Westminster Handbook to Karl Barth*, 125.

16. Angella Son, *Spirituality of Joy: Moving beyond Dread and Duty* (Seoul, South Korea: Jeyoung Communications, 2013).

17. Angella Son, "Agents of Joy as a New Image of Pastoral Care," *Journal of Pastoral Theology* 18, no. 1 (Summer 2008): 70.

18. This is how John Piper summarizes Christian hedonism: "God is most glorified in us when we are most satisfied in him." "We Want You to Be a Christian Hedonist!," Desiring

will, beyond question, experience the same feelings as they parti
this joy-centric worship.[19]

How does our discussion of the joy felt in worshiping God relate to the
primary concern of this book, which is witnessing? Simply put, this joy is
essential. If we believe that mission is first and foremost the mission of God
(*missio Dei*),[20] we must anticipate that joy will characterize his mission. This is
not always communicated in missionary literature. The love and compassion
of God have been greatly emphasized, but references to the joyful mission of
the Triune God are sparse. I wonder what would change in Muslim-Christian
relations if Christians were more aware of this important aspect of mission?
I imagine that they would be inspired by God's delight, pleasure, and joy as
he reaches out to the world as the missionary God. They might even learn
his blissful and energetic dance!

A Joyful Lord

One of the most vivid illustrations of God's joy is the incarnation. A significant
number of the many biblical references to joy allude to this historical event.
Mission historian Scott Sunquist claims the incarnation is "a divine shout
of joy regarding this world of time and matter."[21] Indeed, the birth of Jesus
irradiated the world and the cosmos with joy. Earlier, the Old Testament anticipated the excitement concerning the arrival of the Messiah. In Isaiah 61,
messianic prophecies announced "oil of gladness instead of mourning" (v. 3
NRSV), as well as times of rejoicing and exultation in the Lord. It is therefore
no surprise that the narrative of Jesus's birth is bathed in joy.

Plenty of indicators of joy appear in the biblical narrative of Jesus's birth,
despite the painful fact of Joseph's shame from not being the actual genitor,
the murder of children in Bethlehem, and the forced migration of Jesus's
family to Egypt. The baby in Elizabeth's womb (John the Baptist) leaps for

God website, August 31, 2006, http://www.desiringgod.org/articles/we-want-you-to-be-a-ch
ristian-hedonist.

19. See, e.g., Deuteronomy 12:12; Ezra 6:16; Nehemiah 8:10; Psalm 16:11; Isaiah 51:11;
Jeremiah 33:9.

20. Scott Sunquist defines *missio Dei* as "the mission of God to bring about redemption
of the world." *Understanding Christian Mission: Participation in Suffering and Glory* (Grand
Rapids: Baker Academic, 2013), 7. David Bosch defines *missio Dei* as "God's self-revelation as
the One who loves the world, God's involvement in and with the world, the nature and activity
of God, which embraces both the church and the world, and in which the church is privileged
to participate." *Transforming Mission: Paradigm Shifts in Theology of Mission* (Maryknoll,
NY: Orbis Books, 1991), 10.

21. Sunquist, *Understanding Christian Mission*, 25.

joy at Mary's visit (Luke 1:41). The angel greets Mary with a resounding "Rejoice!" (Luke 1:28 NKJV).[22] Later, she finds words to return this greeting: "My spirit has rejoiced in God my Savior" (Luke 1:47 NASB). The angel of the Lord announces to the shepherds, "I bring you good news that will cause great joy for all the people. Today in the town of David a Savior has been born to you; he is the Messiah, the Lord" (Luke 2:10–11 NIV). Finally, the Magi are "overjoyed" when they see the star pointing them to the place where Jesus was born (Matt. 2:10). *Joy to the World!*

Christians embrace this festive mood at Christmas when they decorate their houses with ornaments and place joy-shaped stocking holders on fireplace mantles. They hum along to Isaac Watts's hymn "Joy to the World" when musical flash mobs surprise shopping-mall customers by performing that song. And when, after Christmas, symbols and trimmings return to their storage boxes, awaiting the following year, this joy often fades away. Believers wait for another birthday of Jesus to experience that same thrill. Recently I had dinner at my dean's house and noticed that the sign "Joy to the World" still hung on his dining room wall. Seeing my surprise (it was February), his wife, Nancy, told me that this year they had deliberately left the sign up when Christmas was over. I like that. It is good to be reminded of this "joy to the world" all year round! *all yr. long*

Likewise, in the Bible, joy does not stop after Jesus's birth. A message of joy issues from the core of Jesus's ministry. The so-called Nazareth Manifesto is often called a declaration of good news (Luke 4:18–19). According to Angela Thomas, the good news is a "message bringing joy."[23] Moltmann promotes this idea: "In the Old Testament, to proclaim a gospel means bringing a message of joy, heralding a victory, announcing salvation. Anyone who proclaims a joyful event is himself the bringer of joy, and is honoured accordingly."[24] Darrell W. Johnson shares the same opinion: "Joy is the dominant emotion of the one declaring the good news, and it is the dominant emotion of those who hear the good news."[25] When there is good news, people rejoice, as God, through his prophet Zechariah, commands his people to do: "Shout and be glad, Daughter Zion. For I am coming, and I will live among you" (2:10 NIV). This exuberant joy was reiterated

22. The Greek behind this greeting literally means "to rejoice."

23. Angela Thomas, *Choosing Joy: A 52-Week Devotional for Discovering True Happiness* (New York: Howard Books, 2011), Kindle edition, location 461.

24. Jürgen Moltmann, *The Way of Jesus Christ: Christology in Messianic Dimensions*, trans. Margaret Kohl (Minneapolis: Fortress, 1993), 95.

25. Darrell W. Johnson, *The Glory of Preaching: Participating in God's Transformation of the World* (Downers Grove, IL: InterVarsity, 2009), 81.

when Jesus, Immanuel ("God with us"), came to dwell on earth (John 1:14). Creation rejoiced because he chose to take up residence on earth (Ps. 96:11–13).

Given that Jesus brought good news, some people wonder if Jesus's life matched what he preached. Did Jesus have a joyful personality? Apparently yes, because he referred to it when speaking to his disciples shortly before his death: "These things I have spoken to you so that my joy may be in you, and that your joy may be made full" (John 15:11 NASB). But is there further evidence of such joy in other places in the Gospels? In her book on joy, Swiss theologian Lytta Basset tries to identify passages where the Gospels specifically mention Jesus's joy,[26] but she finds few.[27] After a more careful look at the biblical texts, however, she finds more joy in Jesus's life than anticipated. Interactions between Jesus and others reveal many happy moments. People who walked with Jesus experienced joy. Take, for example, John the Baptist, who stated that the beginning of Christ's ministry made his joy complete (John 3:29), and recall that "all the people rejoiced at all the glorious things that were done by him" (Luke 13:17 RSV).

Commenting on Jesus's personality, Lebanese writer Jean Maalouf writes,

> Is it conceivable that Jesus, for example, didn't smile at those little children whom He allowed to come and sit down and maybe play with Him? And is it conceivable that He didn't have a friendly smile for His disciples and for all the people who came to Him? And is it conceivable that He didn't laugh with His family and closest friends at life's incongruities? And how, without laughter, could He attend parties, eating and drinking, and mixing with different people?[28]

Theologian George Eldon Ladd agrees when he describes the table fellowship of repentant sinners and Jesus:

> So typical of Jesus's ministry was this joyous fellowship that his critics accused him of being a glutton and a drunkard (Mt 11:18). The same note of messianic joy is heard in Jesus' answer to the criticism that he and his disciples did not follow the example of the Pharisees in fasting. Fasting does

---

26. Lytta Basset, *La Joie Imprenable*, new ed. (Paris: Albin Michel, 2004).

27. The major references to Jesus's joy that Basset found are when Jesus "rejoiced in the Holy Spirit" (Luke 10:21 NRSV) and when at the end of his journey on earth he says to his disciples: "I have said these things to you so that my joy may be in you, and that your joy may be complete" (John 15:11 NRSV).

28. Jean Maalouf, *Jesus Laughed: And Other Reflections on Being Human* (Kansas City, MO: Sheed & Ward, 1996), 12.

not belong to the time of a wedding. The presence of the bridegroom calls for joy, not fasting (Mk 2:18–19).[29]

Unfortunately, church history seldom has focused on Jesus's humor and laughter, picturing him as an emotionless character similar to people in nineteenth-century black-and-white photographs, with stern faces because exposure time was too long to hold a smile. I wonder what would happen to our witness for Christ if we could remember the happy moments that Jesus had on earth and the joy he communicated to those around him.

The residency of Jesus on earth is intermixed with times of joy on the one hand and, on the other, times of temptation, rejection, persecution, and finally martyrdom. The path Jesus walked did not consist of ceaseless joy or nonstop excitement, just as our human path does not. But Jesus's horrific death on the cross could not eliminate divine joy. Jesus knew it would survive, as attested by the author of the book of Hebrews: "For the joy set before him he [Jesus] endured the cross, scorning its shame, and sat down at the right hand of the throne of God. Consider him who endured such opposition from sinners, so that you will not grow weary and lose heart" (12:2–3 NIV).

This joy that Jesus was anticipating was manifested after his death. It is difficult to say whether it is the birth or the resurrection of Jesus that is the most joy-filled event. Missiologist Lesslie Newbigin seems to favor the latter by calling the resurrection an "explosion of joy."[30] To me, Eastern Christian traditions are the most in tune with this vibrant joy—particularly during paschal festivities. I love the ritual practiced by Orthodox churches early on Easter morning, when parishioners knock at the church door searching for the King of Glory. A priest stands behind, ready to open the door. When he does, people greet each other with a resounding, "Christ is risen," while others respond, "Indeed he is risen." As Coptic father Tadros Yacoub Malaty states, "The Holy Week of Easter (Paschal/Passover) begins with joyful processions and ends with joyful celebrations due to the Lord's Resurrection."[31]

Note that the disciples did not feel that joy right away. They first hid behind closed doors, and felt happy only when they grasped what had really happened. I have always been stunned that after Jesus left the disciples on Ascension Day, they "returned to Jerusalem with great joy, and were continually in the temple

29. George Eldon Ladd, *A Theology of the New Testament*, ed. Donald A. Hagner (Grand Rapids: Eerdmans, 1993), 74.

30. Lesslie Newbigin, *Lesslie Newbigin: Missionary Theologian; A Reader*, comp. Paul Weston (Grand Rapids: Eerdmans, 2006), 231.

31. Father Tadros Yacoub Malaty, "The Celebration of the Resurrection and the Rejoicing Processions," trans. Mary Rose, 1999, http://www.st-antonious.org/Downloads/Article%20%20Fr.%20Tadros%20Malaty3.pdf.

blessing God" (Luke 24:52–53 RSV). Why were they so happy at the departure of Jesus? Don't good-byes usually induce more sober feelings, especially if heaven is the traveler's destination? Days earlier, the disciples were frightened, startled, and perplexed. Now, they were filled with joy. As Moltmann so eloquently stated, "Out of the resurrection of Christ, joy throws open cosmic and eschatological perspectives that reach forward to the redemption of the whole cosmos. . . . In the feast of eternal joy all created beings and the whole community of God's creation are destined to sing their hymns and songs of praise."[32] I believe, with Moltmann, that the disciples' joy had gained new heights: "The hymns and praise of those who rejoice in the risen Christ are, as they themselves see it, no more than a feeble echo of the cosmic liturgy and the heavenly praise and the uttered joy in existence of all other living things."[33] The disciples also understood that they were part of the great plan that God had for all things: "The risen Christ does not come just to the dead, so as to raise them and communicate to them his eternal life; he draws all things into his future, so that they may become new and participate in the feast of God's eternal joy."[34]

This explosion of joy was an incredible moment in history. Paul says, "If Christ has not been raised, then our preaching is in vain and your faith is in vain" (1 Cor. 15:14 RSV). What propelled people into mission was the joy of the resurrected Savior and the Holy Spirit, whom theologian John Painter calls the "presence of the absent Jesus." It seems that the joy of the disciples is now complete, as attested by Painter when he says, "In this way the grief of the disciples is turned to become an abiding and indestructible joy (Jn 16:20–24) which is bound to the word of Jesus spoken to prepare them for their witness and work in the world."[35] This is what gave the disciples the courage, the strength, and the boldness to return to their neighborhoods and their communities.

When Jesus left, his disciples were not alone. He sent the Holy Spirit. The references to joy associated with the Holy Spirit are so numerous that they would require an entire chapter. The kingdom of God is a matter of "joy in the Holy Spirit" (Rom. 14:17). Earlier we saw that Jesus rejoiced because he was filled with the Spirit. Acts 13:52 tells us that "the disciples were continually

---

32. Jürgen Moltmann, *The Coming of God: Christian Eschatology*, trans. Margaret Kohl (Minneapolis: Fortress, 1996), 338.

33. Ibid.

34. Ibid.

35. J. Painter, "Joy," *Dictionary of Jesus and the Gospels: A Compendium of Contemporary Biblical Scholarship*, ed. Joel B. Green, Scot McKnight, and Howard Marshall (Downers Grove, IL: InterVarsity, 1992), 396.

ἀled with joy and with the Holy Spirit" (NASB). The effect of the joy flowing from the Holy Spirit is further described in Ephesians 5:18–19, where believers are invited to "be filled with the Spirit, addressing one another in psalms and hymns and spiritual songs, singing and making melody to the Lord with all [their] heart" (RSV). One kind of fruit of the Spirit is joy (Gal. 5:22).

Newbigin best explains why joy is so important for our discussion on witness: "The tomb is empty, Jesus is risen, death is conquered, God does reign after all. There is an explosion of joy, news that cannot be kept secret. Everyone must hear it. A new creation has begun. One does not have to be summoned to the 'task' of evangelism. If these things are really true, they have to be told."[36]

Bringers of Joy

If joy is fundamental to the character of God and of Jesus, and if the gospel is fundamentally news of great joy, then those who bear witness to it are essentially bringers of joy. But what is the nature of the joy that they bring? The Bible guides us here, as in other matters of faith. Indeed, Sri Lankan Christian leader Ajith Fernando claims, "The Old Testament oozes with the theme of joy." But defining the meanings of joy in the biblical context is not simple. Fernando, for example, found twenty-three different Hebrew terms for joy and claims that "in two verses in Zephaniah alone (3:14, 17) seven different words for joy are found!"[37] Painter finds "no less than seven words" to express joy in the Gospels.[38] He finds so many references to this emotion in Luke that he calls it the "Gospel of joy."[39] In his chapter titled "Lucan Joy," Jesuit scholar John Navone proposes ten different Greek expressions used for joy in Luke-Acts.[40]

"Joy" can refer to a sense of belonging to God, eschatological joy, kingdom joy, and many other concepts. It comes in different intensities and forms, such as exuberance, jubilation, or exaltation.[41] I was glad to find an entry titled "joy" in the *Evangelical Dictionary of World Missions*.[42] Its recommendations may be helpful to those who want to learn more about ways to be joyful. The point is, joy is a complex experience, and its complexity is reflected in the

---

36. Newbigin, *Missionary Theologian*, 231.
37. Ajith Fernando, *The Call to Joy and Pain* (Wheaton, IL: Crossway, 2007), 16.
38. Painter, "Joy," 394.
39. Ibid., 395.
40. John Navone, SJ, *Themes of St. Luke* (Rome: Gregorian University Press, 1970), 71–87.
41. Ibid., 71–72.
42. William D. Thrasher, "Joy," in *Evangelical Dictionary of World Missions*, ed. A. Scott Moreau (Grand Rapids: Baker Academic, 2000), 527.

diversity of ways in which Christians interact with others when te
the good news.

Splashes of Joy

The bringers of joy lead others to the source of joy and in so doing experience
joy themselves. Theologian William D. Thrasher writes, "The mission of the
church is to lead the nations to the Source of true joy. . . . The truth that joy
can be found in God's person, work, provisions, rule, and presence is to be
shared with the world."[43] One cannot imagine leading someone to the source
of true joy and not simultaneously receiving splashes of joy. Navone affirms,
"The call to salvation is also a call to joy"; the new experience of the joy of
being saved calls both the new believer and the witness to seek more joy—to
continually seek renewal of joy.[44] Navone states in the same passage that "Joy
is related to the recognition of the present salvation process and experienced
in the measure that one participates in it." Thus, it becomes a matter of not
just hearing about this joy but also participating in it. This joy is infectious.
Moltmann describes the joy that people experience when they meet Christ:
"The first experience that has to be mentioned is the feeling of rapturous joy.
. . . People lift up their heads, possessed by the indescribable joy that we find
in the Easter hymns."[45] When the gospel was preached in Samaria, there was
great joy (Acts 8:8). When the jailer and his family accepted Christ, he was
filled with joy (Acts 16:34). Thus when a person comes to Christ through the
testimony of a Christian, joy splashes in all directions.

Unusual Joy

Does joyful witness include "self-happiness," that is, happiness about one's
own situation? Although Christians don't witness simply to feel good or make
others feel good, that does not mean they can't feel good after witnessing.
Christians have ample opportunity to experience such happiness. In the history of mission, some Christians have thought that witness meant giving up
all pleasure. As noted earlier, however, Jesus himself enjoyed table fellowship
and laughed with people, and many think he was also humorous. However,
joy does not mean that people must be happy all the time to honor God in

43. Ibid.
44. Navone, *Themes of St. Luke*, 73.
45. Jürgen Moltmann, *The Source of Life: The Holy Spirit and the Theology of Life*, trans.
Margaret Kohl (Minneapolis: Fortress Press, 1997), 31.

their witness. We will discuss later how suffering is not dissociated from a joyful life in Christ. Today, even secular literature does not assert that endless happiness is possible or that it is even healthy. The cover of a recent issue of *Psychology Today* shows a smiley face covered by a huge ink spot with the following title: "Happiness? The Upside of Negative Emotions: Why You Need Boredom, Regret, Envy, Anger—More."[46] Scientists now understand that negative moods are not necessarily the opposite of a joyful life.

In spite of that, biblical passages such as "Grieve, mourn and wail. Change your laughter to mourning and your joy to gloom" (James 4:9 NIV), addressed to those who sinned against God and were double-minded, have led some Christians to adopt these attitudes in a permanent lifestyle of mourning or asceticism, perhaps for fear that they could not live a life in complete submission to God otherwise. They also quote a warning of Jesus to the Twelve: "Truly, truly, I say to you, that you will weep and lament, but the world will rejoice; you will grieve, but your grief will be turned into joy" (John 16:20 NASB). I am not trying to ignore these debates. But I believe that it is not joy in general that Jesus condemns, but the joys that separate us from God. It is likely, according to Painter, "that Jesus taught the superficiality of attachment to earthly joys . . . (Mark 4:16 par. Matt. 13:20 and Luke 8:13)."[47] It is possible that some joys are more important than others for our walk with God. If not, then in the passage in Matthew that follows the one cited by Painter, Jesus would not say, "The kingdom of heaven is like treasure hidden in a field, which a man found and covered up; then in his joy he goes and sells all that he has and buys that field" (Matt. 13:44 RSV). One may have to give up some earthly joys to experience a greater joy. Thus an article summarizing a video-recorded interview with Moltmann points out: "According to Moltmann, joy is quite different from fun, which 'is a superficial feeling which must be repeated again and again to last but joy is a deeper feeling of the whole existence.' He further explains that joy can only be experienced with the whole heart, soul and energies, noting that joy is thought to be of divine origin."[48] This feeling that is so unique may be what Jesus described when he said, "Ask and you will receive, and your joy will be complete" (John 16:24 NIV).

Joyful witness also has supernatural aspects that combine with natural joy.[49] Thrasher defines supernatural joy as "a delight in life that runs deeper

---

46. *Psychology Today*, February 2015.

47. Painter, "Joy," 395.

48. "Finding Joy with Jürgen Moltmann," (text introduction to a video of an interview of Moltmann by Miroslav Volf), Yale Center for Faith & Culture, September 24, 2014, http://faith .yale.edu/news/finding-joy-jurgen-moltmann.

49. Thrasher, "Joy," 527.

than pain or pleasure. This kind of joy is not limited by or tied solely to external circumstances. It is not a fleeting emotion but a quality of life that can be experienced in the midst of a variety of emotions."[50] When retracing his journey of faith, C. S. Lewis expresses a similar perspective. He describes an "authentic 'joy'" which is "distinct not only from pleasure in general but even from aesthetic pleasure. It must have the stab, the pang, the inconsolable longing."[51] He wrote, "The subject [of joy] has lost nearly all interest for me since I became a Christian. . . . I now know that the experience, considered as a state of my own mind, had never had the kind of importance I once gave it. It was valuable only as a pointer to something other and outer."[52] Regarding this supernatural joy, one may want to ask whether it is so different that it cannot be measured in an fMRI (functional magnetic resonance imaging) machine. I think it can. Biblical characters rejoicing in the Holy Spirit, for example, displayed verbal or behavioral indicators. Some leaped for joy, others sang, others jumped and danced; all these behaviors can be scientifically observed. What might surprise the scientist, however, is that in the Bible he or she may find joy with narratives related to the script of God—narratives different from the ones the scientist is familiar with.

Amplification of Joy

Joy is for sharing! As a child I was given a small booklet that I read so many times that my mother trashed it because it was completely worn out. I have since tried, without success, to find the name of its author. It contained a story about a small boy who so coveted the sun that he decided to catch it and bring it home to keep it all to himself. On his journey to the sun, he passed beautiful fields and forests, with all sorts of plants, trees, and animals. When he arrived at his destination, he put the sun in a big sack that he had brought with him. On his return journey he passed the same places, but everything looked dark, dull, and dead. Without sun, life had stopped. In wanting to keep the sun all to himself, the boy destroyed its reason to exist: bringing life to the world through its shining. Like the sun, joy cannot be kept in a sack. Theologian Basset talks about an orientation toward joy, a joy shared with God and a joy that cannot exist outside personal

50. Ibid.
51. C. S. Lewis, *Surprised by Joy: The Shape of My Early Life* (New York: HarperCollins, 2002), Kindle edition, location 72.
52. Ibid., locations 237–38.

relations.[53] This relational aspect of joy is a key characteristic of the joyful witness of Christians. Russian Orthodox theologian Sergius Bulgakov writes, "Easter is the joy about the neighbor, as it is proper for a lover to delight in his beloved."[54]

Joy is also communal. The Old Testament talks about celebrations, festivals, and table fellowship. The New Testament also is filled with references to joy shared in the context of community (e.g., John 15:11; Acts 5:41; Phil. 4:1; Col. 1:24; 1 Thess. 1:6; 1 Pet. 1:8–9; 1 John 1:4). Kenneth E. Bailey, a biblical scholar who specialized in Middle Eastern readings of the Bible, eloquently stresses this communal aspect. He identifies joy as characterizing the climax of the famous Lukan parables that are Jesus's response to those who accuse him of eating with the tax collectors and the sinners—in other words, with those whom the Jewish leadership considered traitors and violators of the Mosaic law.[55] Jesus relates the story of a shepherd who searched for one of his hundred sheep, which was lost, and who was filled with joy when he found it (Luke 15:4–7). Bailey describes the shepherd rejoicing, laying the sheep on his shoulder, and sharing in the joy of restoration with his community.[56] Likewise, in his reading of the parable of the lost coin (Luke 15:8–10) Bailey describes the "joy in community over restoration" when the woman finds the precious coin she had lost.[57] Finally, in the parable of the lost son (Luke 15:11–32) Bailey points to the joy expressed in "finding and in celebrating communally the restoration of the one lost."[58]

These three parables emphasize personal joy that resonates with the entire community and is thus amplified. Basset reminds us that the parable of the prodigal son is a parable of inclusion. Joy is an emotion that is best expressed together. Sam Wells, a priest of the Church of England, writes, "The discipline of joy means not just reflecting on your own happiness, your own sense of certainty, exhilaration, and clarity, but also having a community experience, a sharing, walking together, and discovering from one another."[59] A true story from our own time illustrates the same theme as the parables analyzed by Bailey. A few years ago, an Algerian woman who had attended the same Bible study group for years suddenly jumped out of her seat during a meeting and

53. Basset, *La Joie Imprenable*.

54. Sergius Bulgakov, *Churchly Joy: Orthodox Devotions for the Church Year*, trans. Boris Jakim (Grand Rapids: Eerdmans, 2008), 115.

55. Kenneth E. Bailey, *"Poet and Peasant" and "Through Peasant Eyes": A Literary-Cultural Approach to the Parables in Luke* (Grand Rapids: Eerdmans, 1983).

56. Ibid., 146–53.

57. Ibid., 156–57.

58. Ibid., 205.

59. Samuel Wells, *Be Not Afraid: Facing Fear with Faith* (Grand Rapids: Brazos, 2011), 170.

shouted, "I want to follow Jesus." Like one person, the attendees, all North African Christians, jumped up from their seats and danced with joy, ululating and praising God. After the meeting, they all had a big meal together. Splashes became showers as the joy was amplified in the context of a community, which had long been praying for this woman.

Joy as Motivation for Mission

Christian mission of the last couple of centuries has not always been motivated by joy. Hudson Taylor wanted to "save the heathen from damnation."[60] Samuel Moffett advocated for "obedience."[61] Samuel Zwemer, often called the Apostle to Islam, began a long speech pleading for Christians to witness among Muslims as follows: "The Christian watchwords 'Love, Joy, Peace,' are not those of the Moslem world. Instead of joy, the Moslem hearts today are filled with a great sorrow, and instead of peace, the newspapers tell of wars and rumors of wars."[62] Even as Zwemer acknowledges the need for joy, he fails to develop this theme further. He motivates his audience by calling on them to see the great needs of Muslims, describing the compassion of God and pleading for eagerness to defend truth. He often focuses on the urgency of the task.

Have other missiologists chosen "joy" as their central motive? Dutch missiologist Marc Spindler may have woven this theme into his scholarship of mission more extensively than any other scholar. He posits that joy is both at the origin and at the end of the missionary relationship and is, indeed, "the climate of mission."[63] In the final lines of his book on mission he uses the term "joy" to describe the mission of Jesus Christ to humankind. "Joy," he writes, "is the very human 'complement' to the glory of God, the fruit of the Spirit which ripens in the missionary encounter, and which is echoed in heaven, since angels have joy each time a sinner repents (Luke 15:7)."[64] Finally, he adds, "Our mission is not a spiritual imperialism but the sharing of an enormous joy received from above, a work of God, which continues through

60. Paul A. Varg, "Motives in Protestant Missions, 1890–1917," *Church History* 23, no. 1 (1954): 71.

61. Samuel Hugh Moffett, "Why We Go: Recapturing Our Motivation for Missions," *Christianity Today*, November 14, 1994, 53–55.

62. Samuel M. Zwemer, "God's Will for the Muslim World," *Missionary Review of the World*, December 1920, 1089.

63. Marc Spindler, *La mission: Combat pour le salut du monde* [*Mission: Struggle for the salvation of the world*] (Neuchâtel, Switzerland: Delachaux et Niestlé, 1967), 241 (my translation here and in the following notes).

64. Ibid., 239.

us, for the joy of God, for our joy, and for the joy of each human and of all creation in expectation of its fullness."[65] I have embraced Spindler's motive of mission more and more since I first read it. After interacting with people who minister among Muslims over several decades, I have heard all kinds of motives. Many were fear based. Others grew out of a spirit of conquest. Others were motivated by love. Very few were joy driven!

Spindler is not the only missiologist to call for a greater emphasis on joy in mission. For example, Navone, the Jesuit scholar cited above, writes, "The joy of participation in the divine mission ultimately derives from the fact that the disciples belong to God." This "is a deeper motive for their rejoicing rather than their power over demons."[66] Likewise, according to Newbigin, witness is not about making converts but about joy. Given that the church has known the joy of the gospel, she "will indeed—out of love for them—long that they [nonbelievers] may come to share the joy that she knows and pray that they may indeed do so."[67] These examples remind us that joy in ministry does not result from names checked off on a conversion list, or winning the battle over souls between Muslims and Christians, but from sharing the joy that flows from God.

So important is this joy factor in mission that Newbigin wrote,

> There has been a long tradition which sees the mission of the Church pri-marily as obedience to a command. It has been customary to speak of "the missionary mandate." This way of putting the matter is certainly not without justification, and yet it seems to me that it misses the point. It tends to make mission a burden rather than a joy, to make it part of the law rather than part of the gospel. If one looks at the New Testament evidence one gets another impression. Mission begins with a kind of explosion of joy. The news that the rejected and crucified Jesus is alive is something that cannot possibly be suppressed.[68]

Inspired by these statements by Newbigin, Krish Kandiah, president of the London School of Theology, recently wrote an article that urged Chris-tians to connect joy to mission. "Many of our churches," Kandiah lamented, "have failed to make the connection between joy and mission."[69] This con-trasts sharply, he observes, with the experience of the earliest church, for

---

65. Ibid., 240.
66. Navone, *Themes of St. Luke*, 74. See also Luke 10:20.
67. Lesslie Newbigin, *The Gospel in a Pluralist Society* (Grand Rapids: Eerdmans, 1989), 182.
68. Ibid., 116.
69. Krish Kandiah, "An Explosion of Joy: What It Means to Be the Apostolic Church," *Christianity Today*, June 1, 2014, 49.

which (borrowing Newbigin's cherished expression) "Christ's resurrection, the gift of the Spirit, and the bestowal of the Father's authority resulted in an explosion of joy that propelled the church on its mission."[70] He continues, "An apostolic church, therefore, is one that spills over with the same joy that launched the apostles on their mission."[71] This characteristic of joy, its ability to propel people to action, is probably the reason neuroscientists describe joy as an attachment emotion; contrary to shame, which makes people want to disappear from the eyes of others, joy opens us to others. ✓

Eschatological Joy

However, witness may not always result in instantaneous joy. It may at times remain "the joy set before [us]" (Heb. 12:2). Such eschatological happiness characterized the life of many biblical characters and has been embraced by many missionaries. William Carey, a British missionary to India during the late eighteenth and early nineteenth centuries, encouraged Christians "to aspire after heavenly reward via missionary labors." He goes on to say "that that heavenly treasure is the 'crown of rejoicing' mentioned in 1 Thessalonians 2:19."[72]

I could have written an entire book on suffering that I have witnessed in ministry to Muslims. Because there are so few texts about joy in mission, I chose that theme instead. However, the joy that I explore here is not foreign to suffering. As Thrasher observes, the Bible makes it clear that joy "can be experienced in sorrow and trials (Hab. 3:17–19; Rom. 5:3; 2 Cor. 6:10; 1 Pet. 1:6)."[73] Affliction and joy sometimes mingle: "You became imitators of us and of the Lord, for you welcomed the message in the midst of severe suffering with the joy given by the Holy Spirit" (1 Thess. 1:6 NIV). Numerous biblical accounts describe how joy can be found in the most difficult places. When Paul was chained in Philippi, he wrote one of his most popular statements: "Rejoice in the Lord always. I will say it again: Rejoice!" (Phil. 4:4 NIV).

Many missiologists have underlined the unique relationship between joy and suffering in the Bible. Scott Sunquist titled his book on mission *Understanding Christian Mission: Participation in Suffering and Glory*. He explains, "Mission

70. Ibid.
71. Ibid.
72. Travis L. Myers, "Tracing a Theology of the Kingdom of God in William Carey's *Enquiry*: A Case Study in Complex Mission Motivation as Component of 'Missionary Spirituality,'" *Missiology* 40 (2012): 40.
73. Thrasher, "Joy," 527.

is . . . carried out in suffering in this world for God's eternal glory."[74] His words resonate well with the "dialectic of joy and suffering" that Moltmann used to describe the church's experience.[75] In the Bible joy and sorrow sometimes go hand in hand and may even seem impossible to separate. Thus joy is not an antidote to suffering. The relationship between the two is much more complex, I believe, and has been well expressed by missionary-surgeon Paul Brand: "I have come to see that pain and pleasure come to us not as opposites but as Siamese twins, strangely joined and intertwined. Nearly all my memories of acute happiness, in fact, involve some element of pain or struggle."[76]

Thus missiologists of joy are not surprised by suffering. They understand that it is part of the Christian journey. This is what gave me the courage to write this book in the midst of traumatic Muslim-Christian relations. As I wrote this chapter, horrific events took place. In Paris, people were murdered at the *Charlie Hebdo* magazine headquarters and at a kosher store. In Niger, churches were burned. During the same period, two Japanese hostages and twenty-one Coptic Christians were beheaded. A hotel was bombed in Tripoli. Millions of Muslim and Christian refugees are trying to stay alive while facing dire circumstances. Borders between several African countries are riddled with Muslim-Christian conflicts. And the list goes on and on. How can I write about joy in this awful climate, if joy is not merely happy endorphins?

But the tie between joy and suffering is not mere coexistence. "Suffering need not hinder one's joy," Thrasher points out. "In fact, suffering for Christ can even be a cause for rejoicing (Acts 5:41)."[77] Recently the book *The Privilege of Persecution* caught my attention.[78] One of the authors, Carl Moeller, who at the time was president of a ministry for persecuted Christians called Open Doors USA, must have witnessed firsthand the suffering of many Christians in Muslim contexts. Such a title might cause some of us to choke: How can one say that persecution is a privilege? And yet throughout church history there have always been people who believed and understood something of joy wrapped in suffering. Consider the following verse: "But to the degree that you share the sufferings of Christ, keep on rejoicing, so that also at the revelation of His glory you may rejoice with exultation" (1 Pet. 4:13 NASB). Another verse talks about the blessing of persecution, a concept that is not

---

74. Sunquist, *Understanding Christian Mission*, 136.

75. Richard Bauckham, *Theology of Jürgen Moltmann* (London: T&T Clark, 1995), 134. See also "Finding Joy with Jürgen Moltmann" and accompanying video.

76. Paul Brand and Philip Yancey, "And God Created Pain," *Christianity Today*, January 10, 1994, 21.

77. Thrasher, "Joy," 527.

78. Carl A. Moeller and David W. Hegg with Craig Hodgkins, *The Privilege of Persecution: And Other Things the Global Church Knows That We Don't* (Chicago: Moody Publishers, 2011).

too far from the title under discussion: "Blessed are those who are persecuted for righteousness' sake, for theirs is the kingdom of heaven. Blessed are you when people revile you and persecute you and utter all kinds of evil against you falsely on my account. Rejoice and be glad, for your reward is great in heaven, for in the same way they persecuted the prophets who were before you" (Matt. 5:10–12 NRSV). Although I would not encourage anyone to seek persecution to earn more joy or blessing, God seems to give a special kind of joy to those who suffer for his sake.

There are many stories of persecution in Muslim societies. At times the state persecutes, at other times society or family. Although following Christ is sometimes only an indirect cause (more direct causes being cultural insensitivity, economic factors, political turmoil, or wars), persecution is still an important issue for the church in Muslim contexts.

Conclusion

I hope you are more ready to smile when considering witness to Muslims, because joy is central to such witness. The reminder of God's infectious joy may transform the way we look at mission, especially given the many references to joy in the Bible. Verses such as "Always be joyful" (1 Thess. 5:16), "Rejoice in the Lord always" (Phil. 4:4), and "The joy of the Lord is your strength" (Neh. 8:10) are only a few of the most famous. As a body, the Bible's references to joy reveal patterns that highlight characteristics of joyful witness, the heart of God's mission in the world. First, though greatly neglected in the past, joy is a biblical stimulus to missionary work. Second, joy is eschatological—a future hope—but it is also experienced now. Third, joy is divine but is also felt as a human emotion. Finally, joy and suffering are not antagonistic but, like a fabric, form the warp and woof of a beautiful tapestry.

Readers who have no joy in witness will be tempted to fake it and adopt a smiling face, like artists who artificially display emotions with theatrical masks. But God's joy is no gimmick! It flows from a vibrant relationship with him, the source of joy-filled life and witness. The shining face of God irradiates his followers and transforms them into bringers of joy. But joy can also be buried under a mountain of trouble. In my travels across the Muslim world, I have encountered scores of people who have lost feelings of joy. I have attended conferences for mission workers in the Muslim world where there was no reference to the "explosion of joy" or the "divine shout of joy" that we mentioned in this chapter. This is understandable in the sense that some contexts are difficult, discouraging, and even dangerous. Perhaps, as we further reflect on how God's joy is experienced in these dire situations, we will discover fresh models of joy-driven witness, different from those in peaceful and favorable contexts.

For Discussion

1. Is the Triune God joyful? How do you know?
2. What are the characteristics of joyful witness?
3. Give examples of joyful witness in your own life.

2

Muslim-Christian Attachment

People often ask why a Lutheran-born French person like me was attracted to Islamic studies. My response is simple. It all started with ordinary encounters with Muslims. When I was a teenager, a girl who lived a block from my home stopped me on my way to go grocery shopping and asked why I was wearing a T-shirt with the words "Jesus loves you."[1] She was friendly and bubbly. We started a conversation that turned into a friendship. Later we read the Bible and prayed together.

I don't remember thinking, "Wow, I am talking to a Muslim." To me, religion was not the primary lens through which I saw Samira. Although her father was a Muslim, to me she was first a neighbor who turned into a friend. Months later, when attending a mission conference, I met Christians who prayed for "Muslims" and said they "evangelize Muslims." These religious labels bothered me because they objectified Muslims. Even in this book, I am aware of the danger of placing religious tags on people and hope that readers will be able to discover behind them the uniqueness of individuals they encounter. As we all know, people bond with people and not with religious labels, not with religions.

In the previous chapter I wrote about the joyful bond that ties humans with God. We discovered the joy of the Triune God and its impact on creation, including humankind. We identified its infectious nature, ranging from

---

1. I had just decided to follow Christ and was enthusiastic about my new faith!

splashes to explosions. This was necessary to define witness in the Muslim world—in fact, in all the world. We concluded that if God is joyful, our witness also contains sparks of joy. The following chapters will offer examples of how witness in the Muslim world can contain this unique joy. But first we must study the relational context in which joy is diffused. I have chosen to look at ordinary encounters.

Today, scientists are much better informed about the nature of human relations than in ages past. With the use of sophisticated technology, such as fMRI machines, they observe brain activity during emotional communication between two people. What they have discovered about the neurobiological mechanisms of human attachment sheds new light on interpersonal relations, and some of these discoveries are important for understanding ordinary encounters. Surprisingly, joy is an important emotion in such encounters. We must, therefore, invite this emotion into our relationships with Muslims in order to experience healthier relations that may lead to opportunities to share what matters most to us, including our faith in Christ.

Ordinary Encounters

My personal experience described above should remind us all that everyday life offers opportunities to meet Muslims. One does not have to ride the famous Disneyland attraction[2] to realize that today we live in a "small world." Many years ago, studies of acquaintanceship networks revealed that there are probably only six degrees of separation between individuals worldwide. Today, there are even fewer, as the world is increasingly interconnected via social media, migrations, and fast and easy travel systems. As a result, very few places are left where people are not rubbing shoulders with someone from another faith, language, and culture. Christians are perhaps closer to Muslim people than they think. These can even be relatives, classmates, neighbors, or coworkers. It is these kinds of relationships that I call ordinary, and these ordinary relationships can be strengthened through an understanding of attachment theory.

Unfortunately, relationship building, something that should be very natural, is not always easy. Social and political conflicts have recently carved wide and deep trenches between Muslim and Christian communities worldwide. Wars and acts of terror have produced suspicion, anger, and fear between religious communities. In addition, theological differences, sometimes addressed in polemical

2. Disneyland has an attraction called "It's a Small World." Although stereotyping, it shows how the world can be toured in a short time, measured by the duration of the ride.

or hostile ways, have widened these divides.[3] To address these challenging relations, a plethora of books have explored Muslim-Christian relationships in all
corners of the world for nearly fourteen centuries.[4] Scholars have used a host of
concepts from a variety of disciplines to look at what shapes these ties.

Additionally, Christians seek resources in the Bible. Unfortunately, the Bible
does not provide details on how to interact with Muslims,[5] simply because
Islam did not exist in biblical times. Muhammad was born over five hundred
years after the death and resurrection of Christ. Thus Christians are left
with having to draw analogies from other interfaith encounters narrated in
the Bible. Fortunately, these interactions are numerous and range from the
most hostile to the most graceful. On the violent side, Elijah ordered the
slaughtering of the prophets of Baal (1 Kings 18:40), and God ordered Saul
to destroy the Amalekites (1 Sam. 15:3). But God also commanded love for
neighbors, including foreigners.[6] Many peaceful encounters took place, such
as between Solomon and the Queen of Sheba (1 Kings 10). Many Christians
look at the meeting between Jesus and the Samaritan woman as a model of
interfaith encounter. Syrian novelist Mazhar Mallouhi, a Muslim-born follower of Christ, finds this story "one of the most beautiful stories of grace
and love in the Gospels" and describes the encounter as "two thirsty people
at a sacred well, who meet and journey together."[7]

From these biblical teachings and many others, scholars have designed
theories and concepts that have been used in Muslim-Christian relations,
such as the "Convivencia" of the German missiologist Theo Sundermeier,[8]

---

3. The coming of Jesus is good news for Muslims, but his death is not. What first comes to
mind when one thinks of Christian-Muslim dialogue are the heated debates between Muslims
and Christians regarding the doctrine of incarnation. Jesus is deeply respected as a prophet and
the son of Mary, but the question of whether he is the Son of God is almost always polemical.

4. I recommend Hugues Goddard, *A History of Christian-Muslim Relations* (Edinburgh:
Edinburgh University Press, 2000); Nabil Jabbour, *The Crescent through the Eyes of the Cross:
Insights from an Arab Christian* (Colorado Springs: NavPress, 2008); Shirin Taber, *Muslims
Next Door: Uncovering Myths and Creating Friendships* (Grand Rapids: Zondervan, 2004);
Christine Mallouhi, *Waging Peace on Islam* (Downers Grove, IL: InterVarsity, 2002); David
Shenk, *Christian. Muslim. Friend: Twelve Paths to Real Relationships* (Harrisonville, VA: Herald
Press, 2014); and Carl Medearis, *Muslims, Christians, and Jesus: Gaining Understanding and
Building Relationships* (Minneapolis: Bethany House, 2008).

5. Muslims, on the other hand, have plenty of information in their sacred texts.

6. Leviticus 19:18, 33–34 insists that God's people must love their neighbors, including any
foreigners among them. The word "*rea*," used in v. 18, can be translated "friend," "neighbor,"
or "fellow man" (including "enemy," according to some authors).

7. Quoted in Paul-Gordon Chandler, *Pilgrims of Christ on the Muslim Road: Exploring a
New Path between Two Faiths* (Lanham, MD: Rowman & Littlefield, 2008), 86.

8. See Theo Sundermeier, *Konvivenz und differenz* (Erlangen, Germany: Verlag der Ev.-Luth.
Mission, 1995). Sundermeier's reflection on intercultural and interfaith relations was inspired
by the South American concept of *convivencia* used in liberation theology and the peaceful

Joy Was Not Necessarily the First Word That Came to Mind!

Allan Matamoros, Partners International

I still remember, at the end of the eighties, my season of missionary training in my home country, Costa Rica. I took my first "Introduction to Islam" classes in our newly started, first Costa Rican mission society. Even though we were warned not to understand the Muslim world as a monolithic religious and cultural entity, during all of our training time we sensed a pessimistic mood concerning missions to the people of Islam. To be honest, "joy" was not necessarily the first word that came to our minds during that time; probably other valid and very important words like "obedience," "martyrdom," and "suffering" predominated in our thinking and expectations, but "joy" was quite off my list. There is no doubt that we were dealing with preconceptions, fears, and a kind of an inner negative perception about Arabs and Muslims in general.

Then finally we arrived on the mission field and needed a reality check. By living there and exploring the historical ties and similarities between Latin Americans and some of the Arab cultures, we "discovered" what has been one of the beauties of our service living with and among them in Islamic settings.

the "sacred hospitality" of the French Islamicist Louis Massignon,[9] the "inverted perspective" of the Croatian-American theologian Miroslav Volf,[10] the "peace-waging" model of the Australian author Christine Mallouhi,[11] or the

coexistence of Muslims, Jews, and Christians in Andalusia before the Reconquista. He used the German term "*Konvivenz*" (convivence or convivencia) to call people from different faiths to help one another, learn from each other, and celebrate together.

9. See Louis Massignon, *L'Hospitalité Sacrée* (Paris: Nouvelle Cité, 1987). Louis Massignon developed the concept of sacred hospitality after experiencing lavish hospitality from Muslims and studying the concept of hospitality in the Bible, especially in the life of Abraham. To him, hospitality was a sacred practice that Christians needed to adopt in their engagement with Muslims.

10. See Miroslav Volf, "Living with the 'Other,'" in *Muslim and Christian Reflections on Peace: Divine and Human Dimensions*, ed. J. Dudley Woodberry, Osman Zümrüt, and Mustafa Köylü (Lanham, MD: University Press of America, 2005), 3–22. Miroslav Volf referred to the concept of "inverted perspective" to explain that if we consider someone as "the other" in a negative way, we become "the other" to them. In order to improve relationships, Volf suggests that Christians practice listening and understanding what "the other" thinks and feels.

11. In her book *Waging Peace on Islam* (Downers Grove, IL: InterVarsity, 2002), Christine Mallouhi invites Christians who encounter Muslims in times of war to learn from the peaceful encounter between Francis of Assisi and the Sultan Malik during the Crusades.

As soon as we overcame the "fear factor," we "discovered" the immense joy of building mutual, honest, healthy relationships with our Muslim friends—at the end of the day we realized the obvious, that we were dealing with more than numbers and conversions; we were dealing with real people with blood and flesh. We lived then the sometimes painful but surely joyful process of incarnating ourselves in their worldview, sharing together throughout this process our families, time, vulnerabilities, food, laughs, and tears!

Muslims, sometimes more than Westerners, love to talk about faith and religion very often, and then we found that the strength we already had in our "joyful relationships" had prepared for clean and transparent religious conversations with our Muslim friends, a dialoguing experience that helped to release the gospel in such a way that the gospel's own intrinsic power defended its claims and affirmations without our dialogues necessarily becoming battles.

Undeniably, we are facing an extraordinarily difficult season in the Muslim world, but just the power of the gospel bringing peace and reconciliation through joyful relationships between Muslims and devoted Christians can change and catalyze the announcement of eternal salvation and peace through the merits of the Lord Jesus, the One who attracts us to him with immense joy (Jude 24).

"kerygmatic approach" of Lebanese theologian and Islamicist Martin Accad.[12] To these resources, the study of joy in the Bible, associated with findings from neurobiological attachment theory, offers new insight for research on Muslim-Christian relations. Attachment theory specifically looks at ordinary encounters and has found that joy plays a major role in the development of healthy human relationships.

Relational Joy

By observing caregivers interacting with children, attachment theorists learn how people bond with others. They believe that these affective transactions

---

12. Martin Accad explains his kerygmatic approach in "Christian Attitudes toward Islam and Muslims: A Kerygmatic Approach," in *Toward Respectful Understanding and Witness among Muslims: Essays in Honor of J. Dudley Woodberry*, ed. Evelyne A. Reisacher (Pasadena, CA: William Carey Library, 2011), 29–47. After reviewing various models of Muslim-Christian encounters, Accad suggests that in the kerygmatic approach Christ himself is the center of salvation and not religious systems.

provide a template for all future relationships. Humans bond with other people throughout their life span by using a neurobiological attachment structure located in their brain with connections to their body. This genetically formed structure is also shaped by affective interactions with caregivers during the first years of life. It is essentially responsible for the regulation of emotions.[13]

Attachment theorists have discovered that joy is central during relationship building in infancy and childhood.[14] Babies learn the pleasure of being with other human beings through positive emotional transactions with their caregivers. Neuroscientist Louis Colozino explains that "during the first year of life, healthy parent-child interactions are primarily positive, affectionate, and playful."[15] These mutual moments of joy and elation that range from a few milliseconds to several minutes build in children the capacity to experience positive emotions together with other human beings. They learn to feel accepted, loved, and secure in relationships through the pleasant feelings that these relationships provide. These early attachment experiences are remembered nonverbally, as pleasurable and joyful.[16] Thanks to these memories, children can expect other relationships to be delightful.

Positive emotional transactions also expand children's capacity to process joy on their own. At birth, the brain-body[17] structure that processes positive emotion is not fully mature. Babies need to interact with persons who have adult brains, so that the adults can match and regulate the babies' emotional crescendos and decrescendos and amplify their joy. These attuned interactions with their caregivers, via sensory means, act as neuronal stimulations of pleasure centers in the brain. Chemical and hormonal changes in a child's body strengthen the neural pathways between brain structures responsible for processing positive emotional states and the orbitofrontal cortex, a brain structure that the child will use later in life to self-regulate emotions. Schore further explains that these caregiver-child interactions shape the brain systems

13. For a more detailed description of these bodily structures and processes see Allan N. Schore, *Affect Regulation and the Origin of the Self: The Neurobiology of Emotional Development* (Hillsdale, NJ: Lawrence Erlbaum Associates, 1999).

14. Ibid.

15. Louis Colozino, *The Neurosciences of Psychotherapy: Healing the Social Brain*, 2nd ed. (New York: W. W. Norton, 2010), 192.

16. The right brain is dominant during the first three years of life and matures before the left. The emotional brain or social brain, as the right brain is called, stores memories of relational practices shaped by relationships. No one is born with an operational attachment structure. Neuroscientist Allan Schore asserts that "the maturation of the orbitofrontal areas, the brain's central emotion regulating system, occurs completely postnatally, and their development is positively or negatively shaped by attachment experiences." Allan N. Schore, *Affect Dysregulation and Disorders of the Self* (New York: W. W. Norton, 2003), 272.

17. The term "brain-body" refers to the brain with its connections to the body.

responsible for pleasurable social states throughout life. He describes these transactions as follows: "Affective communications of facial expressions, prosody, and gestures with the social environment are central to the experience-dependent maturation of the infant's early developing right brain."[18] If children do not experience these joyful transactions early in life, they will feel insecure in their relationships. Joy is thus a central component of attachment formation. As we will soon see, this has much to do with how we developed genuine trusting and joyful relationships with our Muslim neighbors.

Relational Stress

Unfortunately, instead of joyful transactions, some children experience abuse and neglect, which produce high levels of stress and negative affect. Attachment researchers discovered that abused or neglected children develop insecure and disorganized attachments that make it challenging for them to develop healthy bonds later in life.[19] The lack of feeling joy and elation in the presence of their caregivers impairs the growth of the brain-body structure that processes positive emotions. The role of caregivers during the first year of life should therefore be to minimize stress.[20]

But relational stress (not the product of abuse or neglect) is an inextricable part of life. Children feel emotionally distressed when their caregivers are emotionally unavailable or insensitive to their real emotional needs. According to Schore, this emotional asynchrony produces "shame."[21] Colozino says: "Shame is represented physiologically by a rapid transition from a positive to negative affective state. . . . This shift is triggered by the expectation of attunement to a positive state, only to receive negative emotions from the caretaker."[22] In other words, children sometimes turn toward the caregiver expecting a happy face that matches their internal states only to encounter an unhappy face that does not down-regulate their stress. Shame occurs frequently when toddlers, anticipating a joyful welcome from their caregivers, receive instead negative comments like "Don't touch" or "Don't go there."

18. Allan N. Schore, *Affect Regulation and the Repair of the Self* (New York: W. W. Norton, 2003), 257.

19. From studies conducted in Romanian orphanages, researchers have identified that severe neglect in early infancy disrupts the ability to form healthy attachments. See T. G. O'Connor, R. S. Marvin, M. Rutter, J. T. Olrick, and P. A. Britner, "Child-Parent Attachment Following Early Institutional Deprivation," *Development and Psychopathology* 15, no. 1 (Winter 2003): 19–38.

20. Schore, *Affect Regulation and the Origin of the Self*.

21. Allan N. Schore, *The Science of the Art of Psychotherapy*, Norton Series on Interpersonal Neurobiology (New York: W. W. Norton, 2012), Kindle edition, location 97.

22. Colozino, *Neurosciences of Psychotherapy*, 192.

In infancy, children cannot handle these distressing internal states produced by caregivers. Anyone who has witnessed a baby who suddenly begins shrieking and continues nonstop for an hour knows what it means to say that babies cannot regulate their emotions. They don't experience smooth transitions from high-intensity emotion to low-intensity emotion. They may shift from an exhilarating state of joy abruptly into tears. My mother was well aware of that when she scolded my father for engaging in intense emotional transactions with me just before bedtime: "Stop making her giggle! She will not be able to calm down and go to sleep."

The still face experiment shows how children struggle with emotional regulation.[23] A caregiver plays joyfully with an infant sitting in a baby chair. Abruptly, the caregiver displays an emotionless face (called the still face). The infant often shows surprise, attempts to regain the caregiver's attention, reaches out, utters discontent, cries, screams, and finally collapses in despair. After holding the still face briefly, the caregiver then reengages with the child, in face-to-face joyful interaction. Usually the infant slowly resumes normal interaction and returns to joy. This experiment is very painful to watch, especially the segment in which the child is left alone with his or her emotional distress and cannot figure out why the adult shows that poker face. This little experiment provides vivid evidence that children need adults to match their internal emotional states.

These moments of emotional asynchrony, during which the caregiver does not match the emotions of the child, cause the child stress and rupture the emotional communication. "The good-enough mother of the securely attached infant," however, according to Schore, "permits access to the child after a separation and shows a tendency to respond appropriately and promptly to his/her emotional expressions."[24] Repeated experiences of mutual regulation after stressful moments teach children that relationships with their caregivers can go on after ruptures. We learn from Schore that human beings gain the capacity to build relationships with other human beings when they can experience with their caregivers the joy of being together and reconnection with them after stressful or painful interactions. Experiencing mutual joy is not enough to learn how to form healthy relationships throughout life. One has to learn in early childhood that a broken bond with a caregiver can be repaired. This is how children learn to return to joy when things go wrong later in life.

Thus, by studying human attachment formation, we can better understand the nature of human relations. First, the brain-body structure that allows one

23. Edward Tronick, "Still Face Experiment," (2009), video available at https://www.you
tube.com/watch?v=apzXGEbZht0.
24. Schore, *Affect Regulation and the Repair of the Self*, 122.

human being to connect with others throughout life is shaped by caregiver-child transactions that include emotions such as joy and shame. Second, joy plays a key role in the formation of the bond between caregiver and child as well as in the restoration of the bond after a rupture. Third, the repair of the bond after stressful transactions between caregiver and child allows for the growth of healthy relations. These components of human attachment are all at work in ordinary encounters between Muslims and Christians.

Enjoying Muslims

Through the years, I have taught numerous Muslim-awareness seminars in churches worldwide. Inevitably, participants would say, "We would love to connect with Muslims in our neighborhoods but don't know how." Given that joy is a primary attachment emotion, I recommend the obvious: first start to enjoy Muslims as human beings, to delight in them; this is how the bond will form, as it did when we first learned to attach to our caregivers as human beings. As joy is necessary in the formation of the bond in early childhood, so it continues to be important in the formation and growth of human bonds throughout life.

Unfortunately, I noticed during these same seminars that participants were primarily motivated to connect with Muslims not by delight but by fear, competition, or urgency of the task. Fortunately, compassion and love are now emerging motives, but joy still rarely appears, and as seldom among full-time missionaries to Muslims as among ordinary church members. If God enjoys his creation, does it not seem awkward that his children find no delight in those they evangelize? Furthermore, as joy is so important for healthy relations, it is inconceivable that Christians befriend Muslims for the sake of the gospel without feeling overwhelming joy toward them. When students share their experiences in the Muslim world with me or with their classmates in a class I'm teaching, I often ask: "What joy did you experience?" I put the same question to my readers: can you remember joyful interactions you had with Muslims? If you cannot, you probably never connected with them. If you can, you may agree with Henri Nouwen, who wrote, "True joy is hidden where we are the same as other people: fragile and mortal. It is the joy of belonging to the human race. It is the joy of being with others as a friend, a companion, a fellow traveler. This is the joy of Jesus, who is Emmanuel: God-with-us."[25]

25. Henri J. M. Nouwen, *Bread for the Journey: A Daybook of Wisdom and Faith* (San Francisco: HarperOne, 2006), 38.

Exploration

Joy is an exploration-eliciting emotion. Have you noticed that when tourists are in a sightseeing mood, they display unique behaviors? Their bodies seem to be in starting blocks, ready to move forward, conquer new spaces, and engage with unfamiliar people. The cameras around their necks signal they are eager to capture new visual sensations. Their eyes are wide open. This allows them to marvel at the wonders they discover. They feel enthusiastic, full of energy, and harbor a huge smile. Neuroscientists would say that they are in a sympathetic drive[26] and high on dopamine. Words that come to mind are "seeking," "curiosity," "exploring," "awe," "anticipation," and "amazement."

When we engage with the Muslim world, having a similar attitude will help us greatly. In effect, interest plays a critical role in attachment. According to Schore, "The combination of joy and interest motivates attachments."[27] To connect with Muslims, we must show interest in them and a joyful expectation that we will learn new things from them. Unfortunately, the tourist analogy falls short when one realizes that tourists often connect better to a place than to its inhabitants. Rejoicing over objects and places can help us enjoy a culture but will not automatically cause us to enjoy its people. It is people, therefore, whom we must be interested in and excited about.

In order to form secure bonds with Muslims, we must participate in joyful moments with them. When Christians engage with Muslims, "positive emotions widen the available array of thoughts and actions, thereby facilitating flexibility, exploration, and play. These behaviors in turn promote social bonding."[28] Yes, joyful play associated with interest/excitement should become an integral part of meeting Muslims. Some of the best contexts in which to experience such feelings are ordinary encounters. I naturally connected with Muslim classmates at school, at sport, at work, or in leisure activities. Too often, Christians limit their interactions with Muslims to religious spaces. They forget there are many other ways to meet and enjoy others.

Genuine Joy

There are two kinds of joy. The first is cognitive, basically processed by the left side of the brain. It is often called social joy. The other is affective and is

26. The sympathetic branch of the autonomic nervous system is called the energy-expanding branch. See Allan N. Schore, "Effects of a Secure Attachment Relationship on Right Brain Development, Affect Regulation, and Infant Mental Health," *Infant Mental Health Journal* 22, no. 1–2 (2001): 7–66.

27. Schore, *Affect Regulation and the Origin of the Self*, 97.

28. Disa Sauter, "More Than Happy: The Need for Disentangling Positive Emotions," *Current Directions in Psychological Science* 19, no. 1 (2010): 36.

processed by the right side of the brain. Only the latter, being spontaneous and bodily based, fosters human attachment. Cognitive joy is sometimes used to mask negative emotions with a smile[29] or other playful behaviors for the sake of civility. This faked joy does not have the same infectious effect. For attachments to build, joy must be spontaneous—like a gut feeling. Imagine seeing someone you enjoy and instantaneously feeling joy bubble up in you.

Unfortunately, mission practitioners sometimes approach Muslims with a fake smile. They use relationship building as a strategy to share the gospel with Muslims. Their so-called interest in the Muslim world appears more like an evangelistic marketing technique. When they see Muslims, they mask their negative emotions with a smile and pretend they are happy to see them. They offer to connect with them only because they want to witness. I am all for sharing the gospel, and I support civility, but misunderstandings may occur if Christians smile at Muslims only to evangelize them, because the latter may understand the smile as an invitation to deeper relations. Once a Muslim refuses the gospel, a Christian who has been thus motivated will probably rupture the bond, leaving the Muslim even more confused about the real reasons Christians engage with Muslims. I assume that Christians would be as bewildered if they discovered that Muslims became friends with them only to convert them.

An experience of social joy does not always guarantee that people will attach. Genuine, affective joy is the rule in attachment. This spontaneous and authentic joy is communicated via the right brain of one person and resonates with the right brain of the person to whom joy is being communicated. Right-brain joy is the key to attachment. True joy is not something you can just reason or figure out. One must experience spontaneous joyful emotions originating from a relational context. During interactions with Muslims, joy may suddenly pop up, unexpectedly. One cannot say, "Now I am going to find Muslims pleasant." No one can arbitrarily create happiness by being together with people from another culture (unless happiness is cognitively induced for social purposes). One has to personally be immersed in an unfamiliar environment and feel the spark of joy when it happens. No one can predict when it will happen. It is the path of discovering how one's right brain reacts to the sensory and verbal stimuli in the context of relationship with a Muslim. To those who want to feel the joy of the Muslim world, I can only recommend going and exploring Muslim societies and being open to the joy that will enable them to connect. It may start with a single encounter like the one I had with my neighbor when I was a teenager.

29. Theorists call it a Duchennes smile.

Happy Faces

Facial expressions are important means to convey emotions. I remember walking on the beach when a teenager came out of the water where he had surfed, beaming with excitement. His face radiated with joy. As he walked past me, my face beamed with joy in return. His joy was infectious. I believe that at that moment I experienced the right-brain-to-right-brain affective resonance that child and caregiver experience when they are together and feel nonverbal joy. The cultural display of joy did not matter in this circumstance. Facially communicated joy bypassed words, which was convenient because this teenager did not speak the same language as I do. Was our relationship strong at that point? No! Attachment is a long process that involves more than a one-time affective resonance. But this fleeting positive emotion could have become the springboard for subsequent moments of joy, which could have shaped a bond. I wonder how many of these experiences my readers have had with Muslims. When have our faces beamed with joy in their presence? Can we stop for a moment to recall these memories?

Unfortunately, these days, happy faces of Muslims in the media are in short supply. How can there be mutual sharing of joy if Muslims only get the role of villain in movies and if only their angry faces make newspaper headlines? Recently I googled the word "Muslim" and was shocked by the number of angry faces that appeared in the "image" section. This is strange, because Muslims can be as happy as anybody else on this planet. Unfortunately, most people are introduced to Islam through fearful faces.

Sometimes, at the beginning of a lecture or a church meeting, I ask Christians to think of Muslims and choose a facial expression. I show them a variety of emoticons. Very rarely is the smiley face chosen. That is quite unfortunate for relationship building, because happy faces are inviting, but angry or fearful faces lead to shame-based transactions such as we described earlier. How can someone build healthy relations with Muslims in a context of fear, anger, and terror when few people have memories of joyful encounters with Muslims? Usually relationships start with positive emotional experiences, even if later there might be stress or conflict. In such cases, repairing the relationship will be easier because of the memory of the joyful times of the past. But when people try to initiate connections with Muslims, when all they hear about Muslims is negative, how will healthy relationships ever develop?

The intergenerational transmission of negative feelings regarding Muslims also makes it difficult for non-Muslims to form bonds with Muslims. Terror stories that have been transmitted over generations make it almost impossible to establish healthy bonds, since terror has traumatic effects on human relations. I grew up in France during the Algerian War of Independence. Most young men the age of my brother were drafted. I remember conversations I heard as a child referring to Algerians as enemies. I heard people say, "If you see an Arab, change sidewalks; they might kill you." How do you think this must have shaped my feelings as I resonated at an early age with the fear of an entire country? I was anxious and distant until I met an Arab Muslim girl, with whom I experienced some joy. These positive memories allowed me to form other bonds with Muslims until I was able to experience the entire attachment cycle of joy, shame, and a return to joy with Muslims. Therefore, today, when I speak with anxious people all around the world, I ask them, "Can you get a Muslim smiley"?[30] Besides the angry and fearful faces of terrorists, there are many other faces of Muslims who are like you and me, with no desire to harm Christians but instead are eager to develop friendships with them. You can form healthy bonds with Muslims. I regularly show my students a visual survey filmed in Dhaka, Bangladesh, over a week, in which researchers asked random pedestrians a single question: "Are you happy?" Scores of interviewees share about their daily joys and struggles, many with genuine and spontaneous smiles that are warm and welcoming. As was noted earlier, another video, called the "Happy British Muslims," surprises Christian audiences when Muslims sing along with Pharrell Williams's "Happy." These infectious faces of delight, joy, and elation are often suppressed by communities waging war against each other, since they know all too well the power such expressions have to connect people with each other.

Dyadic Joy

Another important aspect of attachment joy is its capacity to be mutually shared. Self-happiness does not create bonds. Playing alone, enjoying a delicious meal alone, or even using recreational drugs alone—all these experiences eliciting joy that raise the level of dopamine may render life more pleasant but do not contribute to developing human bonds. Dyadic joy,[31] or joy shared with another human being, is what leads to attachment.

Dyadic joy is mutual. When for my doctoral research I interviewed North African Christians in French churches, I noticed that they were making many efforts to enjoy French Christians. But the latter did not always reciprocate.

30. I try to encourage people to draw Muslim faces with a smile because there are many happy Muslims in the world (but media do not often depict "happy Muslims"). Thus Christians have to be proactive and be able to imagine that a smiley can also represent a Muslim person.

31. In social sciences, "dyad" is a technical term for a group of two.

This is not the best recipe for a lasting bond. Both members of the dyad must feel joy. Therefore, when developing bonds with Muslims, we must identify mutually felt joys. Unfortunately, interfaith relationships are sometimes emotionally imbalanced. One person is trying hard to enjoy the other (trying to like her food, appreciate her customs, etc.), but the other is not. Immigrants who want to integrate often make greater efforts to connect in order to be accepted. But this does not necessarily lead to secure bonds, because both members of the dyad must try to find enjoyment in each other. When a relationship is positive for one person in the dyad, this does not mean the two have become securely attached. I have talked to many cross-cultural workers coming back from overseas and saying: "We had such a great time; we laughed with people; we feel really connected; we have become friends." But the words "connected" and "attached" can have diverse meanings and do not necessarily mean securely attached. After their comments, I always ask them to tell stories of mutual joy to assess whether they formed an attachment bond. I then ask if they experienced shame and the return to mutual joy.

I have noticed that in times of cross-cultural conflicts, members of one group tend to forget that the opposite group has the capacity to share joy, laughter, and other positive emotional experiences. This is probably why peacemakers include times of common celebration and play to rebuild broken relationships after wars and conflicts. Joy is not meant to erase all the pain but is a necessary ingredient to repair broken relations. And peacemakers know that every culture has feasts and celebrations that can become spaces for experiencing mutual joy.

The use of the word "dyadic" in human attachment theory, referring to a relationship between two people, implies that attachment takes place one relationship at a time. In childhood, although entire communities can be involved in child rearing, children attach to individuals who are sensitive to their emotional regulatory needs. It is the same with Muslim-Christian relations in adulthood. Have you ever heard people say, "I love Muslims," or "I love the Saudis"? What does this really mean? Bonding occurs with individual people whom you can name. Why do I emphasize this? Because I have seen too many people say, "Oh, I love this culture. I think the people are fantastic!" But they have never even developed one single secure attachment with a person from that country or religion. Attachment takes place one dyad at a time until large networks of relations are formed. A friend of mine, born in a Muslim family, reports that a member of her church made derogative comments about Muslims, saying that she would never trust any. My friend replied, "But I was one of them! Why do you then trust me?" The person replied, "But with you it's different. I have gotten to know you throughout the years." So much was her mind filled with negative images, this church member was not consciously aware that she liked a person from a Muslim background. Once she became aware of it, this changed everything. She realized she could develop bonds with other people from the estranged community. This example comports with my belief that to secure healthier relationships between Muslims and Christians we must start at the micro level, and more specifically with healthy dyadic relationships between Muslims and Christians.

But interfaith and intercultural affective transactions can prove challenging. Anthropological observations highlight that cultures and religions diverge in the ways and contexts in which they display and experience positive or negative emotion. For example, wedding celebrations in certain cultures can be perceived as funerals in others because outsiders don't see the same intensity of joy displayed. Likewise, it may be improper to scream and yell when meeting a friend in some cultures. Anyone observing people welcoming their loved ones in an airport can see differences in the way people from various cultures greet one another. When the intensity or display of joy does not match across cultures, relationships may rupture. There is no universal way to share joy in a relationship.

"Objects" of joy may also differ across cultures and religions. If I asked people from different cultures what they do to enjoy a relationship, the responses vary widely. Some may say, "Going to a baseball game together." Other will say, "Taking a cruise together." And others will say, "Enjoying a meal together." This poses a problem for dyadic encounters. What if the joy that other cultures value is not joy to me? Am I ever going to experience moments of shared joy, or pleasurable moments that strengthen the bond? When I meet a person from another culture and want to develop a bond with her, I often try to find out what she enjoys doing. But doing what the other person enjoys will not bring a secure bond in the long run. Finding these cross-cultural or interfaith spaces where both members of the dyad can say that they truly enjoy each other is the key to developing healthy bonds. It often takes time.

Repair of the Bond

Individuals with joyful and playful personalities may seize more opportunities to connect with Muslims, but it does not mean that they are capable of maintaining long-term relationships. Joyful states are not the only aspects of attachment. Relationships comprise a multitude of stressful moments that must be followed by a return to tranquility and new opportunities to experience joy. Healthy attachment bonds develop only when people are able to repair

Witness as a Lifestyle

John Azumah, Columbia Theological Seminary

Africa is the only continent where Muslims and Christians meet each other on equal footing. That is very much in terms of numbers, in terms of opportunities, in terms of challenges. When we talk about Muslims in Africa, we are not talking about immigrants. We are not talking about aliens. We are not talking about strangers. We are talking about fully fledged citizens. We are talking about people who are not just neighbors but relations, family members, cousins.

And so it is a completely different dynamic when we are talking about Islam and Christian-Muslim relations in Africa. In Africa we don't talk about Islam as just a religious system. We talk about Islam as the faith of my neighbor, a belief of my uncle, sometimes the belief system of my sister, my mother, my parents.

In my situation in Ghana, when we talk about Islam, we sometimes talk about the belief of your members, your representatives in parliament, the faith of your vice-president. . . .

In Africa, when we talk about Muslim-Christians we talk about relatives and family, and the relations take precedent over doctrines. And so, when we

the bond after a shame-eliciting emotional transaction. These aspects of attachment formation provide hope for the restoration of broken relationships.

In effect, not every Muslim-Christian relation is peaceful and joyful. Social and political conflicts have generated attitudes such as stigmatization and prejudice. It is often difficult for Muslims and Christians to attach. Furthermore, today some individuals in certain religious groups are deemed dangerous and cannot be befriended as long as their intentions are harmful. This is the case for Muslims or Christians who build relationships only as a means to attack those with whom they build them. One should not anticipate building healthy bonds with those individuals. But fortunately, there are millions of peaceful Muslims whose ruptured relational bonds with Christians could be repaired.

Relational stress is not caused only by conflict. In fact, conflict will occur whether we want it or not. In my own experience, even when both members of the interfaith dyad have good intentions, religious disorientation, unfamiliar customs, and culture-specific styles of relating can lead to ruptures. For example, I am not as group oriented as some of my North African friends. At

talk about these things in Africa, we talk about people. The most important thing in Africa is people, the second most important thing is people, the third most important thing is people.

So, in a sense, Islam and Christianity in Africa are like two women married to one husband; they bicker, they quarrel, sometimes they fight but they just have to learn to live together. They cannot afford to see each other as enemies. They are at best rivals. And that is how Islam and Christianity are coping in Africa. . . .

Islam and Christianity are both missionary religions. For Muslims in Africa, like Christians in Africa, we take the missionary aspect of our religion very, very seriously. Muslims have no problem believing and stating that Islam is the only true religion. And so they go about their witness without any apologies. And Islam and Christianity were introduced as such to us as missionary religions in Africa. And so for African Muslims and Christians, missions or witness and *da'wah* are essential aspects of our faith.

In fact, witness in an African context is not a course that you go to study. It is not a program that you have to follow. It is not an activity to be carried out. It is a lifestyle. You simply live it!

Quoted from Missiology Lectures 2007, "Toward Cordial Witness among Muslims: An African Perspective," Fuller Theological Seminary (podcast)

times, this has led to relational stress. Allowing each member of the dyad to acknowledge and feel the affective dissonance is not detrimental as long as the repair of the bond follows these ruptures.[32] John M. Gottman, who studied relationships (especially couples) for forty years, says, "It is a misconception that communication ought to be the norm in relationships. What may matter most is the ability of couples to repair things when they go wrong."[33]

Attachment theory provides resources for coping with another kind of relational stress that has preoccupied missionaries for centuries: how to witness in a sensitive manner in other cultural and religious contexts. Missiologists addressed these issues with theories of contextualization, drawing from the example of Jesus's incarnational ministry (John 1). For example, translation of the Bible into local languages has greatly enhanced the communication

32. Schore, *Affect Regulation and the Origin of the Self.*
33. John M. Gottman, *The Science of Trust: Emotional Attunement for Couples* (New York: W. W. Norton & Company, 2011), 14.

of the gospel. I believe that attachment theory provides fresh resources to answer many of these questions. In effect, some contextualization theories have only emphasized form and meaning without taking the affective area into consideration. They recommended that missionaries should eat the same food, speak the same language, and behave the same way as the people they want to reach for Christ. But some missionaries have tried all their lives to adopt these models only to discover that unless one is born in a particular culture, it is impossible to embrace it completely.

This is where attachment comes in handy. It teaches us that people with separate identities can form intimate emotional connections that foster healthy relations. Attachment theory gives cross-cultural workers hope that people from different cultures can live together as long as they know how to engage in cross-cultural attachment. Thus, while contextualization seems more concerned with preventing a rupture of the human bond, attachment theory is more preoccupied with what may prevent the repair of the bond after a relational rupture due to cultural disorientation. It is important to have cultural sensitivity, but if I had to choose between adapting my habits to acculturate and understanding how to regain mutual joy after relational stress, I would prefer the latter.

Fear-Based Relations

As we saw earlier, shame is the primary emotion felt by children who cannot engage in mutual affective regulation with their caregivers. In adulthood, when encounters trigger shame, people may not pursue the relationship unless they have a higher purpose in mind, such as business transactions, religious proselytism, or particular needs. Usually, first meetings should be positive to encourage people to pursue a relationship. So what should be done when initial Muslim-Christian relations today are based on anxiety and fear?

While fear is extremely helpful in times of danger because it allows us to fight back or escape, it can be detrimental to relationships, especially when it is unfounded.[34] We can even become contaminated by the fear of others. One day, I went on a short lake cruise with my sister. The weather was gorgeous, the mountains pristine; everything evoked joy and happiness. I was sitting in the boat when I noticed the eye movements of two couples sitting

---

34. See Evelyne A. Reisacher, "Fear and Muslim-Christian Conflict Transformation: Resources from Attachment Theory and Affect Regulation," in *Peace-Building by, between, and beyond Muslims and Evangelical Christians*, ed. Mohammed Abu-Nimer and David Augsburger (Lanham, MD: Lexington Books, 2010), 157–70.

not far from me. They were staring at something or someone, and their facial expressions revealed they were afraid. Their anxious gazes, the frowning of their eyebrows, and the sudden freezing of their bodies made me curious and anxious. I turned around to discover the object of their fear: a group of veiled women who had stepped into the boat. My fear disappeared as these women reminded me of the many friends that I have in the Muslim world. But without joyful memories, these two couples were left without resources to form a bond with these Muslim women. Safety and tranquility are therefore important components of a relational bond.

Traditional attachment theory has long identified such emotional states. Attachment theorist John Bowlby described ordinary caregivers providing a child with "a secure base from which he can explore and to which he can return when upset or frightened."[35] In attachment theory, the person who provides this safe place is called a safe haven.[36] John Bowlby wrote about "the provision by both parents of a secure base from which a child or an adolescent can make sorties into the outside world and to which he can return knowing for sure that he will be welcomed when he gets there, nourished physically and emotionally, comforted if distressed, reassured if frightened."[37] Schore explains that the secure base is gradually internalized and later accessed when a person is developing relationships in adulthood. Attachment theorist Daniel Siegel adds, "Repeated experiences [of feeling safe] become encoded in implicit memory as expectations and then as mental models or schemata of attachment, which serve to help a child feel an internal sense of what John Bowlby called a 'secure base' in the world."[38] There is now ample evidence from attachment research that the secure base concept plays an important role not only in childhood attachment but also in adult relationships.[39]

Christians who have experienced Muslims as a safe haven are more inclined to connect with them. A friend of mine tells how during riots in a Muslim-majority city, he was pushed to the ground and was in severe danger of being hurt when an elderly Muslim woman dragged him away from the crowd and thereby saved his life. I have myself experienced Muslims as safe havens many times, when I was in danger or when I was sick and needed help from

35. John Bowlby, *A Secure Base: Clinical Applications of Attachment Theory* (New York: Routledge, 2005), 51.

36. Safe haven function: meets the need for security, comfort, and care.

37. John Bowlby, *A Secure Base: Parent-Child Attachment and Healthy Human Development* (New York: Basic Books, 1988), 11.

38. Daniel J. Siegel, *The Developing Mind: How Relationships and the Brain Interact to Shape Who We Are*, 2nd ed. (New York: Guilford, 2012), 91.

39. See, e.g., Everett Waters and E. Mark Cummings, "A Secure Base from Which to Explore Close Relationships," *Child Development* 71, no. 1 (2000): 164–72.

my Muslim friends. When Muslims are experienced as safe neighbors, this can act like a cross-cultural "aha!" moment that may change the perception of an entire people group that has been stereotyped as untrustworthy. When Christians seek proximity to Muslims in times of danger, this signals that there is an attachment bond with them.

However, Muslim-Christian conflicts in several parts of the world are harming this kind of relationship building. Especially today, when images of terror are flashed almost daily on TV and computer screens, the prospect of finding safety in the Muslim world is severely in jeopardy. These founded fears due to the climate of violence and trauma must be acknowledged. How can Christians assume they will find safety when they see terrorists behead Christians in the name of Islam? But these times of violence should not make us forget that, in fact, few Muslims are terrorists.

The majority of Muslims are like you and me. They love their children, visit the sick, argue with family members, and reconcile with them. Christian author Mike Kuhn, who lived for many years in the Middle East, observed, "The primary concerns of most Muslims are similar to ours—raising their children, providing for their children's education, saving for that new car or outfit."[40] Unfortunately, these ordinary Muslims are often mistaken for other members of their community who perpetrate violent acts in the name of Islam. Our task as Christians is to note the differences between individuals. Many condemn violence and can serve as a secure base. For example, Muslims launched the campaign "Not in my Name" after the gruesome attack on Christians by ISIS. Likewise, after the 9/11 attacks in the United States, the *New York Times* published a list of scholars and religious leaders condemning that attack. Women living under Muslim laws joined the campaign: "Bring back the Abducted Girls of Chibok." The Organization of Islamic Cooperation condemned ISIS's threats against and forced displacement of Christians in Iraq. All of these examples show that Muslims are as concerned as non-Muslims about the violence perpetrated by radicals against others.

Conclusion

In healthy attachments, emotional states vary greatly. Periods of tranquility and peace facilitate social activities. Moments of joy and delight help form, grow, and repair the bonds. But it would be detrimental to health to stay in a constant adrenaline high and exuberant joy. Have you been around people

---

40. Mike Kuhn, *Fresh Vision for the Muslim World: An Incarnational Alternative* (Colorado Springs: Biblica Publishing, 2009), 187.

who are always laughing, smiling, or giggling? Their positive energy can wear you out. Likewise, periods of negative emotions need to be regulated. From shame states, the dyad must return to joy and then regain relational peace and tranquility. In his discussion of human encounter, Karl Barth comes surprisingly close to the description given by attachment theory. Angella Son observes that Barth assesses "human beings as 'being in encounter,'" and that he characterizes encounter as "mutuality in looking, speaking, hearing and rendering help . . . [and] subject to an overarching and enveloping principle of joy."[41] She concludes, "To Barth, mutuality is thus the basic form of the human exchanges while joy becomes the ever far reaching life blood in all exchanges of human beings in mutuality."[42]

In chapter 1, we discovered how God's joy is infectious. It is unique in many ways, but diffused in the fabric of human relations. Chapter 2 has offered insight from scientific research on human relations. When comparing the findings of these two fields, missiology and neuroscience, we find a number of similarities between the God-human interaction and the caregiver-child interaction.

First, joy is abundant in the formation and the repair of relational bonds in both cases. Finding delight in Muslims in order to connect with them seems to parallel God's delight in his creatures. Joy is a hallmark of attachment. It should be a mark of our engagement with Muslims.

Second, chapter 1 referred to the radiating face of God (Num. 6:22–27) as a metaphor of God's mission in the world. Likewise, in early childhood, the caregiver's radiating face communicates to the child that human relationships can be pleasurable and delightful. This joy strengthens the relational bond between caregiver and child. In both cases, this kind of caregiving joy seems to transform those who do not yet have the potential to experience it. As children need an adult brain to regulate and amplify their joy, we need God's joy, resonating in us, to experience greater levels of his joy. As disciples of Christ and recipients of his joy, we should bring joy to Muslims, even if they do not yet reciprocate.

Third, joy is not the sole component of relationship building. We discovered how in the Bible, suffering sometimes coexists with joy. Likewise, in human attachment, joy is not distant from relational shame, which occurs in stressful times. Thus, what is important is not that one has continuous joy but rather that joy can return after relational stress, fear, or shame. Shame experiences

41. Angella Son, "Agents of Joy as a New Image of Pastoral Care," *Journal of Pastoral Theology* 18, no. 1 (2008): 62, 64.

42. Ibid., 62. See also Karl Barth, *Church Dogmatics*, vol. 3, part 2 (Edinburgh: T&T Clark, 1960).

are inevitable in our relationships with Muslims; what matters is that they can be followed by joy.

This brief discussion on attachment should encourage us to develop healthier bonds with Muslims. We now have not only the resources of attachment theory but also those provided by divine joy, which uniquely flows from God and invites us to turn our faces toward Muslims and bless them with shalom (peace). As we experience joy, shame, and various other attachment emotions with them, our mutual attachment will grow, our witness will be joyful, and we will live more peacefully together.

For Discussion

1. Identify Muslims in your social network.
2. Describe experiences of joy that you have had while interacting with Muslims.
3. Describe experiences of shame that you have had while interacting with Muslims.

3

Connecting with iMuslims

Imagine you are in Jerusalem on the first Easter morning, joining women who are walking before sunrise toward Jesus's tomb, carrying the spices they had prepared. You arrive and find the tomb empty. Before running back to your community, you text your friends, even tweet the news. The video of the empty tomb goes viral, despite censorship by local authorities. The news is retweeted thousands of times. Then after you have met Jesus and touched his *real-life* body, you send more tweets. These are filled with joy; messages go out on Instagram. "Is that really Jesus of Nazareth? Who is the woman on the left?" In a second, pings resound on smartphones around the world. News of the resurrection reaches your Muslim friends via the hashtag #JoytotheWorld!

Cyberspace is the first environment I chose for investigating joyful witness in ordinary encounters with Muslims. The reason for my choice is simple. Social media have revolutionized the way Muslims interact with each other and the rest of the world. In the past, Christians often found it difficult to meet with Muslims, especially in traditional and conservative regions, where, despite legendary rules of hospitality, foreigners were not always invited into the inner circles of Muslim society, and sex segregation often rendered visits of foreigners to Muslim homes impossible. Later, a modern lifestyle offered fresh opportunities for relationship building in many of these settings, but it is the digital revolution that opened up spaces of encounter that have revolutionized Muslim-Christian relations. Unfortunately, many Christians are still lagging behind in using this formidable mode of communication. It is therefore essential to discuss its use with respect to joyful witness among Muslims.

We can connect with Muslims and engage with Islam through social media in various ways; to do so, we need to understand how the internet shapes new forms of community in Muslim contexts. Since social media may be the first gate through which we engage with the Muslim world, we also need to understand how to respond to the challenges presented by these new forms of communication.

Digital Islam

We live in a global village in which cybercommunication has erased our borders. As Islamicist Barbara Stowasser has written, in the virtual world, "geographical distance has ceased to matter."[1] Muslims and Christians are closer to each other than ever before. I remember exploring Islamic chat rooms on the eve of social media, wondering what Islam had to say about these new forms of communication. Hosts of Muslims were asking their religious leaders whether the internet was lawful or prohibited. Of course, the amusing thing was that they raised these questions using the very same media that they had doubts about. Although some conservative clerics banned the use of social media, most just saw in them a new form of social networking with dangers and opportunities similar to those presented by other media. Today the number of those questions has considerably decreased. It has become normal for Muslims to use the internet. They have gotten used to the entire panoply of digital technologies.

Islam has adapted well to the World Wide Web, which provides unlimited online resources to its devotees. Now one can perform a virtual pilgrimage to Mecca.[2] Religious legal opinions can be accessed online through *dial-a-fatwa* features.[3] According to anthropologist and media scholar Jon W. Anderson, "Islam is represented on-line in a mélange of wire-service news copy, transcribed sermons, scanned texts of the Qur'an and *hadith* collections, advice

1. Barbara Stowasser, "Old Shaykhs, Young Women, and the Internet: The Rewriting of Women's Political Rights in Islam," *The Muslim World* 91, nos. 1–2 (2001): 99.

2. Miriam Cooke and Bruce B. Lawrence write, "Consider the pious Muslim who would like to make the annual pilgrimage to Mecca but does not yet have the time or the money. She may have to content herself with a virtual Hajj for the time being. She can perform the Hajj today via the World Wide Web in a way unimaginable even only twenty years ago" (*Muslim Networks from Hajj to Hip Hop* [Chapel Hill: University of North Carolina Press, 2005], Kindle edition, 20). For a virtual journey to Mecca, see "Mecca 3D: An Interactive Journey to Islam," http://mecca3d.net.

3. "There are e-fatwas being dispensed over the Internet and television programs that have a dial-a-fatwa feature. Some fatwas completely contradict each other, and consumers can literally shop for fatwas that suit their needs." Ranya Tabari Idliby, *Burqas, Baseball, and Apple Pie: Being Muslim in America* (New York: St. Martin's Press, 2014), 91.

and self-help information ranging from where to find *halal* butchers and mosques to matrimonials and cheap travel to prayer-timers and Islamic educational materials."[4] There is such a wealth of online resources that even Muslims sometimes have a hard time finding their way in this maze of information.

Cyberspace certainly provides greater access to Islamic knowledge for Muslims. Gary Bunt, a scholar of online Islam, explains, "As the digital divide is reduced, more people have access through portable devices, the threading of Islamic digital discourse into the wider fabric of Muslim society continues."[5] A good illustration of this is given by a study conducted on a new Islamic website for Chinese Muslims called "The Light of Islam." Chinese sociologist Wai-Yip Ho writes, "'The Light of Islam' has filled the void in establishing its authority in giving guidance and electronic fatwah (religious opinion) for many migrant Muslim workers moving from inland rural to urban coastal China."[6] Like Christians who use the internet for devotions, discipleship, community building, and biblical studies, Muslims become more knowledgeable and devoted through Islamic information they find on the World Wide Web.

But cyberspace also transforms Islam. Amir Ahmad Nasr,[7] a Muslim blogger and author whose understanding of Islam has moved away from conservatism through the blogosphere, organized a conference on new media in which he announced that "for over a thousand years, Islamic scholars have generally maintained significant control over the production, interpretation, and dissemination of Islamic texts and content to Muslim masses throughout the world, [but] now, for the first time ever in human history, that is beginning to radically change. New media—Facebook, WordPress, Twitter, YouTube, and many more online tools—have made publishing and the sharing of content easy and democratized."[8] The internet generates new interpreters of Islam[9] and provides "a more nuanced diversity of views, settings, projects, and expressions of Islam today."[10] Some of these interpretations "significantly

4. Jon W. Anderson, "The Internet and Islam's New Interpreters," in *New Media in the Muslim World: The Emerging Public Sphere*, ed. Dale F. Eickelman and Jon W. Anderson, 2nd ed. (Bloomington: Indiana University Press, 2003), 48.

5. Gary R. Bunt, "Studying Muslims and Cyberspace," in *Studying Islam in Practice*, ed. Gabriele Marranci (New York: Routledge, 2014), Kindle edition, location 4527.

6. Wai-Yip Ho, *Islam and China's Hong Kong: Ethnic Identity, Muslim Networks and the New Silk Road* (New York: Routledge, 2013), Kindle edition, location 2634–37.

7. See Amir Ahmad Nasr, *My Isl@m: How Fundamentalism Stole My Mind—and Doubt Freed My Soul* (New York: St. Martin's Press, 2013).

8. "Islam in the Age of New Media," Freedom House website, https://freedomhouse.org/event/islam-age-new-media.

9. Anderson, "Internet and Islam's New Interpreters," 48.

10. Ibid., 57.

Radio Broadcast in the Muslim World

Shin Sook Kim, Egyptian Theological Seminary and Spiritual Center for Training and Studies

In 1985 I began to work in partnership with an Egyptian pastor to reach out to Muslims through a radio broadcasting program. The program aired in the Middle East and the North African region, with the main offices stationed in Monte Carlo and Cyprus. In Egypt, in cooperation with the radio broadcast program in Monte Carlo, Rev. Reda Adly answered listeners' questions regarding Christianity and prepared Bible studies and sermons for the program. He was the pastor of Azbakia Evangelical Church, in Azbakia, Egypt.

Through the broadcast, some Muslims started to listen to the gospel and became interested in the Bible. They sent letters to the broadcast with their questions about the gospel. In Egypt, Rev. Reda Adly and I responded. When an individual wanted to know about the gospel, we took a three-step approach, consisting of sending three pamphlets. The first answered the question, "What is the Bible?" The second, "Who is God?" The third, "Who is Jesus?" Some individuals accepted Christ through the pamphlets. After a new convert was baptized, our teams would get together to pray for the new believer. These were exciting and joy-filled moments.

At the same time, the radio ministry also taught us how difficult it was to save one soul. Sometimes we were discouraged and wanted to give up when the individual was not serious about his or her spiritual growth or was

challenge the traditional religious authority of the Muslim intellectuals."[11] The internet also stimulates the sharing of "local versions of Islam."[12] As a result, the Islamic scholarly community has been transformed. Christians, similarly, used to learn about Islam through conventional interpretation given by authoritative schools of Islam, but now a whole new pool of knowledge is offered to them through the internet, with many more voices participating in theological debates. The task of getting acquainted with this faith looks daunting, but also promising, as more and more Muslims participate in the conversation about their faith.

In light of all these changes it may take a little more effort to figure out the nature of Islam in the twenty-first century. Less linear thinkers would

11. Wai-Yip Ho, *Islam and China's Hong Kong*, location 2629–32.
12. Cooke and Lawrence, *Muslim Networks*, 24.

forced to leave family or hometown due to his or her beliefs. For those who had to sacrifice their relationship with family and homeland due to their faith, we felt even more responsible to support and encourage them financially, spiritually, and emotionally. In some situations, I had to become a parent-like figure to individuals who had to be sent out of Egypt for safety due to their choice to become a Christian. Despite the difficulties of the ministry, I was happy to participate and felt God's faithfulness through all the encounters.

Over the years, I have continued to encounter and minister to Muslims in contexts outside of the radio broadcast programs. Through these encounters, I have felt and continue to feel God's love, and I feel thankful for the opportunity to serve his kingdom by reaching the Muslim community. One convert who came to Christ through me is Matthew, to whom I have become a mother. As a student of Islamic studies and Arabic language at Cairo University, he began to wonder who Jesus was and why the Bible was considered corrupt. He had many questions about the Bible and Christians in general. His questions eventually led him to us, and we began to study the Bible with him and addressed his questions about Christianity. Through God's blessing, Matthew came to accept Christ. His conversion came at the price of losing his family and country, but he found a new family in Christ and is actively involved in Muslim ministry away from home. He has become a blessing in my life as I have become a mother in faith for him. It is through these joyful instances of witness and ordinary encounters that we see God's meticulous hand at work.

say that we should just go with the flow and interpret Islam as it pops up on the net, in manifold expressions that are sometimes culturally bound. Bunt talks about the development of a kind of Cyber-Islamic environment (CIE).[13] Studying Islam may include identifying how these various zones shape the identity of contemporary Muslims. In the meantime, one may have to be cautious in trying to draw definite conclusions on the nature of the Islam found on the web. We have to take this medium for what it is. John

13. "Cyber-Islamic environment" is another term that I borrow from Gary R. Bunt in *iMuslims: Rewiring the House of Islam* (Chapel Hill: University of North Carolina Press, 2009). He defines CIE as follows: "'Cyber-Islamic Environment' acknowledges diversity among and within different zones in cyberspace that represent varied Muslim worldviews within the House of Islam, all of which present a reference point of identity with a conceptualization of Islam" (1).

Edmiston, president of the Asian Internet Bible Institute, explains that "the web surfer is a self-directed seeker driven by curiosity traveling through a community of hyper-links."[14] Following his description, I would say that the task of Christians is to be able to identify links and nodes that Muslims use to connect with others and make sense of who they are as Muslims. Christians in search of the nature of contemporary Islam must find the sites with the most likes and reads by Muslims to understand whom people follow and what blogs they subscribe to. Coincidentally, an analysis of the web context supports what many anthropologists have observed: there is not one Islam but many Islams, or a multiplicity of faith expressions within Muslim societies.[15] Through surfing cyberspace, Christians will encounter expressions of Islam that reflect the concerns and needs of the contemporary Muslim communities.

But Muslims do not access the World Wide Web only to gain more Islamic knowledge and practice. They also use it to bring about sociopolitical change and transformation. During the Green Revolution in Iran or the Arab Spring in North Africa, "Facebook, YouTube, and Twitter were three significant channels through which a variety of activists and organizations mobilized."[16] Bunt shows that "in Syria, since 2011, the events surrounding the battle between the Assad regime and 'revolutionary' forces has [sic] played out through Facebook, YouTube, Twitter, and other channels. All sides have used the media to make statements."[17] Radical Islamic groups may also use media to bring change. Anderson highlights "websites representing positions of the FIS (Islamic Salvation Front) in Algeria and the Movement for Islamic Reform (MIRA) in Saudi Arabia (which aimed at the Saudi government), both based overseas and both of which moved onto the Internet from using fax machines and other small media to spread their messages."[18] Wai-Yip Ho adds that "one of the most worrying trends is that extremist Muslims are

---

14. John Edmiston, "Missions in Cyberspace: The Strategic Front-Line Use of the Internet in Missions," *International Journal of Frontier Missions* 19, no. 1 (Spring 2002): 13–14.

15. "The survey findings also show that internet use has relatively little influence on Muslims' views of Islam's teachings. Holding other factors constant, Muslims who use the internet are about as likely as those who do not use it to say that Islam is the only path to heaven (rather than saying that many faiths can lead to eternal salvation). Internet users and non-users also are about equally inclined to say that Islam has only one true interpretation." Neha Sahgal, "Among Muslims, Internet Use Goes Hand-in-Hand with More Open Views toward Western Culture," Pew Research Center, May 31, 2013, http://www.pewforum.org/2013/05/31/among -muslims-internet-use-goes-hand-in-hand-with-more-open-views-toward-western-culture/.

16. Bunt, "Studying Muslims and Cyberspace," location 4414.

17. Ibid., location 4520.

18. Jon W. Anderson, "Wiring Up: The Internet Difference for Muslim Networks," in Cooke and Lawrence, *Muslim Networks*, 258.

'misusing' the Internet for the purpose of establishing a terrorist network and inspiration for religious radicalization."[19] Thus social media are playing an important role in influencing Muslim societies today for the best or for the worse. Given that the digital age offers new ways of influencing people and societies, it is worth asking how much the gospel traveling through social media can likewise bring change in people's lives for the good of Muslim societies. Today people share not only the physical world but also a virtual world. I often wonder how much Christians are willing to inhabit that latter world, which also needs the gospel of joy.

Cultural transformation is another important outcome of cyberspace revolution. Corri B. Zoli reports on a campaign on social networking sites regarding the ban on women drivers in Saudi Arabia. Areej Khan, who created the site, wrote, "*We the Women* aims to start a conversation about it. This is a place where you can express yourself freely on the issue. Let's hit the wall and the discussion boards."[20] Zoli underlines that "it is unclear whether this campaign has shifted the discourse on Saudi women driving or not, though signs are pointing to softening official positions."[21] But she also adds, "The important observation for this argument is the recourse to and resourcefulness of Muslims using web technologies to promote and engage transnational public debate, to persuade and to garner support in the public sphere."[22] Many other internet campaigns that are under way may produce long-lasting effects on Muslim cultures. Since virtual spaces can generate cultural transformations, it is valid to ask whether the Christian presence offers values that truly reflect the heart of God. I have talked to too many Muslims who are appalled by family and social practices circulated on the internet that they assume are shaped by Christianized countries.

However, several factors still prevent Muslims from having access to this form of social media (communication). First, in certain regions of the Muslim world, governments censor electronic communication. They have done so several times during recent political events in Arab countries.[23] Second, Muslims may sometimes be afraid to visit certain Christian sites for fear of censorship: they worry that state authorities, hostile to Christianity, may monitor what they are doing and penalize them. Third, language can also be a problem.

---

19. Wai-Yip Ho, *Islam and China's Hong Kong*, location 2640–42.

20. Quoted in Corri B. Zoli, "The Multicultural *Ummah*," in *The Sociology of Islam: Secularism, Economy and Politics*, ed. Tugrul Keskin (Reading, UK: Ithaca Press, 2011), 139.

21. Ibid.

22. Ibid.

23. Rasha A. Abdulla, *The Internet in the Arab World: Egypt and Beyond* (New York: Peter Lang International Academic Publishers, 2007).

Google Translate is not sophisticated enough yet to enable users to carry on meaningful interlinguistic conversations on faith matters. Finally, in certain parts of the Muslim world, few people have access to the internet. Despite the growing presence of "iMuslims,"[24] a recent report issued by the Pew Research Center shows that "globally, internet access varies widely." More specifically, when a survey looked at internet users in thirty-nine Muslim countries across the Middle East, Europe, Asia, and Africa, it found that "internet use varies widely across the countries surveyed, ranging from just 2% of Muslims in Afghanistan to a majority (59%) in Kosovo." Further examples reveal that in "Lebanon, 83% may use internet daily,"[25] whereas in Bangladesh, "11% of Bangladeshis either say they access the internet at least occasionally or own a smartphone."[26] Variations can also be due to age. While 42% of the total population of Tunisia uses the internet, the percentage reaches 66% with Tunisians between the ages of 18 and 34. In Malaysia 55% of the total population uses the internet, with 81% of Malaysians between the ages of 18 and 34.[27] Of course, we can anticipate that these figures will rise in the future when technology becomes more accessible and less costly. In view of these new opportunities, how are we Christians reflecting on, training for, and engaging in this blossoming sphere of interchange? Are we aware that young people inhabit the virtual world in growing numbers and are eager to connect with the world?

We have seen how accessibility and connectivity with Islam have grown exponentially in Muslim communities. Greater democratization of knowledge has led Muslims to investigate both their tradition and other faith traditions. When they do so, "individual authority is enhanced as the individual is given more options for the exchange of information and more ways to reach wide audiences and to elicit trust."[28] But how does digital Islam affect Christians who want to engage in joyful witness? Can digital Islam better help them understand Muslim traditions? Yes, they can, but they need to prepare themselves for potential obstacles that may prevent them from developing a true picture of Islam today. For example, until now, leading academic research in the new field of digital Islam has been mostly in the West, where Islam is a minority

---

24. I borrow the term "iMuslims" from Gary Bunt, media scholar, who proposes a list of thirteen models of iMuslims in his book *iMuslims*, 280.

25. "Though these rates are relatively high, they lag behind the US, where 87% have online access." Pew Research Center, *Internet Seen as Positive Influence on Education but Negative on Morality in Emerging and Developing Nations*, March 19, 2015, http://www.pewglobal.org/files /2015/03/Pew-Research-Center-Technology-Report-FINAL-March-19-20151.pdf, 13 and 21.

26. Ibid., 13.

27. Ibid., 14.

28. Cooke and Lawrence, *Muslim Networks*, 24.

religion.[29] These scholars' perspectives are limited by their geographic and cultural location, and will be the perspectives of readers who rely on their research. However, this is gradually changing. More and more scholars besides Wai-Yip Ho want to understand Islam and Muslim societies in studying their presence on the web.[30]

The overwhelming amount of information online, too, makes it very difficult for those who don't know anything about Islam to select the best information. By just googling the word "Islam" this morning, I came up with 426 million links. Browsing the web without recognizing which nodes and links lead to better knowledge can actually be quite counterproductive. If I were not a scholar of Islam, I would have no idea how to make sense of all the resources available online. As I now daily surf the web for information on Islam, I have learned to bookmark not only scholarly sites but also sites linked with knowledgeable and influential people, to seek online peer-reviews, to listen to conversations among Muslims, and to highlight recurring questions Muslims are asking.

Old frameworks are sometimes shattered when we approach Islam in cyberspace. All at once the infinite worlds of Islam pop up on computer screens. Internet surfers who understand these worlds only poorly should both approach this information with a listening attitude—required of all who want to learn—and interact with it critically, especially when not knowing the assumptions, motivations, and credentials of the web authors.

Having acknowledged the challenges one faces when trying to learn about Islam through the internet, I must admit that the internet has become a great resource for Christians who want to engage with Islam, giving them access to information that was unavailable before. Christians can learn much if they really want to, as long as they have good mentors or personal teachers, or take any of the online classes in Islamic studies offered by a growing number of academic institutions and seminaries. Online courses have opened up amazing ways to connect with students from all around the world, who can richly contribute to the knowledge of their fellow class members as they share from their own contexts.

---

29. Wai-Yip Ho, "Islam, China and the Internet: Negotiating Residual Cyberspace between Hegemonic Patriotism and Connectivity to the *Ummah*," *Journal of Muslim Minority Affairs* 30, no. 1 (2010): 63–79.

30. See, e.g., Heidi A. Campbell, ed., *Digital Religion: Understanding Religious Practice in New Media Worlds* (New York: Routledge, 2013); as well as the web resources, "Virtually Islam: Research and News about Islam and the Internet" at http://www.virtuallyislamic.com; "Research on Middle East, Islam and Digital Media" at http://www.digitalislam.eu; "Online Heidelberg Journal of Religions on the Internet" at http://heiup.uni-heidelberg.de/journals/index.php/religions/.

Interconnected World

Why don't Christians connect more frequently with Muslims? It is so much easier nowadays to make connections. That is what my technology-savvy friends keep telling me. For proof, they show me the plethora of Muslim friends on their Facebook pages. They tweet about current events involving the Muslim world. They share resources on Muslim-Christian relations through YouTube and post pictures of meetings with Muslims on Instagram. One mouse click is sufficient to connect them with the worldwide digital community of iMuslims.

Recently, Amir Ahmad Nasr, the Muslim blogger mentioned above, organized a conference called "The Future of Islam in the Age of New Media," in which each of sixty speakers was given sixty seconds to speak.[31] One of the speakers, Javed Ali, stated, "New generations speak new languages. They no longer just chat; they g-chat, they ping, they text, they pdm, they tweet, they re-tweet, they blog, they upload, they download, they poke. Likewise, Islam speaks a new language. Islam does not speak, Muslims do."[32] Muslim youth use a new language, and "have the microphone for the first time," he added. Have we as Christians become familiar with these new forms of communication with Muslims? I had a conversation with a Muslim teenager recently who asked me: How was life before smartphones? She could not even imagine what this kind of pre–social media era looked like. But when I talk to my missionary friends, I sometimes have the reverse question. They ask what social media look like. They don't know how to communicate with the Muslim cybergeneration. Hence my questions: Are we g-chatting, pinging, texting, tweeting, blogging with Muslims? If we don't adopt these new modes of communication, how will we ever connect with the new generations in Muslim societies?

People rely more and more on social media to nurture their relationships in their social networks. According to a new study from the Pew Research Center, "92% of teens report going online daily—including 24% who say they go online 'almost constantly.'" Although this study only looked at youth in America and not specifically Muslims, it is still relevant as it identifies a trend toward greater use of social media.[33] If we devote so much time and energy to online activities, how much do we spend connecting with iMuslims? Can

31. http://www.amirahmadnasr.com/islamnewmedia/.
32. Ibid.
33. Pew Research Center, *Teens, Social Media & Technology Overview 2015: Smartphones Facilitate Shifts in Communication Landscape for Teens*, April 9, 2015, http://www.pewinternet.org/files/2015/04/PI_TeensandTech_Update2015_040915.pdf, p. 2.

we, as Christians who want to witness to our Muslim friends, intentionally evaluate the time we devote to Muslims when online?

One of the most popular ways to connect with people today is Facebook. According to the study just cited, 71% of all teens in the United States say they use Facebook.[34] The same study reveals that "among Facebook-using teens, the typical teen has 145 Facebook friends."[35] If I were to put this question to Christian teenagers, I wonder what percentage of these 145 friends would be Muslims? Can it be possible to envision that hyper-connectivity could generate more contacts with Muslims? Facebook is not only popular in the United States, since, "Among internet users in the emerging and developing countries surveyed [for a Pew Research Center report], a median of 82% use their internet connections to access social networking sites, such as Facebook, Twitter and other country-specific platforms."[36]

But Christians sometimes hesitate to invite Muslim friends to their Facebook pages. Christians raise many concerned questions about this type of engagement, such as the following: Should I share with them everything I share with my non-Muslim Facebook friends? Even if I am sensitive to their faith, what if they are shocked by conversations held by my other friends? What if the dress code on my Facebook pictures appears offensive to them? What if I cannot answer their questions about my faith? Although all these questions may seem valid, they need not prevent us from availing ourselves of the many new ways cyberspace offers for imagining Christian presence in Muslim contexts. Why not make our Facebook pages Muslim friendly?

Being an authentic believer while inviting people from other faiths is something one learns over time. It means adopting attitudes and behaviors similar to those Jesus practiced when he met the Samaritans or the Romans. It includes displaying interfaith civility. If you invite Muslim friends to your Facebook page, they will also become friends with the rest of your community and may for the first time be able to connect with Christians in a deeper way. Of course, some spaces on social media can be more private than others. Maybe Muslims you meet online will only gradually move into the inner circles of Facebook as trust builds over time. Social media may afford the first time when they are invited to share in the joys, pains, struggles, and religious journeys of Christians. Similarly, Christians will learn about the ordinary lives of Muslims who share their stories, post their pictures, and reflect on their spiritual journeys.

34. Ibid.
35. Ibid., 28.
36. Pew Research Center, *Internet Seen as Positive*, 25. In some countries, however, such as Japan, users prefer other platforms, with the same goal of connecting with others, but with specific features such as greater protection of anonymity, for example.

People often ask whether social media can foster genuine and strong relation-ships. I believe that "in real life" or "in the flesh" relations are still necessary to nurture healthy bonds. Many of my friends have both. Based on attachment theory, face-to-face encounters in a shared physical space are necessary for effective emotional resonance that allows two human persons to experience joy, shame, and the return to joy, as we saw in chapter 2. Nevertheless, social media can foster some level of bonding. They are no longer asynchronous and emotionless. They offer some multisensory experiences, such as visual and au-ditory communication through Instagram, Skype, or chat rooms, for example. These experiences include sharing emotions that are important for developing relationships. I have experienced such sharing through my connections with my Muslim friends in chat rooms or on Skype. There is growing evidence that forming online communities is possible, although they will never totally replace physical encounters. People who meet on the internet often also want to meet off-line. This is confirmed by Doug Lucas, president of the mission organization Team Expansion, who writes, "In seemingly every situation we are seeing, those who perhaps first met on the Internet are creating forums and opportunities that eventually result in face-to-face encounters."[37]

Cyberspace also opens up creative spaces of communication that did not exist before. I recently attended a Muslim gathering of several hundred people in a hotel ballroom. Attendees were for the most part from the Arabian pen-insula. The code of conduct was such that teenage males and females did not mingle. But while seated at tables with their parents they were frantically texting during dinner. I wondered if they were actually texting with the friends at the other side of the room. Social media seem to modify social connec-tions and relational codes. Interconnectedness is certainly changing the ways people communicate with each other, including in religious matters. Take, for example, the case of Muslims who can explore Christianity anonymously online, somewhat like Nicodemus, when he came to see Jesus by night to talk about important religious matters. As authors Mohammed el-Nawawy and Sahar Khamis noted, "Participation in the virtual *umma* can be 'identity-less,' allowing Muslims and non-Muslims to express their views without having to disclose who they are, or where they are coming from."[38]

However, with easier communication, new challenges arise. Without face-to-face connections or social references, how can we know the real identities of those with whom we interact online? How do they know our own identity? How

---

37. Doug Lucas, "The Internet: Tentmaker's Coffeeshop for the Nineties," *International Journal of Frontier Missions* 15, no. 1 (January–March 1998): 31.

38. Mohammed el-Nawawy and Sahar Khamis, *Islam Dot Com: Contemporary Islamic Discourses in Cyberspace* (New York: Palgrave Macmillan, 2009), 116.

can trust be built online? Is it possible to meet harmful people, even terrorists, while browsing social networks online? We hear stories of young people who were seduced into jihad through online terrorist websites. Unfortunately, in a time when jihadist groups, like many others, are using the web to disseminate their ideas, it is possible to inadvertently bump into their ideas online. However, it is also true that millions of Muslims have no desire to even think about causing harm to others and are themselves upset with what violent jihadists are doing today. Most Muslims condemn these practices.[39] Encounters on the internet that lead to harm do not necessarily come from Islam; they may come from non-Muslims. We must be attentive in every encounter.

Ignorance of Islamic tenets may also make Christians insecure as they relate with Muslims online. While in the past, only people with good knowledge of Islam dared to venture into Muslim environments to share the gospel, now anyone can preach freely to iMuslims, without having taken one course on Islam. This can eventually lead to virtual religious cacophony. And although the internet can make it easier to talk freely about contentious ideas, it can also become the vehicle of hateful language toward the religious other. Christian scholar of Islam Martin Whittingham observes that "the rise of the internet increases . . . potential understanding greatly; but it also greatly increases the capacity of believers on both sides to insult or alienate each other."[40] This anonymity that allows for greater freedom to verbally attack is one of the greatest challenges of Muslim-Christian relations on the web. It often undermines respectful interactions that can lead to constructive conversations on faith.

Finally, and not least, there are the boomerang and amplification effects. What is said on the web can have an unexpected and detrimental effect on Christians or Muslims locally and globally. There is ample evidence of the destructive effect of online chats when they are not undertaken with religious civility. On numerous occasions offensive messages or pictures about Islam posted on the internet have inflamed the world. For example, when the American pastor Terry Jones threatened to burn the Qur'an, there were numerous riots in other parts of the world.[41] This would never have happened

---

39. See, e.g., the November 2014 Vienna Declaration titled "United against Violence in the Name of Religion," signed by high-level leaders of major Islamic communities (http://www .kaiciid.org/publications-resources/united-against-violence-name-religion) or British imams condemning ISIS (https://www.youtube.com/watch?v=2Bd0Y6qWmlA).

40. Martin Whittingham, "Christian-Muslim Relations in Britain in Historical Context," in *Naivety and Hostility: Uncovering the Best Christian Responses to Islam in Britain*, ed. Steve Bell and Colin Chapman (Milton Keynes, UK: Authentic, 2011), Kindle edition, location 1246.

41. Paul Harris and Paul Gallagher, "Terry Jones Defiant Despite Murders in Afghanistan over Qur'an Burning," *The Guardian*, April 2, 2011, at http://www.theguardian.com/world/20 11/apr/02/pastor-terry-jones-burning-koran.

the same way a century ago, when news took so much longer to travel. Today, the reaction is immediate and can sometimes be amplified by the lack of interfaith sensitivity and by international conflicts.

I believe that online cross-cultural and interfaith connections require even greater skill than real-life connections. I am dreaming of required classes in intercultural and interfaith studies for all internet users (who would get their license to access the internet only after passing specific tests on culture). When a message is online, it can potentially be accessed by all cultures. This means cross-cultural communication is much more challenging for today's Christian missionaries than for those of the past; formerly, missionaries only had to acquire cross-cultural tools for communicating to one specific cultural context, but now, in crafting their message they must consider the many other internet users from around the world who might encounter the message. Recent research in Japan illustrates how culture shapes the way people surf the web. Gary Fujino, an evangelist and church planter, explains why Japanese social media users prefer local Japanese platforms to Facebook. Japanese sites, he claims, permit anonymity and privacy.[42] He also thinks that the Japanese do not use the internet to "friend" or "unfriend" people. To protect their identity, more than half of all Japanese respondents said that "*not one* of their acquaintances on social networks was a close friend."[43] What we learn from this research is that culture matters and the way people friend or unfriend on social media is also shaped by context.

Today, when a message is posted online, how can one be culturally and religiously sensitive to the entire planet? Impossible! There is no international language that takes into account all religious and cultural sensibilities. Consequently, global conversations are deemed to be at times very conflicting. Hence, the world needs all internet users to conduct themselves online with civility and joy. Specifically, we Christians need to learn new ways to engage with Muslims, and this means we need new rules and new ethics on social media.

Good News on Cyberspace

Muslims and Christians have engaged in theological conversations since Muhammad's lifetime. These conversations have been held in all kinds of

---

42. Gary Fujino, "'Glocal' Japanese Self-Identity: A Missiological Perspective on Paradigmatic Shifts in Urban Tokyo," *International Journal of Frontier Missiology* 27, no. 4 (Winter 2010): 176.

43. Ibid. Here Gary Fujino quotes a 2010 Microsoft survey.

Joyful Witness: A Perspective from Iran

Rev. Sasan Tavassoli, Iranian missionary

We are experiencing some of the most severe persecutions of Christians in the modern history of Iran. We are also experiencing some of the most joyful and exciting days of explosive growth of the church in the history of our country!

In the last few years all Persian-speaking Protestant churches in Iran have been closed down, house-church gatherings are illegal, and a threat to the national security made conversion out of Islam a criminal offense. Christians were arrested and imprisoned. Prominent Iranian pastors were forced to leave the country. In the midst of all of this, we are also noticing that Iran is experiencing the fastest growth of the gospel among Muslims anywhere in the world!

According to a recent finding by Operation World, the house-church movement in Iran is the fastest-growing evangelical church in the world, at a current annual growth rate of 19.6 percent!* Iranians have become some of the most open people groups to the gospel. In this context, one of the most significant tools in fueling the growth of the church is satellite TV.

Although satellite dishes are illegal in Iran, it is estimated that nearly forty million Iranians have satellite TV! For the first time in history, millions of Muslims can now be in the safety of their homes and watch Christian programming. These programs, produced by Iranian Christians outside of Iran and aired in the country through a number of satellite networks, include not only many programs presenting simple and direct presentations of the gospel but also testimonies of conversions, stories of healing and freedom in Christ (especially freedom from addiction, which is a major epidemic in Iran), Iranian worship songs, live programs answering the viewers' questions and praying for their specific needs, and teachings on relationships, marriage, and spiritual growth. Many Iranian Muslims also watch these programs since they find them helpful in dealing with the practical challenges of life and interpersonal relationships in the modern world. Satellite TV has truly become a great platform in engaging a "closed" Muslim country in a positive and constructive way.

*Operation World, "Evangelical Growth," http://www.operationworld.org/hidden /evangelical-growth.

settings: caliphs' courts, divinity schools,[44] mosques, churches, and private homes. For fourteen centuries, these conversations were interrupted only by wars and geographical distance. Today, there are even fewer excuses for failing to talk with each other since social media can more easily bridge conflict and remoteness.

There is only anecdotal research on how Christians interact with Muslims in cyberspace. However, one point is clear: Cyberspace is a unique environment that has its own rules and codes of communication.[45] The internet offers new ways for the gospel to access places it has never reached before. Muslims and Christians can relate to each other free from the limitations formerly imposed by visa denials, limited access to homes, or warring countries. I have heard of online chats between Christian women in Europe and Muslim women in Saudi Arabia. Today, Muslims can read the Bible online, even in places where they cannot find it in their local bookstores.[46] Just as, in the early church, brand-new road systems built by the Romans allowed for easier circulation of evangelists and apostles, so also we should look at the internet as a communication system that transforms our witness among Muslims in a good way. I am all for global digital fibers radiating with divine joy.

The internet also allows "people more freedom of religious choice than ever before."[47] Scholars have noticed that "cultural gatekeepers guarding against the infiltration of foreign and alien values and traditions are by definition insular, xenophobic, and limited. Fortunately, in the age of the Internet, social media, and global reach, they are also on the wrong side of history."[48] It is evident that the internet democratizes religious knowledge. I have had several conversations with Christian organizations that are doing *e-Vangelism*. They all indicate that the digital age has brought extraordinary growth in the number of Muslims investigating Christian websites, chatting with Christians online, and joining virtual communities of faith. Elam, a Christian Ministry reaching out to Iranians, writes on its website: "In 2013, over 90,000 people used Elam's Persian Christian website, Kalameh.com, where they had access

44. Yale Divinity School in New Haven, Connecticut, hosted a Muslim-Christian dialogue which gathered 150 Muslim and Christian leaders in July 2008, http://www.acommonword.com /yale-to-host-interfaith-meeting/.

45. In *New Media in the Muslim World*, Eickelman and Anderson say that those who constructed the internet "built into it open access, flattened hierarchies, freedom of information, and more subtly, notions of transient, purposive connections among people and between pieces of information" (48).

46. As long as they feel secure reading it.

47. Tim Green, "Conversion from Islam to Christianity in Britain," in Bell and Chapman, *Between Naivety and Hostility*, location 1540.

48. Idliby, *Burqas, Baseball, and Apple Pie*, 205.

to 1,000 articles, videos and audio resources to grow in faith."[49] This same ministry developed digital Bibles and developed applications for computers and mobile devices.[50] So popular is the exploration of faith online that the Christian organization visionSynergy has been involved in an internet evangelism network of over two hundred organizations "connecting those using the internet to share the Gospel with Muslims using the Web, chat rooms, SMS, VOIP and other new media expressions, as well as connecting traditional broadcast channels with new media."[51] VisionSynergy writes that "some 6–10 million Muslims monthly visit evangelistic websites run by members of this network."[52]

But sharing the gospel in cyberspace may require a paradigm shift with respect to what online communication is. This, of course, is not new. Throughout history, Christians have adopted new forms of communication that allowed them to share the gospel in more effective ways. *E-Vangelism* is a contemporary example of such a makeover. One may think that, as the Christian Broadcasting Network (CBN) puts it, "The Internet is just one more tool that many ministries are using to reach the world for Christ."[53] But although the CBN welcomes internet evangelism as "casting a new kind of net," I think that this new medium also requires a profound reflection on how the information is contextualized for the web. For example, witness now takes the form of "producing a buzz" about the gospel to Muslims, just like the scenario I shared in the introduction to this chapter. Has this already happened? How many videos presenting Jesus to Muslims have you watched going viral? I have yet to see millions of "likes" for Christian websites reaching iMuslims.

One of the best examples has been offered by two friends, one a Muslim (named Sondos) and the other a Christian (named Michal). They have started a blog together titled *Miss Understanding: Two Faiths. One Friendship*. This blog is clearly defined as "a space where Michal and Sondos will post their reflections—independently and jointly—on what it means to be a practicing Christian and practicing Muslim while building a foundation of mutual respect and understanding."[54] It is obvious that dialogue in this

49. Elam, "Elam's Mission," https://www.elam.com/page/elams-mission.

50. A website for each of the TV programs also enables follow-up and allows interested viewers to learn more. Elam also has a team working daily on internet evangelism and discipleship. They are online live for six hours a day for Bible teaching, worship, and fellowship.

51. VisionSynergy home page, http://visionsynergy.net/digital-ministries/.

52. Ibid.

53. CBN, "Internet Evangelism: Casting a New Kind of Net," http://www1.cbn.com/church andministry/internet-evangelism-casting-a-new-kind-of-net.

54. "Our Story," *Miss Understanding: Two Faiths. One Friendship* (blog), http://www.miss understanding.co/?page_id=190.

case flows from a close relationship in which both authors enjoy each other. As I was looking for the joy factor on this blog, I noticed it at several places both in Michal's and Sondos's postings. For example, after Michal introduced Sondos to a group of Christian students, the latter wrote, "I felt so happy and at peace."[55] To books and oral presentations, interfaith blogs add the dimension of spontaneity and dialogue in real-life situations. They can address current events in real time or include links for questions that make the dialogue more interactive. In a sense it is a dialogue between lives rather than just between ideas.

Although the World Wide Web has contributed considerably to joyful Christian witness, the models of approach have not drastically changed. The conventional way to define models of witness in an interfaith context also applies here, and is worth discussing briefly in order to underline the strengths and weaknesses of those models.

One model is the polemical, according to which the person bearing witness presents a "confrontational argument challenging a particular position."[56] Online polemical videos have proliferated tremendously, especially on YouTube. Though popular, and though attested in some biblical texts, this approach must be viewed as critically as any other. I have observed that in times of sociopolitical conflict between Muslims and Christians, the polemical approach often further escalates conflict without opening up spaces where the religious others can actively and peacefully listen to each other's arguments. Religious reasoning gets overrun with hostile emotions. The atmosphere becomes offensive or defensive, precluding the tranquility needed for reflection on serious matters regarding life and eternity. To see how defensive people become when their faith is attacked, it will often suffice to read the comments viewers write under polemical blogs. Interestingly, Jesus seems much more confrontational in his interactions with people from his own religious group than with people from out-groups, such as Samaritans or Romans who have never heard the gospel. Thus, with the overload of hateful speech on Islam on the internet, one may wonder to what extent a polemical approach truly opens the door to the gospel, especially if it targets religious groups that are already fairly conflicted about Christianity. Would it be possible to challenge theological arguments of Islam without being confrontational? At least, in the midst of confrontational argument, can a Christian express the divine and human joy that we learned about in earlier chapters?

55. "About Sondos," website of Miss Understanding, http://www.missunderstanding.co /?page_id=41.

56. Donald K. McKim, "Polemic," in *Westminster Dictionary of Theological Terms* (Louisville: Westminster John Knox), 211. The word "polemic" derives from the Greek word *polemos* (war).

Cyberspace also hosts a growing number of blogs on Christian apologet-ics. The apologetic approach has been defined as "the endeavor to provide a reasoned account of the grounds for believing in the Christian faith."[57] Blogs or websites taking this approach may provide valuable information on the defense of Christian faith, but it is not always clear that they take into account the centuries of research both on Christian and on Muslim theologies. Fur-thermore, apologetic websites often consist of endless webpages with complex arguments, set in extra-small script, that average internet users (unless they conduct academic research) may not feel inclined to read. It is also noteworthy that for each site offering Christian apologetics addressed to Islam, there is a site offering Muslim apologetics addressed to Christianity and dealing with the same questions.[58] For a neophyte, it becomes a challenging task to compare and contrast the views of these websites. Web designers of apologetics websites should pay attention to the ways people read the internet versus books. Online information flows in unique ways. Users don't study long arguments on endless webpages concerning the Trinity, for example. They want information that is quick, pertinent, and hyperlinked, as they don't mind hopping from one site to another. They also open several pages at the same time, and bookmark some for later use. While they browse for information, they click on "likes" and "dislikes" in manners that may sometimes surprise traditional apologists. Information does not flow the same way today as it did in the past. Therefore, writers of apologetics may have to find ways to contextualize their argument for the web culture. For example, Christians could produce two-minute YouTube videos inviting Muslims to listen to short reflections on daily life in Christ in ways that are relevant to the lives of contemporary Muslims.

Although polemical and apologetic writings on the web often lead to dia-logue at some level, provoking responses and counterresponses, many Muslim-Christian dialogues of a less disputational sort also appear, or are represented in some form, in cyberspace.[59] There are reports, in writing or video, of dia-logue undertaken in physical spaces by Muslims and Christians on a variety

57. Donald K. McKim, "Apologetics," in *Westminster Dictionary*, 15.

58. Compare, e.g., www.answeringislam.org/rebuttals.html (Christian website) with www.answering-christianity.com (Muslim website). Interestingly, someone who favors the Muslim site managed to hack the direct link to the Christian site and inserted the headline "Islam: The True Religion of God Almighty." Although this link has since been disabled, this aptly dem-onstrates that the line between the apologetic and the polemical can be easily blurred, since the defense of one's own position can easily turn into confrontation with those whom one regards as the "opposition."

59. Dialogue is defined as "the process of conversation, especially as representatives of differ-ent religious traditions talk and learn from each other" by Donald K. McKim ("Apologetics," in *Westminster Dictionary*, 77).

of topics: theological, social, artistic, and so on.[60] Likewise, interfaith blogging is a new style of interfaith dialogue, which offers fresh opportunities to
listen to each other in a nonthreatening and nonconfrontational environment.

Following the example of Michal and Sondos writing their blog, Christians could invite Muslims into their daily lives through blogs, videos, and
Facebook. One of the ways my Muslim friends often challenge me when they
talk about Christians is by asking what Christ brings to people's lives. What
an amazing medium we have today that allows us to invite Muslim friends into
our lives, even if we cannot meet with them face-to-face. I am not suggesting
that Christians need to create reality shows about Christian communities,
which may not portray the authentic experiences of followers of Christ. But
I recommend sharing our stories, doubts, surprises, and convictions with
Muslims.

Among the Christians testifying about their faith on the internet today,
many more are converts who were born Muslim than were a few decades
ago. I remember that when I started connecting with the Muslim community,
there were only a handful of published stories of Muslim followers of Christ,
usually in books or articles with very limited circulation. Today, hundreds if
not thousands are sharing their testimony online in various languages, from
various regions of the world.[61] Many have their own websites where they talk
with the world about their faith in Christ. Like other Christians, they adopt
various styles of witnessing, ranging from polemics to dialogue. Whereas in
the past many of these Christians preferred to keep a low profile, now many
are present online and off-line, sharing the gospel openly with the global
Muslim community, without hiding their identity.

In cyberspace, Muslims can now browse the entire gamut of Muslim-
Christian models of witness from their computer or tablet. This certainly
changes the dynamic of interfaith relations. Muslims can hyperlink from one
site to another and thereby move from polemics to apologetics to dialogue.
Like Christians, who often don't know how to make sense of the multiplicity of Muslim discourses on Christianity that they access online, Muslims
may also be puzzled or bewildered as they surf the maze of Christian blogs
and websites on Islam. My question remains the same throughout this book.
Whatever the approach, do Muslims understand the joy that God has when he

60. See, e.g., the panel discussion titled "Evangelicals and A Common Word" at https://vimeo
.com/48603877 or the dialogue between Mehdi Hasan and Ida Glaser titled "We Could Both Be
Wrong about God: Jesus" at https://www.youtube.com/watch?v=Fj27PRF5gEA.

61. See, e.g., the website of MaCasbah at http://www.macasbah.net; La Chaîne Nord-
Africaine (CNA) at http://www.cna-sat.org; or pastor and church planter Hormoz Shariat at
http://hormozshariat.com.

connects with them through Jesus? How do they perceive the delight of God in reaching out to them, and how do they perceive the delight Christians have in connecting with them? It would be very interesting to comprehensively review the existing websites, blogs, tweets, and so on (which I did not have time to do for this book) in search of their joy factor. One may find that certain styles invite joy more than others. Anecdotally, I have found several expressions of joy, especially where websites expressed the joy of human connections. But I also found some very unexciting websites. They don't express the joy and beauty of God. Websites with many "likes" from Muslims are certainly a sign that they enjoy and delight in what they read, watch, or hear. How many Christian websites are millionaires in the currency of "likes"? "Dislikes" may be a sign of relational shame and distance. But content can also signal whether or not there is joy. How can one defend one's faith in Jesus and still communicate that joyful explosion of the incarnation of Christ that we mentioned in chapter 1? In other words, how can divine joy inhabit the web and draw people to Jesus? This question still requires much thoughtful reflection.

While Muslims are developing all kinds of networks to connect with each other,[62] one may wonder how many communities exist online where Muslims and Christians converse. Inviting Muslims into Christian communities of faith has proven difficult in the past. Today, virtual communities[63] offer new forms of religious networking for the sake of worship and witness. I have heard of several online churches in Muslim-majority countries. Other churches, of Muslim-born followers of Christ who meet in physical spaces, post online videos of their church services for everyone to see.[64] Enoch Kim, a missiology professor, researched the value of virtual Christian communities in China. He specifically looked at the benefits of virtual community models for mission.[65] His research on China, the country with the largest number of internet users in the world, amply illustrates the benefits of developing virtual communities for Muslim seekers or followers of Christ. But having underlined the great

62. See, e.g., MuslimSocial.com. The heading under the home page's banner says, "Connect Muslims," and the site states the following invitation: "Come here to build my social network, share ideas, and enjoy other services." See also Ummaland, "a social network for Muslims," www.ummaland.com.

63. In *The Virtual Community: Homesteading on the Electronic Frontier* (Cambridge, MA: MIT Press, 2000), Howard Rheingold calls "virtual communities" the "social aggregations that emerge from the Net when enough people carry on those public discussions long enough, with sufficient human feeling, to form webs of personal relationships in cyberspace" (xx).

64. See, e.g., a series of church services posted online by Algerian churches, https://www.you tube.com/watch?v=EMIy7TUyMTc.

65. Enoch J. Kim, "A New Mission Tool in Creative Access Nations: Christian Virtual Community in China," *International Journal of Frontier Missiology* 27, no. 4 (Winter 2010): 183–88.

potential of virtual communities, one has to remember that not all communities can be safe places on the web. Due to the hostility that Christians currently face in some Muslim contexts, we always need to remember that it is important to protect the privacy and anonymity of Muslim seekers and followers of Christ, unless they decide to adopt an online identity on their own. Unfortunately, Christians are not always wise in their postings. Thus, my rule of thumb is always the same: I must protect the privacy of those who don't want to be identified; I cannot post everything online; I must ask my Muslim friends what I can post about them.

Conclusion

Christian internet users should continue to explore ways to present the gospel to Muslims with joy: How does the gospel become viral among Muslims? When will it get several million hits? How do Muslims visualize Christians through their websites? Do some sites that share the gospel with Muslims need a makeover? Which online Christian profiles communicate the joy of Christ? How many Muslim followers and friends do Christians have? How many "likes" do Christians get from Muslims? What filter do they need to have on their mouths to communicate the love and joy of Christ to the world through social media without escalating existing conflicts? How many Christian sites have Muslim subscribers, and if not many, why? Should Christians hit the tweet button more frequently to express to Muslims the joy Christians have in belonging to Christ? How can Christians be culturally and religiously sensitive in a virtual space with no boundaries? There is so much more to investigate! But the Easter scenario with which I started this chapter summarizes to me the substance of all these questions: Can divine joy and human joy flow through the World Wide Web? I believe it can and should. And, if so, then how can the joyful news of Jesus produce a buzz in Muslim cyberspace? I wish my readers happy surfing in the digital age of Muslim-Christian relations.

For Discussion

1. How do social media provide new opportunities to engage with Muslims?
2. Which stories of joyful encounters through social media in this chapter have inspired you?
3. How will you use social media to engage with Muslims?

4

Joyful Witness through Art

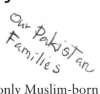

Samira is the only Muslim-born follower of Christ in a small church in Paris. One Sunday I met her after worship and noticed that she was fairly discouraged. Since I knew her quite well, I asked her what was going on. She replied (my paraphrase of her French), "I have been attending this church for a while, but I don't think people care. I feel so lonely and misunderstood. However, each time I feel like leaving, I look at the Bible verses in stylish Arabic calligraphy, hanging next to the pulpit. They make me happy and remind me that there are people who love Arabs in this church." I learned later that this hand-painted calligraphy was a gift from a Lebanese pastor who had preached in this church a few years earlier. He probably did not anticipate that it would become Samira's oxygen supply for her Christian life. This small vignette shows the power of art.

In the past, books on Christian witness seldom referred to the arts. They focused essentially on verbal communication. Thankfully, today there is more interest in the role of multisensory communication in interfaith relations. Art has an important role in Christian faith and witness. Since art is highly valued in Islam as well, Christians can encounter Muslims in new ways through art. Yet sometimes we hesitate to adopt these approaches. As a lover of the arts, I have included personal experiences that support my arguments. I hope the reader of this chapter, who need not be an artist, will find great joy in discovering the multisensory aspect of mission in Muslim cultures.

...e of Art in Islam

I assume that my readers are convinced that art plays a significant role in the historical and contemporary church. But before we can explore ways that it affects their witness among Muslims, we must address the value of art in Islam, given the misunderstandings that seem to have developed recently around this issue. Shortly after 9/11, for example, a church member asked me if Muslims are allowed to listen to music. I was stunned by her question, since some of my favorite artists are Muslim musicians from North Africa, the Middle East, and Central Asia. In fact, my former hairdresser in Paris, while doing my hair, used to hum the tune of the Egyptian diva Umm Kulthum, a Muslim. I concluded that this church person had very little knowledge of Islamic culture and had not yet discovered the importance of music in Muslim societies. The only thing she seemed to know about Islam was that Taliban leaders had recently outlawed music in Afghanistan. Given that it seemed incongruous to give a crash course on Islamic art in the church doorway, I simply recommended that she widen the horizon of her knowledge about Islam and added the proverb, "A little knowledge can be a dangerous thing." Today, I would point her to recent publications on Afghan music that indicate that under the Taliban the censorship of music was not solely due to particular interpretations of the Qur'an and the Hadith, but also to power struggles in Afghan society. Authors like Hiromi Lorraine Sakata, who studied Afghan music for over forty years, confirm that "music has always been a mainstay of Afghan culture,"[1] and John Baily, another ethnomusicologist, describes the rich musical tradition of Afghanistan, such as the charming *ghazal* song genre, commonly employed by people living in the area around Kabul.[2]

Limited knowledge of Islam is not the sole reason why many seem confused about the status of art in Islam. In the last few decades, there has been a rise in attacks on artists by people claiming they acted in the name of Islam, as illustrated by the following list, which is unfortunately not exhaustive. In 1988, Salman Rushdie was forced to go into hiding after the release of his novel *The Satanic Verses*.[3] In 2004, Theo van Gogh was killed after making the movie *Submission* with Ayaan Hirsi Ali. Since 2005, the author of the controversial Muhammad cartoons published in the Danish newspaper *Jyllands-Posten* has

1. Hiromi Lorraine Sakata, "The Politics of Music in Afghanistan," in *Ethnomusicological Encounters with Music and Musicians: Essays in Honor of Robert Garfias*, ed. Timothy Rice (Farnham, UK: Ashgate, 2011), 262.

2. John Baily, "Music and Censorship in Afghanistan, 1973–2003," in *Music and the Play of Power in the Middle East, North Africa and Central Asia*, ed. Laudan Nooshin (Farnham, UK: Ashgate, 2009), 143–64.

3. Salman Rushdie, *The Satanic Verses* (London: Viking, 1988).

lived under police protection. In 2015, caricaturists of the *Charlie Hebdo* satirical magazine were brutally killed in France. In addition to these acts against individuals, the Taliban has engaged in the destruction of ancient Buddhist images in Afghanistan. Finally, as I write this chapter, there are news reports about the looting of the Mosul museum in Iraq by members of the Islamic State of Iraq and Syria (ISIS). Those violent incidents, which have received high media coverage, have shocked the world.

Why would those attackers perpetrate such horrific acts? Is it because, as Islamic "puritans," they want to extirpate art from their society for fear it may steal the stage from God? Or do they fear that the emotional power of art overshadows worship of God? And yet these same puritans do not give up their appreciation for beautifully designed mosques, or for religious artifacts such as the embroidered prayer rugs they use in worship, or for the melodious sounds of the *adhān*, which calls them to prayer. They mistakenly think that by destroying artwork they are faithful to Muhammad, who called for the destruction of all idols and preached against the making of other deities besides Allah (Qur'an 51:51). As a matter of fact, a detailed study of the attacks mentioned above reveals that they were not targeted at art in general but rather at unconventional and sometimes blasphemous representations of the sacred, like the display of qur'anic verses on the naked body of a woman in the movie *Submission*, or Muhammad portrayed as a terrorist in satirical cartoons.

Of course, despite their controversial features, these artworks should never be a reason for killing artists or brutally destroying their work. These iconoclastic acts must be condemned with the greatest firmness. Nevertheless, concluding that Islam is fundamentally aniconic (against the use of images) and against any form of art would be a serious misjudgment. Ample evidence points toward the rich heritage of arts in Muslim societies. For example, the last prophet of Islam has been represented in numerous artworks, such as Mughal paintings and Persian miniatures. Vast audiences of Muslims have acclaimed *The Message*, a 1976 movie chronicling the life of Muhammad. Most Muslims enjoy qur'anic calligraphy, echoing the words of Muslim calligrapher Mohamed Zakariya, who believes it is "a kind of worship, a religious event that prepares one for prayer."[4] Likewise, Muslims appreciate the melodious chanting of the Qur'an, and many are in favor of international contests of qur'anic recitation. Muslims also value the intricately carved wooden Qur'an holders they have at home. They are proud of the pictures of Medina and

4. George Dardess and Peggy Rosenthal, "The Divine Script: The Art of Islamic Calligraphy," *Christian Century*, August 25, 2009, 23.

Mecca hanging in their living rooms. Many would even tune in to *anasheed* music[5] on their radio. And if ever Islamic art would be on the brink of disappearance (which it has never been), Sufis would be quick to remind Muslims of the creative imagination of Islam. Thus, the examples of censorship of art in Islam seem to lie in particular interpretations of the sacred texts, in issues of power—like the ones reported earlier concerning Afghanistan—or in theologically unorthodox practices.

Artistic Controversies in Common

Islam's internal debates concerning art parallel controversies from the history of Christianity. Rarely today do Christians kill over issues related to religious art, as is true for the vast majority of Muslims. Nevertheless, in the past they have often resorted to violence over the place of art in Christian life and worship. For example, during the Byzantine iconoclast periods of the eighth and ninth centuries, Christians argued over whether religious art was valuable or heretical.[6] Christians who disapproved of icons destroyed them and then persecuted their fellow Christians who were iconophiles. Such violence, and even the arguments for violence, strangely resemble what we witness today in some Muslim areas. Christians have also debated the value of musical instruments in worship. Despite their presence in many biblical psalms, they have not always been welcomed in churches.[7] In fact some churches today still believe in using only the human voice for praising God. Likewise, dance has been controversial. Even now some churches include dance in their worship and others do not.[8] At times, churches also condemned controversial representations of Christ.[9] And yet, at other times, Christian societies—like

5. *Anasheeds* are Islamic hymns celebrating the life of Muhammad.

6. Brenda Llewellyn Ihseen, "Smashing God's Face: Art, Theology, and Violence in the Byzantine Empire," *ARTS* 21, no. 1 (January 1, 2010): 40–51.

7. William M. Green, "The Church Fathers and Musical Instruments," *Restoration Quarterly* 9 (1966): 31–42. Certain denominations, such as the Darbist or the Plymouth Brethren, still debate the proper use of instruments in church services. Likewise, musical instruments are usually not used in mosque services but almost everywhere else in Muslim societies.

8. In *The Drama of Dance in the Local Church* (Maitland, FL: Xulon Press, 2005), 87, Emily A. Pardue writes, "The struggles of the Church against religious dances in churches, chapels and churchyards [began] as early as the fourth century. From the twelfth century there [were] dance epidemics in the church and out. . . . In prior centuries church councils and synods ruled against one aspect or another, but it was the Reformation with [its] highly critical attitude toward traditional Church customs that succeeded in suppressing . . . Church dance."

9. Leo Steinberg, "From 'The Sexuality of Christ in Renaissance Art and in Modern Oblivion,'" in *Religion, Art, and Visual Culture: A Cross-Cultural Reader*, ed. S. Brent Plate (New York: Palgrave, 2002), 73–80.

Muslim societies—have produced the most exquisite art. Most of the greatest art in the world is religious art: that of Christians, Muslims, Hindus, Buddhists, and followers of other religions. But each time the church interfaced with new cultural contexts, it faced the question of the validity of using art from other, non-Christian backgrounds.

In fact, monotheistic traditions are so consumed with the belief in the absolute oneness of God that any artistic representation may potentially be a threat. They are very sensitive to the seductive power of art, the possibility that artistic representations will entice people to follow unorthodox philosophies or ideologies. Regardless of the art forms they favor, they also keep a close eye on their artists for fear that the artists will compete with God the Creator. These reactions are partly based on Exodus 20:4–5 (NIV): "You shall not make for yourself an image in the form of anything in heaven above or on the earth beneath or in the waters below. You shall not bow down to them or worship them." Although the Qur'an does not cite these verses directly,[10] Muslim sacred texts express the same aversion toward image worship, albeit with even greater insistence, since the doctrine of the incarnation, absent in Islam, offers more freedom for figurative art. The prohibition of idolatry and the condemnation of image makers, illustrated by Muhammad removing the idols of the Ka'aba and inviting the Meccan pagans to believe in one God,[11] forced Islam to specialize in nonfigural art, although recent scholarship has revealed that human representations have never been completely absent from Islam.[12]

10. In *A History of Islamic Societies*, 3rd ed. (Berkeley: University of California, 2014), Ira M. Lapidus writes, "There is nothing in the Qur'an or early Muslim religious literature to suggest an iconoclastic attitude" (101). Likewise, Richard Ettinghausen, Oleg Grabar, and Marilyn Jenkins-Madina in *Islamic Art and Architecture 650–1250* (New Haven: Yale University Press, 1987) write, "On the aesthetics of painting, sculpture, and other arts the Holy Book is silent" (6). However, in the Hadith literature there are several reports of Muhammad prohibiting the making or displaying of pictures. See, e.g., *Sahih Muslim*, book 37, hadith 148 or *Sahih al-Bukhari*, book 78, hadith 136.

11. The Muslim historian Tabari quotes the words of Umar, the third Caliph of the early Muslim community, who said, "We used to worship idols and embrace graven images until God honored us with Islam." *The History of Tabarī: Muhammad at Mecca*, trans. and annot. W. Montgomery Watt and M. V. McDonald (Albany, NY: State University of New York Press, 1988), 6:65.

12. Göran Larsson refers to this when he writes,

Irrespective of the prohibition against images in the *hadith* literature, reservations against the legality of paintings and the representational arts only date back to late Ummayad or early 'Abbasid times. Archeological materials, book illustrations and miniatures from this period all demonstrate that there is a gap between theory and practice, and it is evident that the prohibition was not put into practice in all parts of the Muslim world. (*Muslims and the New Media: Historical and Contemporary Debates* [Farnham, UK: Ashgate, 2011], 52)

Artistic Enjoyment in Islam

I wish there were more space here to elaborate on the richness of the arts in Islam today. Even as violence against art continues, scholarship about art is proliferating. On my coffee table lies a large, atlas-style book with 640 pages of photos of the arts in the Muslim world—an infinitesimal sample of what has been produced during the fourteen centuries of the existence of Islam.[13] Thus, besides browsing the *Bibliography of Art and Architecture in the Islamic World*,[14] I invite my readers to embark on a personal journey of discovering Islamic art. Visits to prestigious museums and art galleries in major cities of the world will reveal treasures of Islamic art and unveil the artistic heritage of Muslim societies.[15] But those are not the only places to encounter Islamic art. Why not watch movies, theater performances, and videos produced by Muslim artists? And then we should also add mutual encounters with Muslims through culinary or decorative art. Art encounters can take place in a multiplicity of spaces, ranging from the most traditional contexts of calligraphic writings to the more contemporary ones that include Muslim street art. The options are almost limitless if we just have eyes to see and ears to hear.

Encounters through art reveal how much Muslims enjoy art. I have met Muslims, for example, who felt that art enhanced their spirituality. They would agree with Muslim professor Seyyed Hossein Nasr, who said that Islamic art "crystallizes in the world of forms the inner realities of the Islamic revelation and, because it issues from the inner dimension of Islam, leads man to the inner chamber of the Divine Revelation."[16] Other Muslims will highlight the beauty of art, quoting a famous hadith, which says, "Allah is beautiful and he loves beauty."[17] I know very few people who have not been completely mesmerized upon seeing the architectural beauty of some of the prestigious mosques in Iran, Iraq, or Syria, or by the Taj Mahal in India. The ornate calligraphy and graceful mosaics add to the breathtaking design of those buildings. When William Dyrness conducted his research on Muslim devotion in Southern California, he found that "the experience of Muslims

13. Markus Hattstein and Peter Delius, eds., *Arts & Civilisations de l'Islam* (Cologne: Köneman Verlagsgesellschaft, 2000).

14. Susan Sinclair, ed., *Bibliography of Art and Architecture in the Islamic World* (Boston: Brill Academic, 2012).

15. Maryam Ekhtiar, *Masterpieces from the Department of Islamic Art in the Metropolitan Museum* (New York: Metropolitan Museum of Art, 2011). See also Gaston Migeon and Henri Saladin, *Art of Islam* (New York: Parkstone Press International, 2009).

16. Seyyed Hossein Nasr, *Islamic Art and Spirituality* (Albany, NY: State University of New York Press, 1987), 7.

17. *Sahih Muslim*, book 001, hadith no. 164.

with their mosque is often a deeply aesthetic one."[18] He explained, "When asked what role the space of the mosque played in their prayers, respondents, even while rejecting any role for images, made frequent reference to the beauty of the place."[19]

Connecting through the Arts

Art is important because it helps us relate with people through the cultural context that shapes their lives. Indeed, art can be the first link to human connections. Attachment, the concept we looked at in chapter 2, often develops through shared experiences in art or music. I have met Christians fascinated with Muslim music, visuals, or stagecraft long before they met with a Muslim face-to-face. It would seem hard to enjoy art without appreciating at least some facets of the cultures that produced it. To my students who want to move to a Muslim-majority context after their degree, I always recommend that they learn about the art of their destination country. Such preparation is equivalent to stacking up joyful resources that may be accessed in times of cultural shock. Art can never substitute for human connections but will certainly make experiences with unfamiliar cultures more enjoyable and help visitors and nonnative residents see its people through new eyes. Thus, I never visit a Muslim context without appreciating its art, enjoying its aesthetic pleasure, and feeling the emotional resonance and dissonance that signal what links me or distances me from the people I want to connect with.[20] These experiences all contribute to the formation of healthy relations and help to foster better understanding and communication between people of different cultures. Identifying artistic activities that bind people together in a particular culture can also offer new ways to enjoy people. For example, "Music in Afghanistan has always been associated with joyous occasions, such as wedding festivities and the country fairs held over a period of 40 days in the spring."[21]

But in order to participate in the joy of a given culture, it is necessary to identify what people like and what they don't like. Cultures differ in their appreciation of artworks. For example, I have happy memories of the concert of Lebanese singer Fairouz that I attended with Muslim and Christian friends in

18. William A. Dyrness, *Senses of Devotion: Interfaith Aesthetics in Buddhist and Muslim Communities* (Eugene, OR: Cascade Books, 2013), Kindle edition, location 1865.

19. Ibid., locations 1865–72.

20. Cultural dissonances are also part of learning a culture and were addressed in chapter 2.

21. John Baily, "Music and Censorship in Afghanistan, 1973–2003," in *Music and the Play of Power in the Middle East, North Africa and Central Asia,* edited by Laudan Nooshin (Farnham, UK: Ashgate, 2009), 160.

The Stronger the Bridge of Relationship

Dr. Nabeel T. Jabbour, author of *The Crescent through the Eyes of the Cross**

I have lived most of my life with Muslims. They were my classmates, my roommates, and my students. Since the early 1980s I have been sharing this principle: *The stronger the bridge of relationship that you can build with the Muslim, the heavier the truth it can carry.*

Here are a couple of other principles which contributed to relieving me from the pressure and the burden of "doing evangelism."

1. *Sugar Cubes Evangelism.* In Egypt people could buy sugar in two forms, loose sugar and sugar cubes. There were boxes that contained exactly 100 sugar cubes and weighed exactly one kilogram. Let us suppose that I go to a small market in Egypt to purchase a box of sugar cubes and the man tells me that they do not have boxes but there is a big container full of sugar cubes. So I ask the man to weigh for me one kilogram of sugar cubes. He scoops the first 43 sugar cubes, and of course it is not a kilogram. Then he scoops more and more and more until there are 98 sugar cubes on the scale, and it is still not a kilogram. Then, when he puts the last two cubes on, making 100, the indicator shows that exactly one kilogram of sugar is on the scale.

   I used to think that successful evangelism was leading someone to Christ. I gave up on that definition long ago; its shortcomings became especially clear when God put Muslims on my heart. Instead I understand successful evangelism to mean helping every unchurched person I am in contact with to move one little step closer to Christ. That is success. Some people sow in tears and others reap with joy.

2. *Including Jesus.* Some evangelicals assume that successful evangelism means presenting a set of facts to a person and asking that person to commit to these facts or endorse them, as if inviting the person to join a political party. I understand evangelism that leads to conversion as having an encounter with Christ based on true understanding of the gospel. Evangelism means including Jesus in the conversation and playing the role of a facilitator by connecting my unchurched friend with my invisible Lord because of the veil over my friend's eyes.

*For more information about Jabbour, see his website at www.nabeeljabbour.com.

Paris. It is a joyful experience that we remember over and over again, each time we meet to enjoy an artistic event. Such experiences are what bind us together. Common artistic experiences have a way of amplifying joy and strengthening mutual bonds. This also happened to me the first time I accepted an invitation to have coffee at the home of a particular North African woman. She had invited a few of her female friends, and coffee time naturally spilled over to dance. I found out later that women don't have to announce a dance party to spontaneously dance when they are together. When women started to get up from their chairs, I remember holding on to my cup of coffee, frozen with fear, hoping that no one would notice I was there, because I had never danced in their styles before. But, like proper hosts, women invited me to the center of the dance circle. I felt as awkward as Ian Miller, in the 2002 movie *My Big Fat Greek Wedding*, when his fiancée's family pulled him against his will into a frenetic Greek dance. Like me, he stumbled and tripped and looked totally out of place. Today, many years later, after hundreds of celebrations and festivals with Muslim friends, I have to confess that when I hear the first notes of a North African tune, I am up on my feet dancing and whirling with joy. As I reflect on this now, I can see how much I have identified with the culture of my friends. I now can appreciate what they like because of my willingness to enter into some of their joyous forms of art.

Witness through the Performing Arts of Worship

Art can also visibly manifest to others our attachment to God. In biblical texts, for example, spiritual joy is expressed through diverse channels, including dancing, singing and other music, poetry, and so on. Down through the centuries, Christian communities have accumulated new artistic ways of expressing joy as the gospel interfaced with new cultural contexts. I recall one moving spiritual experience during a conference in England. Attendees had gathered around a campfire during the night to listen to the testimony of a Lebanese man who lived in Yemen. I had never heard someone share his journey in Christ with such exquisite Arabic poetry. His testimony lasted for hours, which was so different from the ten-minute testimony sharing I was used to in my own culture. Sitting under the brilliant starlit sky, I hoped this moment would never end. So beautiful were his words that they still resonate in my ears. The proclamation of his faith was beautifully enhanced by his masterful poetic skills. I wish more Muslims could see the manifestation of Christian faith through culturally sensitive art forms like Lebanese poetry.

Hosanna
Hallelu-
74 Ide
I've got the Joy of the Lord!
A Hallelujah song!
Joyful Witness in the Muslim World

Noticing that in the Muslim world the "*taṣliya* is on every lip from morning to night,"[22] missiologist Constance E. Padwick, who lived in Cairo and traveled throughout the Muslim majority world during her lifetime, writes that "the Christian Church should probably hearten herself by greater use, at least in her services, of ejaculations of praise to her Prophet, Priest and King." She recognized that joyful Christian worship has witness potential among Muslims. She therefore recommended that the church make fuller use of the old Hebrew joy cry *Hosanna,* which is the closest equivalent to the *taṣliya*.[23] This cry of joy can come in different artistic forms, conveying a strong message to other faith communities.

Works of Art as Symbols

The science of semiotics reveals the role of signs and symbols in communication. Architecture, for example, can reflect the sacred. Visitors are often struck by the considerable number of mosque minarets in the skyline of Cairo. They are even more surprised when the call to Muslim prayer bursts out of thousands of minarets simultaneously, engulfing the entire city with sacred sound. It is almost impossible to escape the sacredness of the moment, except when one is so used to the sound that it just becomes background noise. One exercise I give in my classes is asking students what symbols remind them of God when they walk or drive to campus for class. In some highly secularized contexts, some students say that they find no remaining human-made religious signs, but only God-made signs such as the human beings they pass on their way to campus, or animals, plants, and the sky. Others say that religious symbols are found in the most profane places or objects as long as their origin can be traced to God, or that they can serve as reminders of the divine.

Architectural symbols can also signify the presence of a community of faith in a specific geographical area.[24] They also provide aesthetic pleasure. If not, why would tourists spend so much time and money visiting sacred sites that may or may not be from their own faith tradition? The visiting of these sacred spaces can also elicit spiritual and emotional experiences. Solomon's temple, for example, became a symbol of joy and pride, not just for the

22. Constance E. Padwick, *Muslim Devotions: A Study of Prayer-Manuals in Common Use* (Oxford: Oneworld Publications, 1996), 165. *Taṣliya* is a form of blessing over Muhammad and his family.

23. Ibid.

24. God's instructions to Moses about the details of the construction of the tabernacle (Exod. 36) and the building of the temple (1 Chron. 28) contain many symbolic materials and images.

people who built it, but for all the nations to which God promised he would hear the prayers they addressed to him during their visit (2 Chron. 6:32–33). Paul later reminded Athenians that God does not dwell in houses or places built by human hands (Acts 17:24). Nonetheless, sacred spaces or buildings served throughout history as physical reminders of invisible realities. Christians therefore should not neglect the nonverbal signs and symbols that in their faith can point Muslims to the Triune God.

But symbols that Christians consider pointers to God do not always speak to Muslims. They may even be completely irrelevant or straight-out offensive. Building cathedrals in Muslim contexts may sometimes elicit the same kind of controversies as the building of mega-mosques in Europe. Leaders of a French church whose neighborhood had turned completely Muslim over a few years faced the issue of the cacophonic meaning of religious symbols. They were discussing the project of erecting a tall cross on their church building. Defining the purpose of the church in their area helped them reach a decision. They not only wanted to serve their congregation; they also wanted to be a witness in the neighborhood. It was decided that instead of putting the cross on the exterior of the building, they would put it inside.[25] Concurrently, parishioners as living "stones" were encouraged to reflect the path of the cross in their daily encounters with Muslims. This church realized that if a visual symbol was the reason why Muslims would misunderstand the gospel, it was better to put it aside for a while and look for another one that would better communicate the message of the cross to them. The Christian community noticed that when it organized activities for Muslims, they were not afraid to walk inside the building anymore. This story shows that if "a picture is worth a thousand words," one must be even more careful of the message any and every "picture" conveys.

In spite of that, Christians should not shy away from using artistic symbols to share the gospel. Admittedly, words are very useful and necessary in Christian witness, because they render communication less ambiguous. But nonverbal elements also produce relevant meaning. Even God made use of multiple modes of communication to "speak" to humans. For example, he "spoke" through his handiwork in creation (Ps. 19:1–6; Rom. 1:20), through tablets of stone "written with the finger of God" (Exod. 31:18 NRSV), and through his word becoming flesh (John 1:14) in the incarnation. Likewise, witness may include nonverbal symbols. In fact, art is a more holistic mode of

25. Qur'an 4:157 is the only qur'anic verse that alludes to Jesus's crucifixion. The general understanding of this verse is that the crucifixion of Jesus did not happen or that someone else died on the cross but not Jesus.

communication that elicits emotional reactions and therefore reaches deeper areas of our being than simply words, as the following example will reveal.

One day, I visited St. Paul's Cathedral with a Muslim friend. At first, she refused to enter the building because her family had told her when she was a child that she might be cursed if she did so. Whether her idea was well founded in the Qur'an or other Islamic teachings is debatable. History shows that Muslims have entered churches on many occasions.[26] But I knew how she must have felt, since there are also Christians who are afraid to go inside a mosque. I was therefore surprised when, after hesitating, she agreed. She had probably become more adventurous because we were set that day to a tourist mode.

As we strolled along the poorly lit church alleys, she suddenly stopped, facing a large painting that I had passed without noticing. I later identified it as *The Light of the World* by William Holman Hunt. The artist depicted Jesus standing outside a closed door and knocking.[27] I immediately related this painting to Revelation 3:20 (NIV): "Here I am! I stand at the door and knock." My friend did not know this biblical passage, although Jesus was not unfamiliar to her from the Qur'an, which portrays him as a prophet. This painting made a deep impression on her. She gazed at it for a long moment. It became the highlight of her visit. Although she rarely wanted to talk about Jesus in our previous conversations, she was ready to share with me how seeing Jesus, standing at the door and knocking, had completely shaken her. A former student of mine recalls that I told this story in class. He admitted years later that he was at first very skeptical. But he changed his mind after he met a Muslim woman who had a similar experience looking at a painting of Christ and becoming a Christ follower.

Strengths and Weaknesses of Artistic Witness

Art creates new spaces of, and for, joyful witness. These spaces are often less threatening than traditional interfaith dialogues during which experts discuss theological issues. I have attended many of these dialogues, where

26. The third caliph, 'Umar ibn al-Khattab, entered the Church of the Holy Sepulchre in Jerusalem. See Amin Maalouf, *The Crusades through Arab Eyes* (London: Al Saqi Books, 1984), 51. A recent book edited by Dionigi Albera and Maria Couroucli titled *Sharing Sacred Spaces in the Mediterranean: Christians, Muslims, and Jews at Shrines and Sanctuaries* (Bloomington: Indiana University Press, 2012) provides further evidence that Muslims and Christians have sometimes shared sacred spaces.

27. St. Paul's Cathedral's website provides a brief description of this artwork at https://www.stpauls.co.uk/history-collections/the-collections/collections-highlights/the-light-of-the-world.

words become the central medium of communication. They are very useful but often limit the breadth of the encounter to the cognitive realm and neglect the affective forms of communication. This is where art becomes significant, since it involves the use of multisensory experiences: tactile, visual, auditory, gustatory, olfactory, spatial, or kinesic.[28] It can render interfaith relations much more fun and playful.

Several years ago, I attended the festival of sacred music in Fes, Morocco. There are many similar festivals around the world. This one was initiated after the first Gulf War in order to promote dialogue between religions. During a weeklong program, participants have the opportunity to attend many events scattered across the city: lectures on art, small concerts in museum gardens, larger evening interfaith concerts with the presence of royalty, and popular concerts on city plazas. I remember a conversation with a Muslim family sitting on the ground next to me during an intimate outdoor Sufi concert that was held after midnight. Their daughter was going through a difficult time. While we were leisurely chatting before the start of the concert, I asked the parents' permission to pray for the girl, knowing how eager Muslims are to receive blessings. They agreed, and as I placed my hand gently on her shoulder, I asked God to shower her with his blessings in the name of Jesus.

Interfaith concerts provide opportunities to explore religious spaces of others through common emotional experiences. During a performance of the gospel singer Craig Adams, with the Voices of New Orleans, I heard Muslims behind me dancing, clapping hands, and singing along resounding hallelujahs, which is an unusual term in their religious discourse. Muslims would rather say, "*Subhan Allah*," "Glory to God," to express praises to God. Music offered these participants the chance to taste new spiritual spaces and broadened the scope of their interfaith experience. I surprised myself by having a similar outburst of joy when the following Muslim performer, Faiz Ali Faiz, sang ecstatic *qawwali* songs.[29] I did not experience it as personal worship, because I could not theologically agree with all the words of the song, but I could still feel joy from the resonance of sounds and rhythms in my body.

One of the reasons why Christians are often reluctant to engage in these types of nonverbal dialogue is precisely the emotional experience I just mentioned. They don't feel that artistic forms can be dissociated from their religious meaning and therefore think that any expression of positive emotion regarding the art of another faith signifies that they have embraced it. In some

---

28. For a more detailed discussion on the role of multisensory experiences in human communication, see the work of anthropologist Ruth Finnegan, *Communicating: The Multiple Modes of Human Communication*, 2nd ed. (New York: Routledge, 2014).

29. *Qawwali* is devotional music performed by Sufis. It is very popular in South Asia.

ways they are right. Art can be tightly associated with the faith tenets in which it is rooted. Some scholars claim that divine law is inherent in forms.[30] If so, then differences in forms can hinder interfaith dialogue. In effect, if calligraphy of the Qur'an is called "a divine script,"[31] how can one use qur'anic-style calligraphy for biblical verses?

However, religious traditions have always borrowed art forms from each other. Design patterns of Byzantine churches are found in early mosque structures. Prayer beads are used in nearly all faith traditions of the world. So, it may not be the artistic form as such that people should be afraid of, but instead, the religious meaning that it conveys to the faith community that adopts it in worship. The questions that differences in artistic form raised for me as I experienced joy at the festival of sacred music are the following: When I am singing along with people from other faiths, can I relate my emotional experience to my own beliefs? Are the other faiths allowing me to borrow their tunes and melodies to express my own faith? Do my behaviors not send a wrong message that eventually prevents me from being a witness for Christ in this community? In other words, can I both enjoy the art of other faiths and share the gospel with their followers? Depending on the meaning and value that faith traditions give to their art, the responses will differ. Symbols that represent in a nutshell the full narrative of a specific faith tradition are probably the most difficult to translate into another religious context, as the earlier example of the church cross revealed.

The difficulty of these questions became obvious to me when a Muslim friend saw a display on my wall of the Lord's Prayer calligraphed in Arabic, which I had bought in Lebanon. Christians have long calligraphed this prayer, which is sometimes mistaken for a qur'anic passage by those who do not take the time to decipher the convoluted tracings of the words. This is exactly what happened with my friend. He made appreciative comments about this calligraphy, thinking it was a qur'anic verse. To him, the art form conveyed more meaning than the words it included. I first could not convince him that it had a biblical meaning. Our conversation eventually morphed into a valuable exchange, once we overcame the initial artistic dissonance. This experience reveals the challenge of dialogue through the arts. On the one hand, the polysemy and subjectivity of art opens more spaces for dialogue, but on the other hand, religions sometimes hijack certain art forms to meet their own congregational needs, rendering interfaith exchanges more difficult.

30. Titus Burckhardt, *Sacred Art in East and West*, trans. Lord Northbourne (Louisville: Fons Vitae, 2001).

31. George Dardess and Peggy Rosenthal, "The Divine Script: The Art of Islamic Calligraphy," *The Christian Century* 126, no. 17 (2009): 22–25.

Besides the question of the emotional impact of art from another faith, we must ask what its spiritual impact is on those who participate for the sake of witness and dialogue. This question has raised animated discussions in my classes. The first came up unexpectedly when I showed a video clip of a *qawwali* concert without informing my students beforehand that performers were Muslims and praising Allah in Urdu. I left out this information intentionally to see what the reactions of the class would be to the rhythms and tunes in the absence of linguistic meaning. While we were watching the performance, one student quietly started sobbing. She shared afterwards that she had never had such an "intense spiritual experience." When I translated the words of the song, she was confused and said, "How is it possible that this song elicited such transcendent joy in me?" I explained to her that in art, religious boundaries become more porous, and definitions more subjective. I added that multisensory dialogue makes many religious people uncomfortable, because emotional experiences may have multiple meanings.

This is evidenced by comments sometimes found below YouTube videos in foreign languages where viewers express how much they have been moved by a video even though they did not understand the language. How can one explain these feelings? In the case of my student, it is possible that the *qawwali* music reminded her of another genre of music that she was more familiar with. Unconsciously she had used that spiritual framework to feel or experience the music I presented in class. This assessment was confirmed when I later read that "*Qawwali* is similar in spirit to American gospel music."[32] Incidentally, my student told me that gospel music was her favorite music.

God has given human beings words but also emotions to connect with him. For example, different people associate a given emotion with different kinds of experiences from their childhood. The emotional states may be the same, but the narratives differ from person to person. Could it be the same with religious experiences? We may share some common emotional experiences through art, but we interpret them through the narratives of our specific faiths.

But what if music, or any art form, in other religious contexts became the medium that spiritual forces that oppose the true God would use to access the lives of people? Would this not discourage Christians from participating in interfaith dialogue through the arts? I remember spending time at the Nizamuddin Auliya shrine in New Dehli[33] with a Christian friend. As we listened to Sufi music played by a lively group of Muslims, she suddenly

---

32. Gini Gorlinski, ed., *The 100 Most Influential Musicians of All Time* (New York: Britannica Educational Publishing, 2010), 317.

33. Nizamuddin Auliya was a prominent Indian Sufi saint in the fourteenth century.

became very nervous and wanted to leave. She told me that she was feeling some supernatural forces that were attacking her soul. She believed that this oppression that she felt came from demons. As we left, we started to reflect on the various ways these feelings of oppression can be interpreted. Those who believe in the existence of demons anticipate encountering demonic forces in objects or art forms. Consequently, they avoid contact with art that may serve as the medium for those forces. Others, who doubt that demons can directly influence people or that demons exist, interpret the oppression they feel in certain religious contexts as a mix of unresolved emotional issues and a lack of spiritual preparedness. This subject has been widely debated throughout church history and will probably continue to be debated in the future.

Contemporary Art

Modern and postmodern contemporary art seems to offer to those who are reluctant to participate in unfamiliar religious artistic experience fresh opportunities to encounter Muslims. In effect, today the ties of art with the sacred realm are much looser than in premodern times.[34] In those times, Seyyed Hossein Nasr explains, certain art forms like qur'anic psalmody and the chanting of the *adhān* (call to prayer) were considered sacred art.[35] Likewise, all pre-Renaissance art, which Nasr calls "traditional art," related to the "necessities of life and spiritual needs of the user of the art," and there was "no distinction between the sacred and the profane."[36]

Although this form of art may still exist in certain regions of the Muslim world, today Muslim artists are much more inclined to investigate new forms of art, outside the strict religious codes of past artistic creation. Their art coincides more closely with what Nasr calls religious art, with "religious subjects in the context of modern civilization, that is, a civilization no longer governed by immutable spiritual principles."[37] This art is not based on "supra-individual inspiration." It is "anthropocentric rather than theocentric."[38] Today, many artistic encounters between Muslims and Christians involve religious art. In effect, not all artists are interested in sacred, or traditional, art. Muslim-born photographer Shekaiba Wakili explains, "Just because you are Muslim it

---

34. Seyyed Hossein Nasr, "Religious Art, Traditional Art, Sacred Art: Some Reflections and Definitions," in *The Essential Sophia*, ed. Seyyed Hossein Nasr and Katherine O'Brien (Bloomington, IN: World Wisdom, 2006), 175–85.

35. Ibid., 176.

36. Ibid., 178.

37. Ibid., 181.

38. Ibid.

doesn't mean that you make Islamic art, whatever that means."[39] Tunisian-born and US-based visual artist Emna Zghal wrestles with a similar issue, stating, "As contemporary Muslim artists, we are questioning what Islamic art is."[40] I think that we should, as Christians, pay more attention to this morphing of the nature of art within Muslim societies, which provides more spaces of encounter, especially to those who do not want to deal with sacred art.

Furthermore, not all artistic encounters between Muslims and Christians have to revolve around art with religious themes. It may be that the joy of the encounter and spiritual exchanges flow from profane art as well. Many artists in Muslim societies would not even self-identify as Muslim artists. They call themselves secular, and some even question the existence of God. They explore all the forms of art that have been neglected by sacred artists. They are also able to mix the sacred and the profane without apologies. For example, Hossein Zenderoudi, an Iranian artist and sculptor, "took modern, abstract styles and used them to express traditional subjects and content."[41] In contrast, Shahzia Sikander, a Pakistani artist, "used a very rigorous and traditional training in miniature painting to express modern and very personal themes."[42] These contemporary artists are worth meeting. They often challenge conventional rules of Islamic art. They explore hip-hop or rap,[43] design Arabic tattoos[44] on human bodies, or create theater or dance companies.[45] Some artists use

39. Quoted in Munir Jiwa, "Muslims and the Art of Interfaith Post-9/11: American Muslim Artists Reach Out to New Yorkers in the Aftermath of September 11," in *Studying Islam in Practice*, ed. Gabriele Marranci (New York: Routledge, 2014), 157.

40. Ibid.

41. Judith Ernst, "The Problem of Islamic Art," in *Muslim Networks from Hajj to Hip Hop*, ed. Miriam Cooke and Bruce B. Lawrence (Chapel Hill: University of North Carolina Press, 2005), 116.

42. Ibid.

43. Although dance has been practiced throughout history in Muslim societies, it was not considered a sacred art and was usually banned from worship in the mosque except in some Sufi orders, such as the Whirling Dervishes. Watch performances of Whirling Dervishes from Turkey at the Festival of Sacred Music in June 2013, at https://www.youtube.com/watch?v=9IoZ4oEIZNs. On the question of dance in Islam, read the section "Islam" in Anne-Marie Gaston (Anjali) with Tony Gaston, "Dance as a Way of Being Religious," in *The Oxford Handbook of Religion and the Arts*, ed. Frank Burch Brown (New York: Oxford University Press, 2014), 189–90. On the question of Hip Hop and Islam, read Suad Abdul Khabeer, "*Rep That Islam*: The Rhyme and Reason of American Islamic Hip Hop," *The Muslim World* 97 (January 2007): 125–41.

44. Hadith literature refers several times to Muhammad forbidding the practice of tattooing. See, e.g., the hadith narrated by Abu Huraira stating, "He [the Prophet] prohibited tattooing" *Sahih al-Bukhari* 5740, at http://sunnah.com/bukhari/76/55. Muslim perspectives vary on this issue according to the level of authenticity and value attributed to these *ahadiths*.

45. While it is often believed that stagecraft is banned in Islam, except for the Shi'i ashura plays that commemorate the death of Imam Hussayn, the grandson of Muhammad, a closer exploration of the role of theater in Muslim Arab societies reveals examples of theatricalized

their skills to become social activists, such as the Iranian-born filmmaker and photographer Shirin Neshat, who challenges the status and role of women in Muslim societies.[46]

Furthermore, as Muslims become followers of Christ, they also create new forms of art. Saïd Oujibou is a Moroccan-born stand-up comedian who lives in France. He draws thousands of people domestically and internationally to his shows, where he addresses societal issues and shares his faith in Christ.[47] Likewise, Farid, an Algerian-born mime who lives in France, fascinates his Muslim audiences as he mimes how he became a follower of Christ.[48] I am afraid that if we bypass these forms of contemporary art, because we focus only on the sacred or traditional Muslim art, we will misunderstand Muslims who live around us. A real transformation of the arts is going on in Muslim societies, and we must take it into account as we meet Muslims.

Art and Conflict

Unfortunately, art does not always elicit joy. It also triggers conflicts. Unconventional or controversial art can sometimes jeopardize Christian witness. Art can escalate conflict or lead to social unrest, as we have discussed earlier. It can also create ambiguity. After serving the Christian community of Constantinople for centuries, the beautiful church of Hagia Sophia in Istanbul became a mosque under the Ottomans. Later, when Turkey became a secular state, it was made a museum. Architecture can sometimes be challenging for faith communities from different traditions that share the same space.

But art can also prevent or appease conflicts and mend broken bonds. Many dialogues with those goals are ongoing. The project CARAVAN, started by Paul-Gordon Chandler, is an initiative that first gathered Muslims and Christians around a festival of the arts in Cairo. The project website explains that CARAVAN is engaged in "peacebuilding through the Arts between the creeds and cultures of the East and West."[49] Another exhibition, this one initiated by Mus-

---

festivals, marketplace storytellings, and a plethora of other forms of theatrical art. See Don Rubin, ed., *The World Encyclopedia of Contemporary Theatre,* vol. 4, *The Arab World* (New York: Routledge, 1999).

46. See Neshat's artwork at http://www.artnet.com/artists/shirin-neshat/ or watch her 2010 TED Talk at https://www.ted.com/talks/shirin_neshat_art_in_exile?language=en.

47. See extracts of one of Oujibou's 2011 shows titled "Liberté, égalité, couscous" (liberty, equality, couscous) at https://www.youtube.com/watch?v=RyJxr3gqOMA.

48. Watch three of his mimes performed with his wife at https://www.youtube.com/watch?v=53sn1-Np21w.

49. According to the CARAVAN website, "CARAVAN develops initiatives that use the arts as a catalyst to bring people of diverse backgrounds and beliefs closer together toward building

lims, came in the aftermath of 9/11. In January 2002, American Muslim artists displayed their works in the Cathedral of St. John the Divine in New York City aiming at "healing wounds" and "building interfaith and intercultural bridges."[50] The exhibition was titled "Reflection at a Time of Transformation: American Muslim Artists Reach Out to New Yorkers in the Aftermath of September 11."

Numerous other events of this kind have been organized to prevent or reduce conflict. The Interfaith Amigos are three clergymen—a sheikh, a pastor, and a rabbi—who tour the United States as a stand-up comedy team. Through their humor, they attract crowds and address sensitive issues that divide communities.[51] Finally, the Brehm Center at Fuller Theological Seminary, in producing the documentary film *unCommon Sounds*, has explored songs of peace and reconciliation among Muslims and Christians. Roberta R. King, who directed the project with Sooi Ling Tan, explains that the research journey brought together "Muslims and Christian scholars, ethnomusicologists, and musicians to explore the contribution of music and the arts in fostering sustainable peace-building."[52]

Jesus in Muslim Art

As they witness, Christians can also highlight biblical themes in the works of Muslim artists. A hadith account reports that Muhammad ordered those who were told to destroy the idols inside the Ka'ba to protect an image of the Madonna and child.[53] Later, "images of the Madonna and the Christ child [were] painted by Mughal artists and collected in folio volumes with other curiosities for the entertainment of the Mughal court."[54] Other works are less biblically faithful, such as the painting representing a Muslim interpretation of Isaiah 21 and showing Jesus riding a donkey next to Muhammad riding a camel.[55] Other pointers to Jesus can be found in poetry. The legendary Persian

---

sustainable peace. We develop, organize, curate and host numerous artistic programs; exhibitions, festivals, lectures, concerts, artist exchanges, collaborations, seminars, symposiums, forums/panels, film screenings, etc." (http://www.oncaravan.org/#!what-we-do/c65z).

50. Munir Jiwa, "Muslims and the Art of Interfaith Post-9/11," in *Studying Islam in Practice*, ed. Gabriele Marranci (London: Routledge, 2014), 150.

51. Pastor Dan Mackenzie, Rabbi Ted Falcon, and Imam Jamal Rahman, *Getting to the Heart of Interfaith* (Woodstock, VT: Skylight Paths, 2009).

52. Brehm Center, Fuller Theological Seminary, "unCommon Sounds," http://www.brehm center.com/initiatives/globalworship/uncommon-sounds/. See also Roberta R. King and Sooi Ling Tan, eds., *(Un)Common Sounds: Songs of Peace and Reconciliation among Muslims and Christians* (Eugene, OR: Cascade Books, 2014).

53. Ernst, "Problem of Islamic Art," 122.

54. Ibid.

55. See Priscilla P. Soucek, "An Illustrated Manuscript of al-Bīrūnī's Chronology of Ancient Nations" in *The Scholar and the Saint: Studies in Commemoration of Abu'l-Rayhan Al-Bīrūnī*

poet Jalal ad-Din Rumi, who is widely read by Muslims and non-Muslims, has written several poems on Jesus. In one of his poems, he writes,

> I called through your door
> "The mystics are gathering
> in the street. Come out!"
> "Leave me alone.
> I'm Sick."
> "I don't care if you're dead!
> Jesus is here, and he wants
> to resurrect somebody!"[56]

A more contemporary example of Jesus in Muslim art comes from the Unterlinden Museum in Colmar, France, which hosts the famous Isenheim Altarpiece, painted by German artist Matthias Grünewald. As a child, I often visited this museum, which is only a ten minutes' drive from where I grew up. In 2012, as I was visiting relatives in the region, I heard about a temporary exhibition in celebration of the five-hundredth anniversary of the Isenheim Altarpiece. As soon as I saw the invitation, I took my camera and made my way to the museum. What I found was amazing. Next to Grünewald's altarpiece the organizers had displayed an artwork from Adel Abdessemed, an artist born in Algeria and based in Europe and the United States. His work consisted of four life-size sculptures of Jesus that resemble the crucified Jesus painted by the German artist: the exact same position of the crucified body of Jesus, without the structure of the cross.[57]

The resemblance was so striking that it called for an explanation. I learned that the material that the Algerian artist used to sculpt the body of Jesus was razor wire and that the artist was inspired by the way Grünewald had depicted Jesus's suffering. In effect, in the original altarpiece, Jesus's body displays the symptoms of ergotism, a disease caused by a fungus growing on grains of rye, which entirely crippled the body of those who were affected by it. This disease caused a terrible plague during the Middle Ages. Grünewald painted this altarpiece for a monastery that welcomed people affected by this sickness. Certainly Grünewald hoped that these sick people would stare at the painting

---

and Jalal Al-Din Al-Rūmī, ed. P. J. Chelkowski (New York: New York University Press, 1975), 107–9. Also see a picture of this painting in Christiane Gruber, "The Koran Does Not Forbid Images of the Prophet," *Newsweek*, January 9, 2015 (http://www.newsweek.com/koran-does -not-forbid-images-prophet-298298).

56. Jalal ad-Din Rumi, *The Essential Rumi: New Expanded Edition*, trans. Coleman Barks with John Moyne (New York: HarperCollins, 1996), 201.

57. The artwork is called *Décor*.

and receive healing, such as the people of Israel who had been bitten by snakes and who lived after looking at the bronze snake lifted up in the desert (Num. 21:8–9). Adel Abdessemed does not claim to be a Christian, but I wonder if he was not touched by the identification, in Grünewald's painting, of Jesus with the suffering of people. That may explain why he portrayed Jesus sculpted from industrial-grade razor wire, as a modern symbol of the plagues of physical violence, torture, and displacement. As a Christian, I could easily imagine under Abdessemed's painting a label with the following inscription: "He took up our pain and bore our suffering . . . he was pierced for our transgressions, he was crushed for our iniquities; the punishment that brought us peace was on him, and by his wounds we are healed" (Isa. 53:4–5 NIV).

Conclusion

Christians have more opportunities than they can imagine to build relation-ships with Muslim individuals and communities through art. As we have seen in this chapter, despite the fact that certain art forms have been prohibited at certain times in the history of Islam, the majority of Muslims throughout the centuries have enjoyed art and even used it in worship. As Christians engage with Muslims, they will discover a religion with a rich artistic heritage. They will meet artists who express their faith in manifold ways and grapple with similar questions regarding the interface between art and religion. We have learned here that a growing number of Christians enjoy meeting Muslims through the arts. I hope that this chapter has stimulated a wide number of readers to explore these spaces where relationships are formed through shared emotions generated by artistic experiences. I am not a professional artist, but I could not imagine Muslim Christian relations deprived of aesthetic pleasure.

For Discussion

1. Discuss the role of art in your witness for Christ among Muslims.
2. How would you define interfaith dialogue through arts (what are the strengths and weaknesses of this approach)?
3. Currently, Muslims are becoming more and more aware of the positive role that art is playing in connecting individuals and transforming so-cieties (exhibition in Cairo, photography of Iranian women, etc.). Can you share other examples from your own context?

5

Thinking Green in Sharing
the Gospel

The other day, I had a friendly conversation with a Muslim woman. We were envisioning how the earth would look a hundred years from now. Like me, she was alarmed by the continual environmental catastrophes that, according to some analysts, may have human causes. She was as worried as I was about the future of her family and friends and shared her plans of changing her eating habits and acting more responsibly in avoiding products and practices that would harm the earth. Her environmentally friendly approach struck me as an excellent illustration of the ways to engage in joyful witness. There was something I could share with her about my understanding of God's creation and how God interacts with the world, as we will see below.

I started writing this chapter on Earth Day, which commemorates the beginning of the modern environmental movement in 1970. Twenty years later, in 1990, two hundred million people in 141 countries observed Earth Day in some way.[1] Today countless ecological movements around the globe seek to address contemporary menaces to nature. Many organizations whose core missions are not primarily ecological have now included ecological recommendations in their mission statements. Countries are changing laws to

1. Earth Day Network, "Earth Day: The History of a Movement," http://www.earthday .org/earth-day-history-movement.

Four Important Lessons

Moussa Bongoyok, Biola University

I became a follower of Christ when I was twelve years old. I felt such a deep peace and joy that I could not resist sharing my faith with people around me. Since then, I have continued to share the gospel with my Muslim neighbors. I have followed four essential principles over the years.

First, whoever has really encountered Christ as his or her Savior and Lord has a story to tell. When Jesus comes into someone's life, he transforms the person. It may not be a radical transformation, but one cannot be born again and continue to think and live the same way (Cf. 2 Cor. 5:17; Col. 3). People around the convert start to notice changes and ask questions. These are golden opportunities to tell one's story.

This is where the second principle intervenes: prayer is essential. We need God's direction as to what to say, how to say it, and when. We also need to pray that the Lord will touch the lives of those to whom we tell our story of faith, open their spiritual eyes, and help them to realize only Jesus can give them eternal life. Prayer must continue even when they commit their lives to the Lord as they navigate through various joys and challenges.

Third, friendship and love yield more results than confrontation. Although apologetics still has its place in some circumstances, it is far better to develop friendship with Muslim neighbors, to show them Christ's love in our actions, and to create an environment where we can communicate the gospel in a friendly and peaceful way. Then they are likely to be more receptive.

Fourth, I learned that immediate follow-up is critical. Though similar in some ways on the surface, Islam and Christianity are also profoundly different. The new believer has a lot to learn about basic questions like: Who is God? What is the true nature of Jesus Christ? How should I pray? How should I read the Bible? How can I grow in Christian faith? How should I share the gospel? In addition, we must remember that Muslims usually live communally. Isolating the new believer is disastrous. We must help him or her grow spiritually, and even reproduce himself or herself spiritually in the light of 2 Timothy 2:2 and in a context of Christian fellowship.

protect the earth. From local projects started by individuals to global projects run by major international organizations, many seem to lean toward an eco-friendly lifestyle.

If, once a year, our calendar reminds us that it is important to think of the earth and its well-being, what about our own religious communities? Do Muslims and Christians share this concern? What can we learn from environmental activism? How does it relate to the joy-thread running through this book? Is caring for the earth part of witness? And if it is, how does it relate to witness among Muslims? Environmental issues are indeed connected to witness, and I invite this current generation of Christians, who seriously worry about the future of our planet, to consider new ways to engage with Muslims through interfaith initiatives for the good of our world. Considering joyful witness in the context of ecology can also help us reflect on how Muslims perceive the Triune God we worship by the way we deal with the world God has created.

Ecology and Mission

Missional discourse increasingly includes environmental discussions. It is now common to find entries under the term "ecology" in encyclopedias of Christian mission. With the media packed with coverage of ecological challenges, Christians, with the rest of the world, are increasingly concerned about the fate of the planet. Thus, Gerry Breshears, professor of systematic theology, starts an article on ecology and the ecological movement with a somber statement about the degradation of God's earth, extinction of species, environmental destruction, alteration of energy-exchange systems, and the pollution of land, water, and atmosphere systems.[2] "Meeting human needs," he asserts, "without caring for the earth is not only impossible, but unbiblical. . . . Earth-keeping must be a worshipful activity, an act of praise to the Creator. Reverence for God must include appreciation of all his creation."[3] Concepts of Christian witness that incorporate love of the earth are now addressed in seminary curricula. Even in classes on Muslim-Christian relations this topic becomes increasingly relevant.

Similarly, Christian movements are putting the issue of ecology on their agenda. The Cape Town Commitment, drafted in 2010 by a team led by missiologist Christopher Wright, includes an article regarding creation care titled "We Love God's World," which states, "We cannot claim to love God while abusing what belongs to Christ by right of creation, redemption and

2. Gerry Breshears, "Ecology, Ecological Movement," *Evangelical Dictionary of World Missions*, ed. A. Scott Moreau et al. (Grand Rapids: Baker Books, 2000), 296.
3. Ibid.

inheritance."[4] The confession clearly encourages Christians to care for the earth, take ecological responsibility, engage in environmental advocacy, and exercise responsible dominion and stewardship. The missional call is clearly outlined by the authors. Creation care is under the lordship of Christ. Sharing the gospel, therefore, cannot be conceived without paying attention to the earth. The mission mandate of the Cape Town Commitment concludes, "Integral mission means discerning, proclaiming, and living out, the biblical truth that the gospel is God's good news, through the cross and resurrection of Jesus Christ, for individual persons, and for society, and for creation."[5] Witness entails a real concern for God's earth.

It is not surprising, therefore, that eco-theology has been gaining favor among Christians.[6] According to Richard D. Calenberg, a professor of world missions, "The redemptive purposes of God include not only humankind but also the created order."[7] Consequently, it seems natural to look at the earth from a missional perspective. Calenberg argues for including in mission theology a "doctrine of stewardship of the earth and its resources."[8] He also lists examples of how, through liberation theology, churches have more clearly articulated that mission includes care for the earth, thus promoting new definitions and practices.[9] As stewardship of the earth gains more importance in mission theology and practice, many more topics will need to be addressed, especially in regard to interfaith initiatives.

Joyful Creation

Does Christian witness with a focus on creation care also radiate the joy that we described in chapter 1? It does indeed! The gospel to which Christians bear witness is expressed in the Bible, and the Bible often describes the joy that the Creator feels about his creation. After vividly describing God making the earth, mountains, springs, birds, plants, trees, moon, sun, animals, and so

---

4. *The Cape Town Commitment: A Confession of Faith and a Call to Action*, Lausanne Movement, 2011, http://www.lausanne.org/content/ctc/ctcommitment, under "We Love God's World."

5. Ibid.

6. World Council of Churches, "Christian Authors Address Eco-theology, Ethics and Climate Change," March 5, 2015, http://www.oikoumene.org/en/press-centre/news/christian-authors -address-eco-theology-ethics-and-climate-change.

7. Richard D. Calenberg, "Creation," in Moreau et al., *Evangelical Dictionary of World Missions*, 240.

8. Ibid.

9. Ibid. Calenberg further explains earth care by saying, "Creation and salvation have been merged into a struggle for political justice, economic equality, and ecological responsibility."

on, Psalm 104 concludes, "May the Lord rejoice in his works" (v. 31 NIV). Theologian John Piper remarks that God takes pleasure in his creation.[10] He delights in it (Gen. 1:3, 9, 12, 18, 21, 25, 31). The theme of joy is interwoven with the theme of creation in the poetic descriptions of hills clothed with gladness (Ps. 65:12), fields jubilant and trees singing with joy (Ps. 96:12), mountains bursting into songs (Isa. 55:12), deserts being glad (Isa. 35:1), and meadows and valleys singing and shouting for joy (Ps. 65:13). What a joyful concert of praises to God that emanates daily from this earth! The whole creation celebrates God's actions: "Shout for joy, you heavens; rejoice, you earth; burst into song, you mountains! For the Lord comforts his people and will have compassion on his afflicted ones" (Isa. 49:13 NIV).

The Bible states that God found that what he made was good (Gen. 1:31). William Dyrness explains that the word "good," which has an ethical and aesthetic meaning in the creation narrative, "echoes the joy that Scripture elsewhere says accompanied God's creative work."[11] The link between the goodness of God and ecological concern is further elaborated in an article titled "The Joyful Environmentalists," in which journalist Andy Crouch describes two environmentalists, Eugene Peterson and Peter Harris, who "think of creation care not as an onerous duty but a natural response to the goodness of God."[12] In effect, according to the same conservationists, creation care should not be seen as "an attempt to 'save the planet'" but as a "response to who God is."[13] Although that article ends by observing that the "marker personality trait among environmentalists is anxiety," it also argues that "the Christian approach is very different: it is celebratory and grateful and hopeful."[14] As we consider current ecological damage or environmental disasters, we should remember how the goodness of God's creation and his great pleasure in it can make us joyful environmentalists.

We talked about the joyful noise emanating from the earth in praises to God. But creation today also utters sounds of sadness and deep sorrow. The earth is feeling the pain of destruction and abuse. In several instances, the Bible describes the suffering of creation awaiting its restoration with eager longing, wanting to "be delivered from the bondage of corruption" (Rom. 8:19–21 NKJV). Other passages describe the groans, the cries, and the pain

---

10. John Piper, "The Pleasure of God in His Creation," February 8, 1987, http://www.desiring god.org/sermons/the-pleasure-of-god-in-his-creation.

11. William Dyrness, *Let the Earth Rejoice: A Biblical Theology of Holistic Mission* (Eugene, OR: Wipf and Stock, 1998), 22. See also Psalm 148:3–5.

12. Andy Crouch, "The Joyful Environmentalists," *Christianity Today*, June 2011, 31.

13. Ibid.

14. Ibid., 32.

of creation (Rom. 8:22). As we look at the grim situation of the earth's environmental health, it is not very different from what these verses describe. In effect, the earth seems to be suffering and longing for better times. It is an important matter to consider as we think of witness: how can the earth radiate God's joy when it is carrying the wounds of an abusive humanity?

Indeed, there should be joy in the relation between God's earth and human beings. In dialoguing with Muslim scholar Badru D. Kateregga, Christian author David Shenk explains, "The witness of the Bible is that the earth with humans on it is very good. It is to be enjoyed. . . . God wants us to enjoy his creation and give thanks for it."[15] I enthusiastically agree! I enjoy God's creation. I delight in his works whether I am in a familiar environment or traveling around the globe, including the Muslim world. My camera is in continuous shooting mode as it attempts to capture the manifold expressions of God's creation. My computer is overloaded with pictures of the Creator's artistic designs. The immeasurable universe, like the infinitesimal world, reveals God's mind-blowing creativity.

However, although human beings are called to enjoy God's creation, the Creator remains the ultimate source of joy. Christians are not pantheists who revere nature; instead, they adore the Creator. Even at times when creation falters, joy remains, like in the following passages: "Though the fig tree should not blossom, and there be no fruit on the vines, thought the yield of the olive should fail and the fields produce no food, though the flock should be cut off from the fold and there be no cattle in the stalls, yet I will exult in the Lord; I will rejoice in the God of my salvation" (Hab. 3:17–18 NASB). Likewise God says to believers, "Though the mountains be shaken and the hills be removed, yet my unfailing love for you will not be shaken nor my covenant of peace be removed" (Isa. 54:10 NIV). The true source of joy is God, although he has also created many things for humans to enjoy.

This brief reminder of the joy God experienced when he created the earth and the joy radiating from creation reminds us that God's joy is a mark of Christian witness. We can now easily see that creation is not left out of this joy. As we engage in joyful witness, we cannot neglect the delight God expresses not only in creating human beings but also in all creation. This joy should powerfully stimulate us to steward the earth. If we remember God's joy when he contemplated his works, the goodness of God's creation, and the longing of creation to be delivered from suffering, we will certainly feel a greater motivation to care for the earth. We will also reflect on how we, as

15. Badru D. Kateregga and David W. Shenk, *A Muslim and a Christian in Dialogue* (Harrisonburg, VA: Herald Press, 2011), 123.

Christians, can bless Muslim communities by preventing the destruction of the environments in which we all must live. Muslim-Christian conflicts have sometimes devastated these environments, for example, by spoiling forests, polluting water and air, depleting natural resources needed by Muslim populations, or harming the natural systems on which their agriculture or other kinds of production depend. We will also carefully evaluate our lifestyle to be sure that it reflects the relationship we tell Muslims we have with the Triune God.

Ecology in Islam

What does the Qur'an say about creation? Does Islam invite its followers to care for the earth, just as Christianity does? Like the Bible, the Qur'an affirms that God created the heavens and the earth.[16] Although the creation narratives of the two texts differ on some points, they share common themes, and both claim that God[17] is Creator. For example, the Qur'an states, "Allah is the creator of all things" (13:16).[18] This passage resonates surprisingly with Psalm 24:1, which emphasizes that "the earth is the LORD's, and everything in it," because he is the One who formed everything. The Qur'an further states that "He is Allah, the Creator, the Evolver, the Bestower of Forms (or Colours). To Him belong the Most Beautiful Names: whatever is in the heavens and on earth, doth declare His Praises and Glory: and He is Exalted in Might, the Wise" (59:24). Reviewing the theological themes of the Qur'an, John Renard found that references to "God's nature and relationship to His Creation" are the "second-most numerous category of theological texts."[19] The Qur'an is replete with references to creation that remind believers of God's work.[20] Some passages also invite creation to praise God, albeit in a more toned-down manner compared to the Bible, where the praises of creation are so joyfully

16. Compare Qur'an 7:54 with Genesis 1:1.

17. I have chosen to use "God" for "Allah," since in most English translations, Muslims would use the word God. I understand that although there is only one God, the Qur'an and the Bible sometimes describe that God differently.

18. *The Holy Qur'ān*, trans. Abdullah Yusuf Ali (Ware, UK: Wordsworth Editions, 2000). All quotations from the Qur'an are from Yusuf Ali's translation unless otherwise indicated.

19. John Renard, *Islamic Theological Themes: A Primary Source Reader* (Oakland: University of California Press, 2014), 3.

20. Fazlun M. Khalid writes, "The Qur'ān speaks of creation (*khalq*) and it contains two hundred and sixty one verses where this word is used in its various grammatical forms derived from the root *kh l q*. These verses contain references to the human world; to the natural world of the Earth, from trees to turtles, from fish to fowl; and to the sun, stars and skies." "Islam and the Environment, Social and Economic Dimensions of Global Environmental Change," in *Encyclopedia of Global Environmental Change*, ed. Peter Timmerman (London: Wiley, 2001), 5:334.

expressed. The following qur'anic passage provides such an example: "Seest thou not that it is Allah whose praises all beings in the heavens and on earth do celebrate, and the birds (of the air) with wings outspread? Each one knows its own (mode of) prayer and praise. And Allah knows well all that they do" (24:41).

To Muslims, creation contains signs of God, as underlined in these qur'anic verses: "Verily in the heavens and the earth are Signs for those who believe. And in the creation of yourselves, and the fact that animals are scattered (through the earth), are Signs for those of assured Faith. And in the alternation of Night and Day, and the fact that Allah sends down Sustenance from the sky, and revives therewith the earth after its death, and in the change of the winds—are Signs for those that are wise" (45:3–5; see also 16:10–17). These passages show how Islam gives importance to God's creation. Inspired by these texts on creation, many Muslims develop a real passion to care for the world. In a document drafted for the International Union for Conservation of Nature, Islamic environmentalists emphasize this by saying that "vitally important, as the social functions of all things are, the primary function of all created beings as signs of their Creator constitutes the most sound legal basis for conservation of the environment."[21] These qur'anic passages resonate with biblical passages that talk about signs of God in creation. For example, "The heavens are telling of the glory of God; And their expanse is declaring the work of His hands" (Ps. 19:1 NASB). Another well-known passage says, "Ever since the creation of the world his [God's] invisible nature, namely, his eternal power and deity, has been clearly perceived in the things that have been made" (Rom. 1:20 RSV). Although Muslims and Christians differ in several areas on their understanding of how creation reflects God, these statements contain intersecting perspectives that allow for interfaith initiatives toward global conservation. Muslims, like Christians, have a strong sense that God is to be honored and worshiped as the Creator.

Thus, even though the joy-thread is not as clearly expressed in the Qur'an as in the Bible, Muslims also find reasons to care for the earth. According to Nawal Ammar, who has written extensively on ecology and Islam, Muslims have the duty "to enjoy and use the bounties of the earth" (Qur'an 31:20; 67:15). I have traveled with Muslim friends who display the same enthusiasm as I have when they look at God's creation. They remember Muhammad, their final prophet, who one night looked toward the majestic sky of Arabia

---

21. Abou Bakr Ahmed Ba Kader, Abdul Latif Tawfik El Shirazy Al Sabbagh, Mohamed Al Sayyed Al Glenid, and Mouel Yousef Samarrai Izzidien, *Environmental Protection in Islam*, IUCN Environmental Policy and Law Paper No. 20, rev., World Conservation Union, 1994, http://cmsdata.iucn.org/downloads/eplp_020reven.pdf.

and said: "In the creation of the heavens and the earth, and in the alternation of Night and Day, there are indeed signs for men of understanding."[22] I remember landing one night in a country bordering the land where Muhammad stood when he said this. My plane had arrived late at night in Amman, Jordan. While my host was driving me to her home, I stared at the sky and was stunned by the beauty of the desert night, illuminated by millions of glittering stars. With the psalmist, my heart burst out joyfully, "He counts the number of the stars; He gives names to all of them. Great is our Lord and abundant in strength; His understanding is infinite" (Ps. 147:4–5 NASB). It is not surprising, when one looks at the majestic sky, that God warned people not to worship creation instead of the Creator (Deut. 4:19).

We all, Muslims and Christians, marvel at creation. Among Muslims as among Christians, poets express this marvel with particular emotional force. Frederick Denny reminds us of a favorite hadith of Sufis which explains why God created the universe: "I was a hidden treasure, and I desired to be known; therefore I created the creation in order that I might be known."[23] Muslim Sufis have excelled in praising God for his creation. As the filmmaker and poet Mahmood Jamal says, "The Sufi poet feels justified in praising earthly beauty, because it reflects the Ultimate Beauty of the Creator."[24] For instance, Ahmad Jam, an eleventh-century Iranian poet, wrote,

> Whatever I see, I see the Beloved's beauty;
> Wherever I look I see His creation.
> Wherever I look, I see Goodness;
> Whatever is beautiful is the Beloved's beauty.
> Every form that is beautiful in the world
> Is only a sign to the Beloved's beauty.[25]

This celebration of God's works has even led some Muslims to express joy in creation care. Christian scholar of Islam David L. Johnston reports on research conducted by Anna M. Gade, a professor in environmental studies in Indonesia who shows that in environmentally friendly Islamic boarding schools, creation care and green Islam were promoted through "the emotional/ affective impact of songs and poetry extolling the beauty of God's creation

---

22. Hadith narrated by Ibn 'Abbas in *Sahih Bukhari*, book 78, chapter 118, hadith 239, http://sunnah.com/bukhari/78/239.

23. Frederick Mathewson Denny, *Introduction to Islam*, 4th ed. (New York: Routledge, 2016), 216.

24. Mahmood Jamal, ed. and trans., *Islamic Mystical Poetry: Sufi Verse from the Early Mystics to Rumi* (London: Penguin Classics, 2009), Kindle edition, location 542.

25. Ahmad Jam, "Wherever I Look," in Jamal, *Islamic Mystical Poetry*, location 1124.

and the joy of joining him in caring for it."[26] But as in the biblical narratives, so in Islam, the exaltation of creation should never replace the adoration of the Creator. Nawal Ammar states, "It is essential to underscore the issue that in Islam to consider nature or other creatures as sacred is in direct opposition of the Tawhid perspective, which views only God as sacred and only Allah to be worthy of worship."[27] Like Christians, Muslims wrestle with the question of whether creation, which suffers abuse and neglect, will ever be restored. Many believe in an eschatological liberation of creation. But this belief in a future recovery should not demotivate Muslims and Christians who want to care for the earth today.[28]

As we have seen, the Muslim teaching about creation can potentially stimulate Muslims to address environmental issues. It was not my intention to compare the creation texts in the Bible and the Qur'an in depth. Nevertheless, Christian and Muslim perspectives reflect common concerns that allow us to sit together and address some of the most challenging environmental issues that the world is facing. As Christians, we can contribute to reflection on creation care by highlighting aspects of our theological basis for creation care that diverge from Islam. In Christianity, God is not just one, as in Islam, but also triune. The work of Christ and the Holy Spirit, as a basis of environmental endeavors, is missing in Islam. The Trinity is a contribution that Christians can uniquely offer to this world. Nor does Islam see the consequences of Adam and Eve's disobedience to God as devastating to humanity, as the Bible does. In the Qur'an the original sin did not disrupt the relationship between humans and their environment in the same way as in the Bible. Although, in the Qur'an as in the Bible, Adam and Eve were expelled from paradise after their disobedience, they could still please God afterward through devotion and obedience to him as well as good works. Christians believe human beings need

26. David L. Johnston is particularly interested in the question of "divine mandate for human stewardship" as announced on his website titled *human trustees* (http://www.human trustees.org/about-us). He quotes Gade's research in one of his blogs titled "Islam and Ecology: Finding Today's Pulse," October 13, 2012, http://www.humantrustees.org/blogs/faith-and-ecology /item/76-islam-and-ecology-pulse.

27. Nawal Ammar, "Islam and Deep Ecology," in *Deep Ecology and World Religions: New Essays on Sacred Ground*, ed. David Landis Barnhill and Roger S. Gottlieb (Albany: State University of New York Press, 2001), 195.

28. Frederick M. Denny, a professor of Islamic studies, writes, "Muslims envision heaven as a beautiful garden which the Qur'an describes in many places. If life on earth is preparation for eternal life in heaven, then the loving care of the natural environment would seem to be appropriate training for the afterlife in the company of God and the angels in an environment that is perfectly balanced, peaceful, and verdant" ("Islam and Ecology: A Bestowed Trust Inviting Balanced Stewardship," Forum on Religion and Ecology at Yale, 1998, http://fore.yale.edu /religion/islam/).

a Savior. This changes the approach to creation care. Without the redemptive work of God in Christ, neither humans nor creation can be restored. While Christians, like Muslims, discern a call to engage in good works to heal the planet, they first have to recognize that the heart must be transformed by the saving work of Christ.

Caretakers of God's Earth

According to the biblical narrative, when God created Adam and Eve, he gave them a cultural mandate. They should be fruitful, increase in number, fill the earth, and subdue it (Gen. 1:28). Although the nature of this role as subduer has been debated throughout church history, it is clear that God foresaw a strong relationship between nature and human beings. Humans were called to be caretakers. Unfortunately, this mandate has sometimes been misunderstood, with detrimental consequences for the earth, especially when human beings practice earth stewardship in a domineering manner. When God appointed Adam and Eve to have "dominion" over the world, he did not mean that they should abuse or destroy it. Since many Christians misunderstand dominion, Gerry Breshears explains, "If we really believe the environment we inhabit is the handiwork of God and that we have been given responsible stewardship for it, then we will be zealous to protect and preserve what the Creator has put in our trust. We will see ourselves as God's stewards rather than owners."[29]

Christian Sri-Lankan author Vinoth Ramachandra carries the reflection even further. He claims that we can understand stewardship only when we understand creation as a gift: "Respect for the natural order, an order not alien to human beings but a shared realm of creaturely dependence, flows out of this recognition that we receive the world as a gift, not as a possession."[30] He describes human worship as "part of a cosmic act of praise that the whole creation, consciously or unconsciously, offers to its Creator."[31] Ramachandra suggests that the word "stewardship"[32] is not adequate. He prefers an attitude of gratitude toward nature, "recognizing that our dominion (as the unique bearer of the *imago Dei*) is exercised as part of a 'fellowship of creation,' hierarchically ordered toward the fulfillment of God's purposes."[33]

29. Breshears, "Ecology, Ecological Movement," 297.

30. Vinoth Ramachandra, *Subverting Global Myths: Theology and the Public Issues Shaping Our World* (Downers Grove, IL: InterVarsity, 2008), Kindle edition, location 2453.

31. Ibid., location 2460.

32. Ramachandra refers here to the traditional theological definition of "stewardship" as "human responsibility toward the nonhuman creation." Ibid., location 2461.

33. Ibid., location 2464.

When we consider, like those authors, that we don't own creation, that we
have deep connections with it, that it is a gift, and that it brings joy to the
heart of God, we will certainly consider it from a new perspective. We will
feel a greater motivation for empathetic caretaking. Furthermore, as we
consider our Muslim neighbors, we also wish the best for their environment, which is also God's creation. This is important to underline, especially
nowadays when Muslim and Christian communities are divided in many
places in the world. As countless human beings are killed in conflicts, we
often don't think of the environmental consequences. We ought to spend
more time not only praying for Muslim peoples in general but also asking
God to protect their nature, their air, their water, their natural resources,
because after all, their environment also ultimately belongs to God, the
Creator.

The Qur'an also acknowledges that the earth has been created for humans
to enjoy: "And He [Allah] has subjected to you, as from Him; all that is in
the heavens and on earth" (45:13). Authors like Fazlun M. Khalid, founder
of the Islamic Foundation for Ecology and Environmental Sciences (IFEES),
even contend that God created everything on earth as a gift to humans.[34] But
that gift entails conditions: "It is decidedly not something that one runs and
plays with."[35] Islamic thinking clearly emphasizes that humans cannot turn
away from creation. Ammar writes, "The whole universe is one single system
created and united by Allah. Looking at the universe with such a perspective
where all creatures are connected reveals common principles in Islam and
deep ecology."[36] But, although the Qur'an describes a close tie between human
beings and creation, it recognizes that they have different roles and statuses.
Adam is called a *khalifa* (vicegerent), or trustee of God. He has a specific
responsibility toward nature. The term *khalifa* reflects the responsibility given
by God. It is interpreted by environmentalists as an invitation to Muslims to
be better caretakers of the earth, as in the following declaration on one of
their websites: "This is . . . a call to Muslims to live up to their responsibilities
as guardians (Khalifa—Qur'an 6:167) of Allah's creation and work towards
leaving a livable earth for future generations."[37]

34. Fazlun M. Khalid, "Islam and the Environment," in *Encyclopedia of Global Environmental Change*, vol. 5: *Social and Economic Dimensions of Global Environmental Change*,"
ed. Peter Timmerman (Chichester, UK: John Wiley & Sons, 2002), 337.

35. Ibid.

36. Ammar, "Islam and Deep Ecology," 197.

37. This declaration is posted on the website of the Islamic Foundation for Ecology and
Environmental Sciences (IFEES), which is a charity based in the United Kingdom and according to the same website "dedicated to the maintenance of the Earth as a healthy habitat for all
living beings" (http://www.ifees.org.uk).

In his dialogue with Christian leader David Shenk, mentioned earlier, Muslim author and professor Badru Kateregga writes, "The superior position man holds in the eyes of God makes man an authority over all God's creation."[38] But humans should not overstep the limits, he says, and not misuse nature.[39] Likewise, David L. Johnston reminds us that for Muslims, "He [God] has placed humankind on earth as trustees of his good creation, and thus accountable for how they use (or abuse) its natural resources, which are meant to be shared equitably among themselves, with particular concern for the poor and marginalized."[40] Indeed, Islam recognizes that humans can misuse their responsibility toward creation. Ammar explains, "The role of humans as Khalifah, vice-regent, on earth is to better it and improve it and not spread evil and destruction."[41] In her view, God created the earth so that humans can be tested to see whether they will perform the good to which they are called. Khalid, too, sees the earth as a "testing ground of the human species."[42] Thus, according to these arguments, man-made environmental disasters may indicate that humans have abandoned their desire to please God.

Although there are differences between Muslim and Christian interpretations of the command God gave humans to care for the world, this shared concern about creation will make it possible for Christians to work with Muslims on environmental issues. The desire to care for the earth brings us closer, since it focuses our attention on the "this-wordly" aspect of the kingdom of God. Christians are aware that, like other dialogues of life, those that occur in the context of interfaith initiatives can stimulate fresh kinds of encounters between Muslims and Christians. In his brief article on Muslim-Christian dialogue, Charles A. Kimball explains that "'dialogue in community' and 'the dialogue of life' are inclusive categories concentrating on practical issues of common concern."[43] Earth care falls under these categories. Kimball explains that these kinds of dialogue encourage common action. As we engage in common initiatives with Muslims, who also care for the earth, our encounters take on an ordinary aspect. Kimball was right when he said, "Another important

---

38. Kateregga and Shenk, *Muslim and a Christian*, 39.

39. Ibid., 39–40.

40. David L. Johnston, "Qatar Going Green," *Human Trustees* (blog), November 5, 2012, http://www.humantrustees.org/blogs/faith-and-ecology/item/78-qatar-green.

41. Ammar, "Islam and Deep Ecology," 199.

42. He explains, "The tests are a measure of our acts of worship (ihsan) in its broadest sense. That is living in a way that is pleasing to Allah, striving in everything we do to maintain the harmony of our inner and outer environments." Khalid, "Islam and the Environment," 335.

43. Charles A. Kimball. "Muslim-Christian Dialogue," Oxford Islamic Studies Online, http://www.oxfordislamicstudies.com/article/opr/t236/e0567.

My Encounter with Abdul

Caleb Chul-Soo Kim, Africa International University

Abdul was living in a humble Muslim community of northern Kenya. Despite extreme poverty, he was always proud to be a faithful Muslim. When I began my ministry in his neighborhood in the early 1990s, he was very disturbed with my presence there. He sometimes expressed his dislike of me even with some harsh words. Having watched my services for about two years, one day he called upon me at my local church. He did not want to enter the church compound, which was *haram* for him. So I went out to meet with him, and to my surprise I had a quite pleasant conversation with him. We greeted each other nicely for the first time, and even pleasantly exchanged our different views on afterlife and other religious issues. All of a sudden he said, bluntly yet in a concerned tone, "Mr. Kim, I now believe that you are a good man. But I am very sad that you will go to hell because you are a Christian!" A bit stunned for a moment, I maintained my calm and suggested that he read the Bible. Surprisingly, he agreed and received a copy of the Swahili New Testament. He said that he would read it because of our friendship! After that interesting encounter, he invited me to his humble house, and even asked me to pray for his sick son. I asked him if I could pray in the name of Jesus, and to my surprise again he was happy to let me do so, saying, "We love Jesus too." Although his understanding of Jesus was different, Abdul was one of my first Muslim friends who taught me about who Muslims are and how they sincerely follow their religious traditions in the context of ordinary life. Through him and other Muslim friends like him, I *learned Muslims*, not just Islam. Since then I have met and befriended innumerable Muslims who are just like us, caring about family, fearing God, and struggling with so many challenges in varied life settings. Abdul didn't come to Christ by the time I left for my first home assignment, and sadly I did not hear further of his life journey. But I still treasure our friendship in my memory.

function of dialogue in community is difficult to measure: organizers often express the hope that it will stimulate more intentional and informal daily interaction between Muslim and Christian neighbors."[44] Just like Jesus, who struck up conversations with people on issues that deeply mattered to them

44. Ibid.

and often identified crucial needs of society, we, as Christians, may find that when we engage with Muslims on environmental issues, we have the opportunity to share God's joy for the world.

Green Islam

Although creation narratives seemed to predict a bright future for creation, with caretakers who are given a clear mandate to do their job well, we live in a world in which we must admit that humans have abused these responsibilities. Instead of being good caretakers of this world, they have brought much mischief to it. Thus, like Christians, Muslims have understood the environmental challenges and developed a growing interest in adopting ecological practices. Islamic eco-news is increasingly buzzing on the internet. Islam has become green.[45] Muslims draw from their sacred texts valuable lessons about earth care. Denny explains, "There is, in the Qur'an and in the teachings and example of the Prophet Muhammad . . . much with which to construct an authentic Islamic environmental ethic that both sustains what Muslims have achieved traditionally in this direction and leaves open a wide avenue for creative and innovative solutions in the contemporary context."[46]

As a result, a plethora of Muslim earth-care movements and organizations have been created in many countries around the world. Ammar explains, "Islam recommends a clear path to achieving the equilibrium between use and protection [of the earth], namely action."[47] Islam regards actions focused on care of the earth as actions of devotion to God. Ammar points out that throughout history these actions have taken many forms.[48] In our own time, IFEES,[49] based in Birmingham, England, promotes understanding of environmental issues; publishes *Eco-Islam*, a newsletter devoted to ecology; and provides guidance and resources for Islamic communities.[50] The vision of another group called

45. The word "green" can have many meanings in environmental discussions. The implication here is that Muslims are increasingly becoming concerned about creation care as drawn from their own religious texts.

46. Denny, "Islam and Ecology."

47. Nawal H. Ammar, "Islam and Deep Ecology," in *Liberating Faith: Religious Voices for Justice, Peace, & Ecological Wisdom*, ed. Roger S. Gottlieb (Lanham, MD: Rowman & Littlefield, 2003), 556.

48. Ibid.

49. "About IFEES," www.ifees.org.uk.

50. Sophie Gilliat-Ray and Mark Bryant, "Are British Muslims 'Green'? An Overview of Environmental Activism among Muslims in Britain," *Journal for the Study of Religion, Nature and Culture* 5, no. 3 (2011): 292.

Green Muslims is "to be a source in the Muslim community for spiritually-inspired environmental education, reflection, and action."[51]

Islamic ecological organizations often like to use the word "jihad" to describe their undertakings.[52] For example, they talk about jihad against litter in major cities.[53] Denny, referring to the color green as a symbol of Islam, says that it also "provides a charter for a green movement that could become the greatest exertion yet known in Islamic history, a 'green jihad' appropriate for addressing the global environmental crisis."[54]

This green jihad influences many areas of life. For example, Muslims are increasingly concerned about animal welfare.[55] There are also new earth-friendly trends in mosque architecture. More and more eco-mosques are being built. The Cambridge Mosque Project states on its website, "This building will be truly inclusive, sustainable, safe, secure and respectful of the neighbourhood."[56] In an article titled "Is the Dubai Desert about to Go Green?" John Vidal reports that by 2030, "Dubai will have cut its carbon emissions by 29%, switched 30% of its $100bn a year economy to renewable energy, 'clean coal' and nuclear, and initiated a plethora of energy- and water-saving initiatives."[57] All these

51. Green Muslims home page, http://www.greenmuslims.org.

52. According to *The Oxford Dictionary of Islam* (ed. John L. Esposito [New York: Oxford University Press, 2003], 159–60), the word "jihad" is "from the Arabic root meaning 'to strive,' 'to exert,' 'to fight'; exact meaning depends on context. May express a struggle against one's evil inclinations, an exertion to convert unbelievers, or a struggle for the moral betterment of the Islamic community. Today often used without any religious connotation, with a meaning more or less equivalent to the English word *crusade* (as in 'a crusade against drugs')."

53. See, e.g., the "Clean Medina" video which promotes Jihad against litter in the city of Birmingham, UK (https://www.youtube.com/watch?v=VZdNqJ9WGFg). The BBC website in an article titled "Clean Medina-the Jihad on Litter" by Nick Booth, reported on that initiative at http://www.bbc.co.uk/birmingham/content/articles/2007/09/19/clean_medina_feature.shtml. Other phrases seen on the web are "jihad against pollution," "waging a green jihad," or "jihad against waste."

54. Denny, "Islam and Ecology."

55. Ammar helps us better understand the Islamic view that shapes the attitude of Muslim environmentalists toward animals:

The Prophet has forbidden the beating of animals on the face, and prohibited the throwing of stones at animals. He has recommended that every care should be taken when slaughtering animals. It is forbidden to make animals the objects of human sports or entertainment. The Prophet asks humans to feel within their souls the pain animals feel and avoid all practices that torture and frighten living beings. The Prophet says about using animals in game, "A sparrow that was used just for entertainment would on the day of judgment complain to [God] against the person who did so just for fun." (Ammar, "Islam and Deep Ecology," 202)

56. "Cambridge Announces Plans for Eco-Friendly Mosque," *Islam Today*, July 17, 2010, http://en.islamtoday.net/artshow-229-3720.htm.

57. John Vidal, "Is the Dubai Desert about to Go Green?," *Guardian*, October 24, 2013, http://www.theguardian.com/environment/2013/oct/24/dubai-desert-green-renewable-energy.

initiatives seem very familiar to the Christian community, which undertakes similar projects around the world, all for the good of the planet.

David Johnston shows "how Shari'a is also used by a growing number of Muslims to promote earth-friendly practices and lobby for government regulations that protect the environment."[58] To him, "the Shari'a is now a symbol for 'green Muslims.'"[59] Muslim environmental organizations, for example, debate over "the Sharia-compliance of genetically modified crops."[60] Recently, firms in the United Kingdom announced Sharia-compliant green energy projects.[61] But environmental activists also work through grassroots movements. In April 2015, Masoumeh Ebtekar, head of the Department of Environment of the Islamic Republic of Iran, in celebration of Iranian Women's Day, gave a speech in which she highlighted the major role that women are playing in protecting the environment.[62] She is a 2006 Laureate of the United Nations' Champion of the Earth Award. She has "helped establish thousands of environmental groups led by women seeking change."[63]

Although we witness the growth of these green movements, or green jihads, in the Muslim world, the world is increasingly interconnected, and it will not be surprising to see Christian and Muslim environmentalists rubbing shoulders more often. For some Christians, these encounters will essentially result in interfaith initiatives that potentially can heal creation on a larger scale. Two are better than one! For other Christians, these ordinary types of encounters may offer opportunities to create stronger bonds, with opportunities to point toward the resources found in the Triune God and participate in his joy.

58. David L. Johnston, "Intra-Muslim Debates on Ecology: Is Shari'a Still Relevant?," *Worldviews: Global Religions, Culture, and Ecology* 16 (2012): 219.

59. Johnston, "Qatar Going Green."

60. Qur'an 15:19 advocates "balance in nature." Other qur'anic verses to consider in this discussion are Qur'an 30:30 and 4:117–19. For example, Mohideen Abdul Kader, the vice-president of the Consumer Association of Penang, Malaysia, wrote, "Islamic scholars must be wary of being manipulated by the biotech industry to give religious legitimacy to its products, and realise how aggressively this industry is trying to penetrate foreign markets" ("The GM Controversy," *Eco-Islam*, no. 8 (June 2011): 2, http://www.ifees.org.uk/wp-content/uploads/20 15/04/newsletter_EcoIslam8.pdf.

61. "Sharia-Compliant Green Energy Investment Project Is 'World's First,'" BusinessGreen website, http://www.businessgreen.com/bg/feature/2346770/sharia-compliant-green-energy -investment-project-is-worlds-first.

62. "UNESCO Celebrates the Iranian Women's Day," UNESCO Office in Tehran, http:// www.unesco.org/new/en/tehran/about-this-office/single-view/news/unesco_celebrates_the _iranian_womens_day#.VUzuUM6d6fQ.

63. Brennan R. Hill, *World Religions and Contemporary Issues: How Evolving Views on Ecology, Peace, and Women Are Impacting Faith Today* (New London, CT: Twenty-Third Publications, 2013), 332.

Interfaith Perspectives

In each of the two faith traditions there are followers who desire to partner with followers of the other tradition in environmental projects. For example, the Green Muslims announce that they are "committed to collaborating and partnering with organizations interested or already engaged in issues related to the environment."[64] Several Christian scholars interested in Islam have chosen ecology as their major research topic. Johnston's book *Earth, Empire and Sacred Text: Muslims and Christians as Trustees of Creation*[65] is of particular interest since, as a Christian scholar, he is interested in the health of the planet, with a particular focus on how Christians and Muslims can partner in earth care. He encourages Muslims and Christians to embrace a common ethics deriving from their creation theologies in order to foster environmental change. His blog is a valuable resource for Christians who want to understand how to engage with Muslims on ecological issues.[66]

Thus, religious leaders underline the important role that religious communities can play in earth care. They promote environmental projects for the obvious reason that religions have a large sphere of influence and through their authority can impact large groups that can make changes for the good. Recently, United Nations secretary-general Ban Ki-moon emphasized this very fact when he said, "Religious leaders, we the peoples need your moral leadership to address climate change."[67] Muslims welcome such invitations. Johnston reminds us that Seyyed Hossein Nasr, in *Religion and the Order of Nature*, "argues that the worsening ecological crisis cannot be solved without people of faith coming together and pooling their spiritual resources which center on the sacredness of nature."[68] Johnston adds that contemporary Islamic thinker Mawil Izzi Dien also believes that "our planet's woes can only be addressed through a concerted effort by people of all faiths."[69] Muslims

---

64. "Partners and Collaborators," Green Muslims website, http://www.greenmuslims.org /programs/partners.

65. David L. Johnston, *Earth, Empire and Sacred Text: Muslims and Christians as Trustees of Creation* (London: Equinox, 2010).

66. David L. Johnston, *Human Trustees*, http://www.humantrustees.org/about-us/david -l-johnston.

67. Ban Ki-moon, Twitter post to The Climate Group, April 28, 2015, https://twitter.com /ClimateGroup/status/593088325692616704.

68. Seyyed Hossein Nasr, *Religion and the Order of Nature* (Oxford: Oxford University Press, 1996), cited in Johnston, "Intra-Muslim Debates on Ecology," 222.

69. Johnston, "Intra-Muslim Debates on Ecology," 223. Izzi Dien's book *The Environmental Dimensions of Islam* (Cambridge: Lutterworth, 2000) devotes almost half of its content to an Islamic theology of environmentalism and over a half to Islamic ethics and the use of Shari'a in ecology, with a particular focus on the legal tool called *maslaha*, or public benefit.

understand that effective changes will benefit not just their communities but also non-Muslims. Several interfaith conversations have been undertaken to rally forces around the conversation about the planet. For example, the Interfaith Declaration on Climate Change states, "Our vision is to repeat the message over and over that the religions of Earth stand as one behind strong and immediate limits to climate changing emissions of 'greenhouse gasses,' predominantly CO2."[70] In 2008, the National Association of Evangelicals sponsored a talk titled "A Christian and Muslim Dialogue on Creation Care" at the World Bank in Washington, DC, which discussed, among other topics, the ethics of evangelism and *da'wa*.[71] The World Council of Churches has started several interfaith initiatives, including Muslim leaders in ecological projects, as when it recently issued a call for action on climate change.[72]

These initiatives may be slowed down, however, because some adherents of both faiths are not motivated to participate. Some believers in both traditions think humans can do nothing to restore creation because it will be renewed only eschatologically. Others resist participating because they believe they are not responsible for environmental problems; they contend that the problems arise from the actions of those who don't believe a Creator exists and who therefore feel less motivated to care for the earth. Nawal Ammar, for instance, shows that some Muslims "see the harm that is done to God's creation as being the consequence of the non-Muslims," who have lost sight of the sacred and acted with greed and hunger for power. Other Muslims blame some forms of disempowerment of Muslim nations coupled with Western corruption.[73]

Conclusion

Both the Qur'an and the Bible provide resources to inform earth stewardship and uniquely shape the motivations of those who want to bring healing to the earth. Christians should be stimulated to care for the earth because God

70. "Vision," website of the Interfaith Declaration on Climate Change, http://www.inter faithdeclaration.org/vision.html.

71. Rick Love, "The Ethics of Da'wa and Evangelism: Respecting the Other and Freedom of Religion," talk given at the World Bank, June 2008, http://www.worldevangelicals.org/resources /source.htm?id=529. In Islam, *da'wa* means inviting someone to embrace the Muslim faith.

72. "Interfaith Statement on Climate Change: Climate, Faith and Hope; Faith Traditions Together for a Common Future," World Council of Churches, September 21, 2014, https:// www.oikoumene.org/en/resources/documents/general-secretary/joint-declarations/interfaith -statement-on-climate-change.

73. Nawal Ammar, "Islam and Deep Ecology," in *Deep Ecology and World Religions: New Essays on Sacred Ground*, ed. David Landis Barnhill and Roger S. Gottlieb (Albany: State University of New York Press, 2001), 206.

delights in it, because humans have received it as a gift to enjoy, and because there is a deep fellowship between creation and human beings. Joy is clearly reflected in creation.

In both traditions, humans are responsible for caring for the earth. Yet today, instead of rejoicing, the earth is hurting in many places. Both Muslims and Christians know that they have sometimes been unfaithful to God's calling to guard the earth. They need to evaluate their practices in light of what their sacred texts teach. To Christians the cultural mandate clearly shows that they should see creation as a gift. They do not own creation. It belongs to God. Therefore, they must understand that they should not only care for their immediate environment but also respect contexts in which Muslims live. If God owns the earth and has given it to humans to enjoy, there is no reason why Christians should neglect ecological challenges of other faith communities. We must acknowledge and assess the ways that we have hurt Muslim environments. We have to repent for resources that we have not shared with Muslims in a manner that honors God.

The Qur'an and the Bible share enough creation themes to spark shared projects in the protection and use of the earth. Two faith communities are better than one for solving the gigantic environmental problems we face. The task of earth care offers Muslims and Christians opportunities to meet in ordinary encounters. In these encounters, Islam takes on a human face for Christians and vice versa. As war and conflicts rage between Muslim and Christian communities in many parts of the world, creating insurmountable barriers, it is important to create these spaces of tranquil encounters where people peacefully work together for the good of the world. When Muslim and Christian youths are planting trees together to protect the earth, they are less likely to harm each other.

Since this book is primarily written for Christian readers, I end this chapter with insights for them. Joy is a key characteristic in God's creation. Joy is an emotion that propels people forward. It gives them the energy to do what seems otherwise tedious or even impossible. Remembering God's joy about his creation should help us engage with greater confidence in eco-friendly behaviors.

We should think carefully about how we treat our own parts of the world but also other parts of it, where Muslims live, for example. Their land is God's land, the land he created and delights in. How are we using or misusing the resources with which God provided Muslims as they moved to these lands? How do we partner with them in ways that honor God as faithful trustees of the earth?

As we engage with Muslims on environmental issues, we should never forget that, although many signs point to God in his creation, the perfect sign is Jesus Christ. To truly understand God's purpose for the world from a biblical perspective requires a meticulous reading of the New Testament. Jesus was chosen before the creation of the world (1 Pet. 1:20). Colossians 1:15–16 (RSV) reminds us that Jesus "is the image of the invisible God, the first-born of all creation; for in him all things were created, in heaven and on earth, visible and invisible, whether thrones or dominions or principalities or authorities—all things were created through him and for him." Joyful witness places Jesus at the center of the environmental discussion.

As we follow Jesus, we respect and please God in caring for his works. In other words, we are stating, by adopting new behaviors, that we are thankful for what God has entrusted us with. But we also recognize that the roots of the environmental issues are deeper than may appear to nonbelievers. It is good to ponder the following statement made by Patriarch Bartholomew of the Eastern Orthodox Church: "We believe that the roots of the environmental crisis are not primarily economic or political, nor technological, but profoundly and essentially religious, spiritual and moral. This is because it is a crisis about and within the human heart."[74] And to Christians, unlike Muslims, the crisis of the human heart can be resolved only when a person acknowledges what Jesus Christ has accomplished. The following verses from Colossians give us the clue: "For in him all the fullness of God was pleased to dwell, and through him to reconcile to himself all things, whether on earth or in heaven, by making peace through the blood of his cross" (Col. 1:19–20 RSV).

For Discussion

1. What do the Bible and the Qur'an say about earth care? How does this shape Muslim-Christian relations?
2. Can you identify Muslim-Christian environmental projects related to earth care that you may want to join?
3. How can Christians engage in joyful witness among Muslims as they address local and global environmental issues?

74. "By His All-Holiness Ecumenical Patriarch Bartholomew at the Conferral of an Honorary Doctorate in Sociology from the Izmir University of Economics," February 9, 2015, http://www.ec-patr.org/docdisplay.php?lang=en&id=2005&tla=gr.

6

Caring for the Needy

A few years ago, I was in Cairo, staying at the home of friends while they were abroad. One morning I heard a knock on the door. I opened the door and saw a veiled elderly woman asking if my friends were home. I invited her in; she entered but did not sit down. She seemed to be in a hurry. She asked if I had some food that I could share with her. I opened the fridge and handed her what I found, a carton of eggs. She put her arms around my shoulders and started sobbing out of gratefulness. It felt like I had given her the world. She then explained. She had six young children. Her husband died and left her with no resources. She had found a cleaning job that provided just enough money each day to feed her children. The previous day her son had fallen from a flat rooftop on which he had been playing with friends. Since he had been taken to the hospital, she had missed a day of work and had no money to buy food. This is why she came, hoping my friends would help. As she ended her story, the Lord's Prayer came to my mind: "Father . . . , give us this day our daily bread" (Matt. 6:9, 11 RSV). How often do I forget, amidst consumerism, that not everyone has bread daily? Today, as I write these lines, some people will have nothing to eat, not even breadcrumbs.

In Christian witness words are not enough. Caring deeds are also important, and joy is intrinsic to care. Muslims, too, care for others, including the needy. Unfortunately, human caregiving has sometimes divided religious communities, especially when motives are misunderstood. Both Muslims and Christians have addressed these tensions, but as the needs of our world grow, we must see how Christians and Muslims can address them together. As we care for one another, we may discover that estranged relations can turn into ordinary encounters.

Biblical Reflections

From Genesis through Revelation, the Bible is replete with references about caring for human needs. A few key texts will suffice: the Mosaic laws, the Sermon on the Mount (Matt. 5–7), the Nazareth Manifesto (Luke 4:16–21), the practices of the early church (Acts 2:44–47), and the recommendations of the apostles regarding human caregiving (e.g., James 2:14–26). These passages may be summarized, as Jesus did, in the twofold commandment to love God and love one's neighbor (Mark 12:30–31). To paraphrase the author of the Epistle of James, faith without deeds is dead (James 2:26). Thus, there is no Christian witness without caring for the needs of others. It may start as simply as sharing a carton of eggs with a Muslim woman, moving overseas short term to help after a natural disaster, moving long term to work with a non-governmental organization, or even being a voice for the poor in politics. ✡ Churches are called to be diaconal communities, ministering to the needs of their members and others. The New Testament often shows churches sharing resources and serving others (e.g., Acts 2:44–45). Although the use of the Greek word *diakonia* (service) in the biblical context has been interpreted variously, it is clearly an important concept.[1] The verb *diakoneō* (to serve) is even applied to Jesus, who came to serve and not to be served (Mark 10:45). In the numerous testimonies I have heard from Muslims who have become followers of Christ, they often said their lives were touched by the generosity and hospitality of Christians. It is also my experience that Muslims often look at whether my life, as a Christian, matches what I profess. My words are usually not sufficient. As a missionary who worked in Algeria said many years ago, in Muslim contexts "the messenger is as important as the message."[2] It is not enough to preach; Muslims have to see our faith through our lifestyle, our compassion, our good deeds. That is how we say Jesus has transformed our lives and is worth embracing. Christian scholar of Islam J. Dudley Woodberry conducted research that corroborates this thesis on the conversion of

1. How this term should be understood is often debated. Does it mean service or mission? Are some Christians called to preach the word, others to perform good deeds? How does *kerygma* (preaching) combine with *diakonia* in an individual's life?

2. Charles R. Marsh, "Sharing Our Faith with Muslims," in *Encountering the World of Islam*, ed. Keith E. Swartley (Tyrone, GA: Authentic Media, 2005), 304.

Muslims. He writes that "respondents ranked the lifestyle of Christians as the most important influence in their decision to follow Christ."[3] In other words, Muslims do not want to see a gap between what people say and how they apply it to their daily lives. Muslims are touched by the love of Christians, their moral conduct, and their peaceful attitude. Recently, I talked with a Muslim-raised Moroccan believer who said that the only reason his Muslim mother, otherwise suspicious of Christianity, accepted that he was a follower of Christ was that his life was so deeply transformed by the message of the gospel.

As in other places around the world, there is currently an ocean of need in Muslim societies. As Christians we can address these needs, starting in our neighborhoods. When I lived in Paris, I met poor Muslim migrants with vital needs. Although the Christian ministry I had joined focused primarily on the spiritual needs of Muslim-background believers, we also spent time caring for those who had barely enough to eat. I devoted much of my time to driving people to job interviews, helping newcomers find housing, teaching French, and cooking meals. Sometimes ministry can mean offering a glass of water in the name of Christ. Likewise, many churches around the world are reaching out to migrant workers and refugees. Since some Muslim migrants have plenty of resources, they, too, are helping their needy coreligionists.

Other Christians feel the need to look beyond their neighborhoods. They are moved by the needs of Muslims they see on the news or during travel abroad. A scan of almost any news source reveals that in many places human beings hurt deeply. Thus, at Urbana 12, the 2012 meeting of InterVarsity Christian Fellowship's triennial student missions conference, sixteen thousand attendees assembled caregiver kits for people living with HIV and AIDS in several African countries. Countries with large Muslim populations also have huge needs. The Christian humanitarian organization World Vision lists the Syrian refugee crisis, Iraq displacement, the Somalian drought, and the South Sudan conflict among the top humanitarian crises in 2015.[4] According to Amnesty International, there are over 4 million refugees from Syria, and 7.6 million Syrians are displaced.[5] In many African countries, the violent acts of al-Shabab and Boko Haram have led to the deaths of tens of thousands of

3. J. Dudley Woodberry, Russell G. Shubin, and G. Marks, "Why Muslims Follow Jesus: The Results of a Recent Survey of Converts from Islam," *Christianity Today*, October 24, 2007, http://www.christianitytoday.com/ct/2007/october/42.80.html?start=1.

4. Chris Huber, "Top Humanitarian Crises to Watch in 2015," World Vision, last updated September 21, 2015, http://www.worldvision.org/news-stories-videos/top-humanitarian-crises-2015.

5. *Amnesty International Report 2014/15*, Amnesty International, 2015, 2, http://www.amnestyusa.org/pdfs/AIR15_English.PDF.

Reaching a Muslim's Heart through Her Feet

J. Dudley Woodberry, Fuller Theological Seminary

In the days leading up to 9/11/2001, fighting in Afghanistan between the various sectarian *mujahideen* groups and then the Taliban resulted in thousands of refugees pouring down into neighboring Peshawar, Pakistan. There they were squashed into tents and mud hovels in refugee camps in intense heat and with poor sanitation. Our oldest son, with his family, had set up a humanitarian aviation and communication agency in that city to serve throughout Afghanistan. My wife, Roberta, went there during the school year to teach our grandchildren and other children of aid personnel, and I commuted there between teaching intensive courses at Fuller Seminary.

Conditions at one camp were harsher than at others; so Roberta and her class took school supplies to the students so they had more than just black slates with chalk. Another group of aid workers imported thousands of sandals for the children who ran around with bare feet on the rough and

civilians, abductions of hundreds, and insecurity and fear for countless others.[6] A plethora of secular and faith-based organizations have resources available to fill needs in these Muslim contexts—needs caused by war, politics, lack of resources, unjust social structures, and natural disasters.

A few years ago, when a tsunami hit Indonesia with devastating force, in the Muslim-majority region of Banda Aceh there were numerous reports of how Christians and Muslims started to partner together for relief work, despite previous conflicts. In Breueh, an Island of northern Sumatra, Christians started to reach out to Muslims, helping them rebuild their village. The nature of their relationship was transformed for the better. As reported in *Christianity Today*, Christians, who first feared they would be persecuted by Muslims, "discovered that Banda Aceh people are not so bad," and added, "We now live in each other's minds. Grace can walk through open doors."[7] Thus, besides meeting basic needs, Christians also experience new kinds of encounters with Muslims, often for the good.

Compassion and human care have characterized Christian engagement among Muslims. Christians have felt compelled to show their attachment

6. Ibid., 6.
7. Tony Carnes, "Walking the Talk after the Tsunami," *Christianity Today*, March 1, 2006, 66.

parched ground. But they decided that they would also wash their feet as Jesus had. Our daughter-in-law joined the group. For a week they washed every foot with antibacterial soap, "anointed" it with oil, and silently prayed for the child, then gave each of them new sandals, a quilt, and a shawl, plus a twenty-kilogram bag of flour for every family.

At first the sores, pus, "pink eye," and dirt were revolting, but then our daughter-in-law felt a deep love as she silently prayed, "Dear Father, this little girl looks like she does not have anyone to care for her. Let my touch feel to her as if you were touching her. May she remember how you touched her this day, and may she seek after you hereafter. Thank you that those who seek you will find you." Many looked up and shyly smiled.

Sometime later a teacher in one of the tents used for a refugee school asked her class, "Who are the best Muslims?" A girl raised her hand and replied, "The *kafirs*" (a term meaning "unbelievers" that is often used by Muslims for Christians). After the teacher recovered from her shock, she asked, "Why?" The young girl replied, "The Muslim fighters killed my father, but the *kafirs* washed my feet."

---

to God by feeding the hungry, giving the thirsty something to drink, hosting strangers, providing clothes to those in need, caring for the sick, and visiting the prisoner (Matt. 25:34–40). Anyone reading books on mission among Muslims will find countless accounts of acts of human caregiving that have impacted Muslim-Christian relationships for the good. Following God's call to care for the sick, the orphans, the widows, and the poor, Christians have established hospitals, schools, and orphanages as integral parts of their witness. Some of these good deeds have touched the heart of rulers in Muslim lands. A nineteenth-century report of missionary work by the Arabian Mission in the Arabian Peninsula stated: "The king has made repeated calls on our medical personnel."[8] Today, likewise, one can find manifold Christian ministries tending to economic, health, and educational needs throughout the Muslim world. I could give numerous examples for each of these mission practices from my travels around the Muslim world. Christians are caring for the needs of Muslims in many parts of the world, as illustrated by the Kasr el-Dobara Church in Cairo opening its doors to care

8. Gerrit D. Van Peursem, "The Arabian Mission and Saudi-Arabia," *Muslim World* 38, no. 1 (January 1, 1948): 10.

for the injured after the demonstrations during the Egyptian Revolution,[9] or by Christians caring for refugees.[10]

Touched by the needs of others, Christians have also issued statements and developed theological models that address these issues. In the Manila Manifesto, from the Lausanne Movement, Christians are called to "demonstrate God's love visibly by caring for those who are deprived of justice, dignity, food and shelter."[11] Thus we are called to adopt these same practices as we live among Muslims, in order to demonstrate God's love. The same manifesto affirms that "good news and good works are inseparable." Muslims can easily understand this approach, since in their own faith tradition they are also called to good deeds. Actually, Muslims are quite surprised if they encounter Christians who share the gospel only with words, since in their own faith tradition there is no separation. Later, the Lausanne Movement generated the Cape Town Commitment, with a similar emphasis on human caregiving. It invites Christians to "love the world's poor and suffering."[12] It is good to remember, in a world that is often divided along religious, ethnic, or cultural lines, that this love knows no boundaries. Jesus constantly crossed these lines while he was on earth. Likewise, despite what separates Muslims and Christians, it may be that God asks us to forget the divisions to reach out to those who hurt. Bryant L. Myers, professor of transformational development at Fuller Theological Seminary, has reflected and taught extensively on these questions and states that development, "from a Christian perspective, is a theological act every bit as much as it is a technical problem-solving act."[13] According to Myers, "Poverty is about relationships that don't work, that isolate, that abandon or devalue."[14] He then suggests, "Transformation must be about restoring relationships, just and right relationships with God, with self, with community, with the 'other' and with the environment."[15]

9. Jonathan Westmark, "Egypt's Christians Provide Lessons in Faith," *The Clarion*, Bethel University, February 15, 2012, https://www.bethel.edu/news/clarion/articles/2012/february/egypt-christians.

10. See how World Relief partners with churches to help Syrian and Iraqi refugees at http://www.worldrelief.org/refugee-crisis/.

11. Manila Manifesto, article 8, Lausanne Movement, July 1989, http://www.lausanne.org/content/manifesto/the-manila-manifesto.

12. "The Cape Town Commitment: A Confession of Faith and a Call to Action," Proceedings from The Third Lausanne Congress on World Evangelization, which took place in Cape Town, South Africa (October 2010), point C, under section 7 titled "We Love God's World," 2011, https://www.lausanne.org/content/ctc/ctcommitment).

13. Bryant L. Myers, *Walking with the Poor: Principles and Practices of Transformational Development*, rev. and updated (Maryknoll, NY: Orbis Books, 2011), Kindle edition, location 1414.

14. Ibid., location 1980.

15. Ibid.

Joy of Helping the Poor

Overwhelming needs, hopelessness, and suffering may lead Christians to think that human caregiving brings only stress and weariness. Does caring for those in need involve joy, or is it only a religious duty that generates no positive emotion? Joy can run through human caregiving just as it can run through the witness we bear while engaging with people in social media, art, and earth stewardship. Many biblical passages talk about the blessings of giving, though not all use a word translated "joy." Giving, in the Bible, is seen as something good and positive, rather than cumbersome. "It is more blessed to give than to receive" (Acts 20:35 NIV), "God loves a cheerful giver" (2 Cor. 9:7 NIV), abundant joy can overflow in copious liberality (2 Cor. 8:1–5), and giving brings much joy to the heart of those who receive (Phil. 4:10–20). It also delights the heart of God (Heb. 13:16).

In a study of the well-being of humanitarian workers by the Headington Institute, we learn that caring for one's own needs is not enough, because it will "never yield true joy or peace."[16] Researchers of the institute then suggest, "It is a paradox—we best refill our own cup of contentment and joy when part of the effort goes towards pouring out some for others. Those who give to others set in motion a cycle of blessing that often includes feelings of satisfaction, fulfillment, and a clear sense of purpose."[17] This joy has also been observed by scientific studies of the brain. Research on unselfish acts conducted at the National Institute of Neurological Disorders and Stroke in Bethesda, Maryland, reveals that charitable giving activates the brain's reward and pleasure centers, which release dopamine, a neurotransmitter involved in pleasurable feelings.[18] When people are generous and donate for good causes, their bodies respond with joy. After looking at this evidence, therefore, it is difficult to imagine that joy is not associated with giving.

Hospitality

One cannot talk about caring for the needs of others without addressing the theme of biblical hospitality. From biblical accounts of hospitality, we learn that the giver must also be able to receive. One cannot care properly for the

16. Lisa McKay, *Spirituality and Humanitarian Work: Maintaining Your Vitality*, online training module 6 (Pasadena, CA: Headington Institute, 2010), 30.

17. Ibid.

18. Jorge Moll et al., "Human Fronto-Mesolimbic Networks Guide Decisions about Charitable Donation," *Proceedings of the National Academy of Sciences of the United States of America* 103, no. 42 (2006): 15623–28.

needs of others if one has not received help from others. The Bible clearly
highlights this fact when it tells us that Moses exhorted the Israelites, "You
are to love those who are foreigners, for you yourselves were foreigners in
Egypt" (Deut. 10:19 NIV).

As we will see below, hospitality is a practice that includes giving and receiving. Often it starts with a meal. In the English language, one talks about
"enjoying" food. Although hospitality can sometimes be experienced as a
burdensome duty, it can also produce much joy. I have experienced firsthand
how joyful some of these times together can be in Muslim-majority countries.
I am reminded during these times that God's generosity toward the generations
preceding Christ portrayed in Acts 14:17 was a form of joyful hospitality. In
that verse, Paul and Barnabas remind the inhabitants of Lystra, "He [God]
did good and gave you from heaven rains and fruitful seasons, satisfying your
hearts with food and gladness" (Acts 14:17 RSV). One of my uncles was a
farmer, and I know what this generosity of God meant to him. I often saw his
face light up as rain, long hoped for, was announced in the weather forecast,
or when we harvested his fields together in the summer.

Hospitality and Christian witness are strongly linked. In the context of
Muslim-Christian relations, various authors have deeply cherished this practice. Louis Massignon, for example, a Roman Catholic priest and scholar
of Islam, points us toward the theme of sacred hospitality by reflecting on
the story in Genesis 18 concerning Abraham, who hosted three strangers
who had been sent from God.[19] This biblical story has shaped Massignon's
encounter with Muslims tremendously. Incidentally, the Qur'an has a similar
story of Abraham receiving guests and feeding them a fat calf (51:24–37). I
have always been moved by the way Massignon, during the Algerian War of
Independence, supported the peaceful Algerian demonstrators who had been
attacked and killed on October 17, 1961: "Massignon tried to recover bodies
discarded in the River Seine to provide proper Islamic burials."[20] Following
in Massignon's footsteps, many Catholic missionaries in Muslim contexts
have adopted this same approach and used hospitality as their mission motivation and practice.

Amos Yong, a professor of theology and mission, commenting on the 9/11
aftermath in the United States, remarks on "the massive mobilization of disaster relief, the charitable efforts and commitments of people, and the many
acts of unrelenting kindness, all of which brought together people across

19. Louis Massignon, *L'Hospitalité sacrée* [*Sacred hospitality*] (Paris: Nouvelle Cité, 1987).
20. Gordon Oyer, "Louis Massignon and the Seeds of Thomas Merton's 'Monastic Protest,'"
Merton Annual 26 (2014): 85, http://www.merton.org/ITMS/Annual/annual26.aspx.

traditionally divided religious lines," including Christians and Muslims.[21] This is for him also a form of hospitality. Missiologist Tobias Brandner underlines an important characteristic of biblical hospitality, when he discusses the "dialectic of hosting and visiting" in the Bible.[22] As a paradigm of Christian witness, he explains, "to offer hospitality to the stranger is to welcome something unknown and vulnerable into our life-world, to create space for something foreign, to offer room, to accommodate, care for, and protect the alien."[23] Thus, as we exercise hospitality, we must always remember that we need to accept hospitality from others. In visiting churches worldwide, I have seen that some Christians struggle more than others with this idea. It seems sometimes easier for them to offer hospitality to Muslims than to become the guests of Muslims. It probably requires more humility and vulnerability than to be the host, who by definition can always maintain some form of power and control in his or her role of giver.

This reflection on hospitality in Muslim contexts engenders new missionary models. Brandner, interestingly, proposes that missionaries should come as guests and strangers and thus "express the highest level of respect and value to their hosts. A guest accepts the rules of the host and enters the alien environment as somebody who wants to learn what it means to live there and what challenges are to be faced. Guests come with a healthy curiosity, with respect for the local culture, and with questions rather than answers or solutions."[24] I tend to agree with him. I have seen too many Christian workers have just the opposite attitude and find themselves estranged in the very places where they want to serve because they were not ready to act like guests.

Hospitality is an important paradigm in witness in the Muslim world because it reflects the nature of the Triune God we serve. Hospitality is not merely an "economy of exchange."[25] It is best expressed as the final words of a biblical verse that invites Christians to "heal the sick, raise the dead, cleanse those who have leprosy, drive out demons" (Matt. 10:8 NIV). This verse ends with "Freely you have received; freely give." Consequently, the person who gives does not necessarily await something in return. It is interesting to notice that Muslims, while lacking the crucial belief in God's grace offered freely

---

21. Amos Yong, *Hospitality and the Other: Pentecost, Christian Practices, and the Neighbor* (Maryknoll, NY: Orbis Books, 2008), 2.

22. Tobias Brandner, "Hosts and Guests: Hospitality as an Emerging Paradigm in Mission," *International Review of Mission* 102, no. 1 (2013): 95.

23. Ibid., 96.

24. Ibid., 97–98.

25. Silas Webster Allard, "In the Shade of the Oaks of Mamre: Hospitality as a Framework of Political Engagement between Christians and Muslims," *Political Theology* 13, no. 4 (2012): 420.

in Christ, also claim that the righteous should give freely without expecting anything in return.[26]

According to the biblical narrative, God has extended perfect hospitality. Missiologist Cathy Ross, who has reflected extensively on the hospitality paradigm in mission, writes, "Jesus modeled powerlessness and vulnerability by being a guest in our world, by letting go and being among us in our place and space."[27] Thus, our witness as hosts and guests consists of inviting others to experience the same hospitality we experienced when we came to God. Unfortunately, the resistance that I have seen to Muslims in several parts of the world renders this attitude almost impossible unless we embrace it with the grace of God. Too many wars and prejudices have created hard feelings and shields of protection that sometimes prevent Christians from being vulnerable. They are afraid of taking relational risks. However, Brandner, who has helped those involved in mission to think about hospitality toward Muslims, talks about evangelism as "inviting others to experience the redemptive hospitality of God."[28] Thus, it is not just our hospitality that we want to extend. Instead, we want to show Muslims how God extends generosity, compassion, and hospitality in the biblical narrative. Hospitality is a recurring theme in Christian mission conferences. In 2012 the triennial mission conference Urbana, mentioned above, adopted the theme "the great invitation to God's banquet table." Participants were called to join this table set up by God and in turn invite others to join in the feast. Nowadays hospitality may not seem as critical for survival as it was for bedouins who lived in the desert and depended on generous hosts to feed and protect them, but it is still as critical for people's salvation. In effect, without joining God's banquet table, Muslims will not experience the fullness of what the Triune God has offered to humanity.

What Challenges?

Despite the joy of caregiving and the biblical invitation to care for others, Christians have encountered unique challenges in applying these principles in Muslim contexts. Today—and this was also true in the past—we hear allegations that Christians care for Muslims, but with manipulative motives.

26. See Qur'an 76:8–9: "And feed with food the needy wretch, the orphan and the prisoner, for love of Him [saying] we feed you, for the sake of Allah only. We wish for no reward nor thanks from you" (Pickthall translation).
27. Cathy Ross, "Hospitality: The Church as 'A Mother with an Open Heart,'" in *Mission on the Road to Emmaus: Constants, Context and Prophetic Dialogue*, ed. Cathy Ross and Stephen B. Bevans (London: SCM, 2015), Kindle edition, location 2045.
28. Brandner, "Hosts and Guests," 100.

Christians are sometimes accused of doing social or humanitarian work as undercover evangelism to convert Muslims, especially in places where proselytism is outlawed.[29] Muslim scholar Abdul Rashied Omar underlines "heightened religious tensions resulting from the contentiousness of certain Christian aid agencies accompanying the U.S.-led wars in Afghanistan and Iraq."[30] He calls these activities "aid evangelism" and believes that "the activities of such groups have reinvigorated the debate over whether it is ethical for philanthropical activities and humanitarian service to be undertaken with the primary intent to proselytize."[31]

Both faith traditions have discussed these issues vigorously in the past. A 1976 conference in Chambésy, Switzerland, led to some tough declarations that strongly urged "Christian churches and religious organizations to suspend their misused *diakonia* activities in the world of Islam."[32] What the word "misused" means here is left open for discussion. As a result of these tensions, some Christians hesitate to do humanitarian work in Muslim contexts. Elizabeth Ferris of the Brookings Institution, who studies the international community's response to humanitarian crises, says that faith-based organizations "are doing everything they can to avoid charges of proselytism and to keep missionary work separate from the humanitarian work."[33] As a result, prospective missionaries sometimes wonder how they can serve God in a Muslim context when they have a strong desire both to proclaim and to care through acts of compassion.

How should Christians, then, act if they do not want to use humanitarian work as a cover for illegal mission work or as a means to get a visa, but at the same time want to be able to associate *kerygma* (proclamation) with *diakonia* (caring)? This question is regularly raised by young Christians who want to work in Muslim-majority countries but struggle with what it means to witness in these contexts. Experts who have dealt with this issue have offered several answers. Reverend Richard Sudworth suggests a "cruciform ethics" to help Christians avoid being "in the business of 'twist and sell,'—offering

29. Several Muslim countries have laws forbidding proselytism.

30. Abdul Rashied Omar, "The Right to Religious Conversion: Between Apostasy and Proselytization," in *Peace-Building by, between, and beyond Muslims and Evangelical Christians*, ed. Mohammed Abu-Nimer and David Augsburger (Lanham, MD: Lexington Books, 2010), 184.

31. Ibid., 179.

32. This excerpt from the *Christian Mission and Islamic Da'wah: Proceedings of the Chambésy Dialogue Consultation* is quoted in *World Christianity in Muslim Encounter: Essays in Memory of David A. Kerr*, vol. 2, ed. Stephen R. Goodwin (New York: Continuum, 2009), Kindle edition, location 5730.

33. "Christian Aid Groups Tread Lightly in Muslim World," National Public Radio, last updated August 12, 2010, http://www.npr.org/templates/story/story.php?storyId=129155780.

one thing and manipulating those we are with, only to slip them something else."[34] He believes in a "practice that is informed by the self-giving love seen on the cross." He explains, "Jesus gave and gave, and continues to give whether we receive that grace or not."[35] Thus, we should not feel a need to collect data on how many people turned to Christ. Jesus healed people, and not all devoted their lives to God. The most important thing is to give, like God, who gives joyfully.

Great Anglican scholar of Islam Kenneth Cragg, after reporting the various tensions and challenges that participants faced at the Chambésy Consultation, invites Christians to compassion rather than imperialism toward Muslim countries. He concludes, "Experience of mutual mission, which is what the Chambésy Conférence set out to understand and relate, can best yield its lessons if we lift its tensions and its debates into experience of the common earth and our mutual humanity. For that is the sphere of our humility and the arena of our relevance."[36] When Muslims understand that we care because we share in the same humanity, we don't have to defend as vehemently the reasons behind our caring.

Christian Islamicist J. Dudley Woodberry defines mission as *kerygma* and *diakonia*. In other words, he believes the good news is shared in words and deeds and that the two cannot be dissociated.[37] This recommendation, coming from a scholar who has lived and ministered in Muslim-majority countries as diverse as Iran, Saudi Arabia, Indonesia, Egypt, Afghanistan, Pakistan, and so on, can only be received with great appreciation by those who want to serve through words and deeds.

Today many mission models refuse the tension and dichotomy between ministry of proclamation and ministries of caring for the poor and needy. They don't want a "separatist" attitude with respect to the relationship between sharing the gospel and development.[38] Numerous international consultations have provided resources to address this issue.[39] Missiologists have also proposed models that are currently being used in contexts where Christians want to engage in humanitarian work in the name of Christ. Holistic mission is one

---

34. Richard J. Sudworth, "Holistic Responses in Multicultural Birmingham," in *Between Naivety and Hostility: Uncovering the Best Christian Responses to Islam in Britain*, ed. Steve Bell and Colin Chapman (Milton Keynes, UK: Authentic, 2011), Kindle edition, location 2799.
35. Ibid.
36. Kenneth Cragg, "Us and Ours," *International Review of Mission* 66 (April 1977): 175.
37. J. Dudley Woodberry, "Toward Mutual Respectful Witness," in Abu-Nimer and Augsburger, *Peace-Building*, 171–78.
38. James W. Gustafson, "The Integration of Development and Evangelism," *International Journal of Frontier Missions* 8, no. 4 (October 1991): 115.
39. Ibid.

of them. Interserve International, a Christian organization working in several Muslim-majority contexts, explains on its website that its call toward holistic or integral mission combines the practical expression of the gospel with verbal proclamation. More specifically, it states that "integral mission or holistic transformation is the proclamation and demonstration of the gospel."[40] To this organization, social involvement and proclamation are not two separate tracks. Proclaiming the gospel has social consequences, and social involvement highlights the transformative power of the gospel of Jesus. A person working predominantly in Muslim-majority countries illustrates the effectiveness of this holistic approach: "We see Muslims' attitudes to Christians change as we work among them, to the extent where those in positions of authority tell us: 'We need more people like you, with integrity and a commitment to the poor.'"[41] "Integral mission" is another concept that emerged from the integration of proclamation and service. The Latin American Theological Fellowship was first to define this missional approach championed by missiologist C. René Padilla.[42] These models that call for a great fusion of *kerygma* and *koinonia* have given greater confidence to Christian workers that their mission engagement can impact Muslim societies for the good.[43]

These ideas regarding new ways to combine deeds and words in mission have recently permeated a great number of international mission statements. The Cape Town Commitment, for example, says, "Such love for the poor demands that we not only love mercy and deeds of compassion, but also that we do justice through exposing and opposing all that oppresses and exploits the poor."[44] Other mission documents, such as the World Council of Churches' Affirmation on Mission and Evangelism, refer to mission seeking justice,

40. "Holistic Ministry amongst Muslims," Interserve International, https://www.interserve.org/story/102-holistic-ministry-amongst-muslims.

41. Ibid.

42. This is how Padilla describes integral mission: "It is focused on crossing the frontier between faith and no faith, not only in geographical terms, but in cultural, ethnic, social, economical and political terms, for the purpose of transforming life in all its dimensions, according to God's plan, so that all people and human communities may experience the abundant life that Christ offers them." In C. René Padilla, "What Is Integral Mission," Del Camino Network For Integral Mission in Latin America, http://lareddelcamino.net/en/images/Articles/what%20is%20integral%20mission%20cr%20padilla.pdf.

43. Pervaiz Sultan, "Mission from the Perspective of a Pakistani Christian," http://cca.org.hk/home/ctc/ctc08-12/10_pervaiz_sultan61.pdf. Sultan, who is principal of St. Thomas's Theological College in Karachi, also wrote a thesis titled "The Role of the Church of Pakistan in Development" while attending the Oxford Center of Mission Studies. See also Peter Kuzmič, "Integral Mission in a World of Violence," in *Justice, Mercy and Humility*, ed. Tim Chester (Carlisle, UK: Paternoster, 2003), 150–61.

44. "The Cape Town Commitment: A Confession of Faith and a Call to Action," Proceedings from the Third Lausanne Congress on World Evangelization, which took place in Cape

healing, and wholeness of individuals and communities.[45] The 2012 World
Council of Churches statement on mission and evangelism includes affirmations on "participating in God's ongoing work of liberation and reconciliation by the Holy Spirit" in order to attain justice, peace, and reconciliation.
This work includes "the restoration of right relationships between God and
humanity and all of creation." It also "requires a commitment to struggle
and resist the powers that obstruct the fullness of life that God wills for all,
and a willingness to work with all people involved in movements and initiatives
committed to the causes of justice, dignity, and life."[46] The Sabeel Ecumenical
Liberation Theology Center is an example of a group that has borrowed ideas
about working for justice, peace, and reconciliation from the Latin American
context and applied them to the Palestine-Israel context.[47] Likewise, a group of
Palestinian Christian leaders and theologians drafted the "Kairos Palestinian
Document," emphasizing the need for a theology of love and solidarity with
the oppressed and a call for justice and equality.[48]

J. Dudley Woodberry reminds us that

> Jesus . . . indicated that there are times when the deed alone is appropriate,
> as when he [Jesus] healed a leper and then said, 'Tell no one' (Matthew
> 8:1–4). . . . Yet as has been noted, the example and commission of Jesus
> includes word and deed as part of witness. . . . A biblical understanding
> of the answer to poverty and injustice is *shalom* (or *salam*)—peace that
> expresses human well-being and health, including their spiritual and ma-
> terial aspects, and reconciles created beings with God and each other. . . .
> This involves lifelong "transformational development" toward the recovery
> of our identity as created in the image of God and a calling to be stewards
> who care for the world and our neighbors.[49]

However, caring for others can sometimes be dangerous. Christians are
not immune to tensions, conflicts, and violence perpetrated in some Muslim-

---

Town, South Africa (October 2010), point C, under section 7 titled "We Love God's World,"
(2011), https://www.lausanne.org/content/ctc/ctcommitment).

45. *Together towards Life: Mission and Evangelism in Changing Landscapes*, World Council
of Churches, September 5, 2012, https://www.oikoumene.org/en/resources/documents/com
missions/mission-and-evangelism/together-towards-life-mission-and-evangelism-in-changing
-landscapes.

46. Ibid., 7.

47. See the home page of Sabeel, http://www.sabeel.org.

48. "Kairos Palestine Document: A moment of truth: A word of faith, hope and love from the
heart of Palestinian suffering," December 11, 2009; https://www.oikoumene.org/en/resources
/documents/other-ecumenical-bodies/kairos-palestine-document.

49. J. Dudley Woodberry, "A Christian Response to Chapters on Interfaith Dialogue," in
Abu-Nimer and Augsburger, *Peace-Building*, 208.

Touching the Heart of a Refugee

Kathryn Kraft

A few weeks ago, I was sharing with a friend at my church in London about my research with churches in Lebanon. As Rupen Das described in a post several months ago, many churches in Lebanon are providing assistance including food, blankets, clothing, or education, to refugees, most of whom are from Syria. They also engage refugees in a variety of other social and religious activities within the everyday life of the church. Churches are doing this as an expression of Christ's love for all people, and out of an understanding of what it means to be "Church" in the world today.

Then I told my friend that one of the most interesting things about how churches are assisting refugees, is that they are doing more than just providing life-saving material aid. There is a deeper element to what they are doing. For example, even though most Syrian refugees are Muslim, new friendships are being built between them and Lebanese Christian church members. For many, this is the first time they become friends with someone of a different religious tradition. In addition, refugees are learning new skills and having the opportunity to engage in different types of activities than they ever did back home. These might include literacy, artisan crafts, or the Bible. In all these ways and more, churches are seeking to meet the most urgent and deeply-felt needs of the refugees they serve.

My friend then commented, "So in other words, the churches are doing good work, but they aren't having any kind of spiritual impact?"

To which I responded in protest: "No! This is spiritual impact!" I sensed a degree of hope and joy when refugees described the assistance they were receiving from churches, and surely there is something inherently spiritual about hope and joy!

Kathryn Kraft, "Touching the Heart of a Refugee" (blog),
Institute of Middle East Studies, June 12, 2015,
https://imeslebanon.wordpress.com/author/katiworonka/.

majority countries. Today, some Christians serve in war-ridden areas of the Muslim world. They went to Muslim areas out of compassion, but not all the people they met understood their good intentions. I could list many examples, ranging from Christian workers killed as they provided

help after a flood in Pakistan,[50] to Christian medical workers murdered in
Yemen,[51] to Egyptian Christians killed in Libya,[52] to a Korean pastor killed
in Afghanistan,[53] to French monks killed in Algeria,[54] and the list could go
on and on. These people, unfortunately, became entangled in wars that
were not theirs. They may have been killed not because they were Christians
but rather because they are symbols of the enemy or the invader, even if
in reality they were not belligerents. According to the Aid Worker Security
Database, there has been a drastic increase of attacks on humanitarian aid
workers, "since 2006, most of the violence has occurred in Afghanistan,
Sudan, Somalia and Pakistan, all predominately Muslim countries."[55] Even
though faith-based organizations may not have been necessarily singled out,
Abby Stoddard, a researcher on international humanitarian action, adds
that it is "reasonable to assume that organizations with a clear Christian
identity face an additional layer of vulnerability."[56] Thus, those who care
for Muslims today may have to pay a high price in some regions. Should
they not care anymore? Those who work in hostile environments must be
more thoughtful and consider if they are willing to pay the price of such
involvement. It they go, they should be aware that it might not be an easy
path.

Muslim Caring

Muslims, like Christians, excel in human caregiving. Anyone with Muslim
friends has experienced how generous, hospitable, and caring they are. In
sermons, I have heard Christians say that if Jesus had told the Good Samaritan parable today, he would have used a Muslim and the parable might have

50. "Pakistani Taliban Kills Three Foreign Christian Aid Workers," Open Doors, August
27, 2010, https://www.opendoorsusa.org/newsroom/tag-news-post/taliban-killed-three-chris
tian-relief-workers-in-pakistan/.
51. Ted Olsen, "Three American Missionaries Killed in Yemen," *Christianity Today*,
December 1, 2002, http://www.christianitytoday.com/ct/2002/decemberweb-only/12-30
-13.0.html.
52. "Islamic State: Egyptian Christians Held in Libya 'Killed,'" BBC News, February 15,
2015, http://www.bbc.com/news/world-31481797.
53. Ted Olsen, "Afghanistan Kidnappers Kill Hostage as South Korea Debates Mission
Work," *Christianity Today*, July 26, 2007, http://www.christianitytoday.com/ct/2007/julyweb
-only/130-41.0.html.
54. John W. Kiser, *The Monks of Tibhirine: Faith, Love, and Terror in Algeria* (New York:
St. Martin's, 2002).
55. Scott Neuman, "Christian Aid Groups Tread Lightly in Muslim World," *NPR*, August
12, 2010, accessed at http://www.npr.org/templates/story/story.php?storyId=129155780.
56. Quoted in ibid.

been called "The Good Muslim."[57] Muslim generosity starts in the home. I have had memorable meals at Muslim friends' houses, during which leaving my plate empty meant that I was still hungry, and since I did not understand the rules, my hosts would keep saying in colloquial Arabic, "*Sidi, sidi* [more, more]," while piling more food on my plate. I could share a flurry of stories about the generous hearts of Muslims. They range from lavish hospitality, to a Muslim flying from overseas just to visit me when I was in the hospital, to Muslims stopping at the roadside to help me change a flat tire. I have even seen local Muslim leaders coming to my church in Paris and asking if we had any poor people they could help.

I started this chapter with a story in which I was at center stage, caring for the needy, but a few days later, the situation was reversed when I visited a Muslim family in a poor neighborhood of Cairo. When I arrived at their house, they welcomed me with a royal meal. I knew that what they served me was the equivalent of their week's food consumption. Their hospitality was exceptional. I was traveling at that time with a friend, who realized she did not have her diabetes medication. As soon as they found out, one of the sons of the family ran out to a store through the back door and came back with her medication. As hosts, they showed exemplary sensitivity to our needs.

This shows that Christianity does not have a monopoly on helping the needy. Like other faith traditions, the Qur'an contains numerous references to caring for others.[58] *Zakat* (compulsory almsgiving) and *sadaqa* (voluntary almsgiving) are important ways for Muslims to share their resources. The Qur'an explains, "The alms are only for the poor and the needy, and those who collect them, and those whose hearts are to be reconciled, and to free the captives and the debtors, and for the cause of Allah, and (for) the wayfarer; a duty imposed by Allah. Allah is Knower, Wise" (9:60; Pickthall trans.). It is evident from this list that Muslims are invited to care for those in need in their society. They are also called to care for the orphans (Qur'an 4:2), to free the captives, feed the hungry,[59] and visit the sick.[60] Muhammad, the last prophet

57. See, e.g., Alastair Lawson, "NYC Hails Muslim 'Good Samaritan,'" BBC News, December 18, 2007, http://news.bbc.co.uk/2/hi/south_asia/7149916.stm; or Idrees Ali, "Nigeria: A Modern Day 'Good Samaritan' Story," *Common Ground Blog*, May 20, 2014, https://www.sfcg.org/nigeria-a-modern-day-good-samaritan-story/.

58. Qur'an 2:3; 2:83; 2:177; 2:184; 2:215.

59. Sahih Bukhari, vol. 4, book 52, hadith 282.

60. These lists are strangely similar to certain biblical statements, such as Jeremiah 7:5–7: "For if you truly amend your ways and your doings, if you truly execute justice one with another, if you do not oppress the alien, the fatherless or the widow, or shed innocent blood in this place, and if you do not go after other gods to your own hurt, then I will let you dwell in this place, in the land that I gave of old to your fathers for ever" (RSV).

in Islam, also practiced and recommended generosity and hospitality during his lifetime. Numerous hadiths report the importance of turning favorably to one's neighbors. In one hadith, for example, Abu Huraira reported that Muhammad said, "Whoever believes in Allah and the Last Day, should not hurt his neighbor and whoever believes in Allah and the Last Day, should serve his guest generously."[61] I have quoted only a few references to the generosity of Muslims in their sacred texts. Someone reading the Qur'an and the Hadith will find a plethora of other, similar recommendations.

During religious festivals, Muslims pay special attention to the needy. Last Ramadan,[62] I found the website of a Muslim magazine titled *The Message*, which featured an article titled "The Joy of Caring and Sharing."[63] It said, "Caring and sharing should be part of a Muslim's personality and they should exemplify this throughout the year, in all aspects of daily living."[64] This joy of sharing is so ingrained in the practices of Ramadan that a Christian friend of mine who used to be Muslim answered in the following way when I commented on her depressed face during a Christian festival: "I am sad because I miss times like during Ramadan, when people in my neighborhood would come to my home and offer me a huge piece of meat for me and my children." I am not telling this story to underline that Muslims are more generous than Christians during festivals. I have many Christian friends who open their doors or go to needy neighborhoods to serve food during Christmas or Easter. Rather, I want to emphasize that Muslims are not very different in the ways they share, give, and care. They have very big hearts when it comes to helping others.

This deep concern for the needy has resulted in the founding of countless Islamic charitable organizations. One of them, Islamic Relief USA, raises money for the major crisis zones in the world. Islamic Relief USA's work ranges from addressing humanitarian crises, to providing emergency relief, to establishing and administering education and health programs, and more.[65] Foundations such as the Alwaleed Philanthropies Foundation support community development, disaster recovery, women's empowerment, and so on.[66]

61. Sahih Bukhari, vol. 8, book 73, hadith 158.

62. Ramadan is the yearly fast observed by Muslims. It lasts a lunar month.

63. Mahbubur Rahman, "The Joy of Caring and Sharing," *The Message*, December 31, 2014, http://messageinternational.org/the-joy-of-caring-and-sharing/.

64. Ibid.

65. See the website of Islamic Relief USA (IRUSA), http://www.irusa.org, for the kinds of work the Islamic Relief Fund does. The Islamic Relief Fund International is an independent nongovernmental organization founded in the United Kingdom in 1984. Its US branch was founded in 1993.

66. See "Building Bridges. For a Better World," under the "Who We Are" tab of Alwaleed Philanthropies, http://www.alwaleedphilanthropies.org/who-we-are.

Recently the magazine *The Economist*, which is published in London, included a full-page advertisement from this organization offering grants for philanthropic initiatives.[67]

Young Muslims are also increasingly attracted to helping the poor. Disappointed by the society of consumerism, they embrace a different lifestyle. Major Muslim singers are attracting crowds and donating money for the poor. A prominent R&B singer, Maher Zain, who is a Swedish-Lebanese Muslim, gives numerous concerts to raise funds for refugees or to combat poverty.[68] As an artist, he regularly goes on humanitarian missions. Another Muslim singer, Sami Yusuf, wrote a charity song titled "Hear Your Call" to raise money for children's emergency relief in Pakistan after the 2010 flood.[69] All profits of the song went to a UN-sponsored charity called Save the Children. Sami Yusuf wrote on his website, "We cannot remain indifferent to what's turning out to be the biggest emergency on our planet today. . . . Donations have to pour in with the belief that they'll reach the needy. After God, only through your help can the victims still hope, and only through your generosity can they dream for a safer future."[70] In order to renew the motivation of Muslims to care for others, the same singer released another song called "Healing." The lyrics say, "Heal and you will be healed / Break every border / Give and you will receive / It's nature's order."[71]

Muslims sometimes direct this caring attitude toward Christians. Episcopal priest and author Paul-Gordon Chandler relates that during the Egyptian Revolution, while there was much unrest in the city of Cairo, Muslims protected him: "One night, our apartment building was attacked by mobs of armed looters nine times. Each time, our Muslim neighbors sheltered us all from harm."[72] Likewise, Christian scholar of Islam Joseph Cumming relates how, having committed to live among the poor in Mauritania, he and his wife were deeply transformed, and their lives were protected by Muslims on several occasions: "We rented one room (then, after our children were born, two rooms) in a house with two local

67. *The Economist*, May 16, 2015.

68. See, e.g., "Press Release: Maher Zain to Perform in Dublin," Human Appeal, October 14, 2013, http://humanappeal.ie/media/press-releases/press-release-maher-zain-to-perform-in -dublin/#.VUxVUM6d6fQ.

69. "Sami Yusuf - Hear Your Call (Official Video)," YouTube video, 4:27, posted August 28, 2010, https://www.youtube.com/watch?v=-7s4Jf1U0d4.

70. Sami Yusuf, Hear Your Call website, http://www.samiyusufofficial.com/pakistan/doc /appeal.html.

71. Sami Yusuf "Healing," http://lyricstranslate.com/en/sami-yusuf-healing-lyrics.html.

72. Paul-Gordon Chandler, "Behind Egypt's Revolution," *Christianity Today*, March 7, 2011, http://www.christianitytoday.com/ct/2011/marchweb-only/behindegyptrevolution .html?start=2.

Muslim families, with no running water or electricity, and sharing an outdoor latrine with our neighbors. More than once, through the years, our wonderful Muslim neighbors saved our lives."[73] Recently, after a church bombing in Peshawar, Pakistan, "200–300 Muslims and Christians united and gathered to make a human chain around a church in Lahore."[74] Likewise, Christians formed a human chain around Muslims as they prayed during the Cairo protests.[75] All these examples show how Muslims are also extending their help to Christians. I found it important to share them because I still meet Christians who do not believe that these things happen and consequently are more reluctant to trust and engage in ordinary encounters with Muslims.

Two Are Better Than One

It is not uncommon today to see Christian organizations partnering with Muslims to care for the needy, realizing that the needs are too big to be addressed by just one faith tradition. World Vision, for example, has contact with Muslims in several Muslim-majority countries. Chawkat Moucarry[76] describes the relational dynamic between World Vision staff and Muslim coworkers operating in a number of Muslim-majority countries as follows: "Providing orientation on Christianity and Islam to all our staff has been a fascinating experience, as we engage on faith issues and learn from each other about our respective faiths and often about our own! Without ignoring the distinctive beliefs of each tradition, the common ground we have enhances our work for the good of the communities we serve."[77] These encounters

---

73. Personal website of Joseph Cumming, http://www.josephcumming.com.

74. Aroosa Shaukat, "Human Chain Formed to Protect Christians during Lahore Mass," *Express Tribune*, October 6, 2013, http://tribune.com.pk/story/614333/muslims-form-human-chain-to-protect-christians-during-lahore-mass/.

75. "Images of Solidarity as Christians Join Hands to Protect Muslims as They Pray during Cairo Protests," *Daily Mail*, February 3, 2011, http://www.dailymail.co.uk/news/article-1353330/Egypt-protests-Christians-join-hands-protect-Muslims-pray-Cairo-protests.html#ixzz3aU88eDLj.

76. Moucarry explains further how he envisions his role: "Firstly, it is important to build bridges and therefore identify the common ground we have with people of other faiths. We are all human beings and we must relate to one another at this level regardless of religious backgrounds. As we develop trusting relationships, we can find common ground." "World Vision Broadens Global Focus with New World Religions Specialist," *Christian Today*, September 22, 2006, http://www.christiantoday.com/article/world.vision.broadens.global.focus.appointing.world.religions.specialist/7715.htm.

77. Chawkat Moucarry, "A Plea for Dialogue between Christians and Muslims," Lausanne Movement, 2010, http://www.lausanne.org/content/a-plea-for-dialogue-between-christians-and-muslims.

sometimes provide opportunities for witness. Christian author and professor David W. Shenk reports an encounter between Islamic militants and Christian teams in post-tsunami rebuilding projects in Banda Aceh: "The [Hizbullah] commander slept in the same room with the pastor, and they became friends! One evening around the evening meal, the commander began to weep. He said, 'When I think of what we have done to you, and how you reciprocate with love, my heart has melted within me!' He confided to the pastor, 'I have discovered that you Christians are good infidels.'"[78]

Some people may think that partnering on certain projects could challenge the integrity of Christian organizations. It need not. After a deep and thorough reflection on Christian witness and transformational development, Bryant Myers ends his book *Walking with the Poor* by saying, "We must take great care that we point, not to the effectiveness of our development technology, but to the fact that the good deeds that create and enhance life in the community are evidence of the character and activity of the God of the Bible, the God whose son makes a continuing invitation to new life and whose spirit is daily at work in our world."[79] Thus, as we engage with Muslims in caring for the needs of humanity, we will always, as Christians, have a distinctive interpretation of what it means to care for the needy, since that interpretation flows from our understanding of the mission of the Triune God in this world.

Conclusion

On my coffee table lies a picture book of humanitarian action in war. It shows portraits of people living in war zones, like millions do, and those who try to help them.[80] Several chapters deal with Muslim-majority countries. I can leave this book on my table and enjoy the professional pictures, or I can open up my home, offer hospitality, and step out to meet those in need. The proclamation of the gospel is not dissociated from helping the poor and the needy. They actually go together.

Several models have been developed to guide Christians as they live their Christian witness—with a harmony of words and life—in Muslim communities. Unfortunately, there may be people who care for the wrong reasons and

78. David W. Shenk, "The Gospel of Reconciliation within the Wrath of Nations," *International Bulletin of Missionary Research* 32, no. 1 (January 2008): 3. The word "infidel" is sometimes used by Muslims to identify Christians, although the referent of the term is not always clear from the qur'anic texts that use it.

79. Myers, *Walking with the Poor*, locations 6987–91.

80. Paul Grabhorn, *Seeking Light: Portraits of Humanitarian Action in War* (New York: Viking, 2015).

sometimes even cause prejudice against the local churches in Muslim lands. This is why I believe we must think very seriously about Christian witness and how it radiates out of our hospitality, generosity, and human caring. Christians should not be shy in explaining to those who ask that they care in the name of Christ.

Muslims can be as generous as Christians. Their sacred texts call them to care for the needs of others, just as the Bible calls Christians to do so. I encourage those who are involved in Muslim contexts to become familiar with the Muslim theology of human caregiving. But as we think about Muslims' practices and initiatives in this area, we must also ask ourselves, as Christians, if we are willing to accept their hospitality and care, if needed. I believe that if we want to deeply engage in ordinary encounters, help cannot be unidirectional. Even Jesus was open to accepting water from the Samaritan woman (John 4).

Christians should also remember that human caregiving includes joy, despite all the challenging questions we have addressed here, ranging from controversial conversations on aid evangelism to Christian aid-workers being killed in Muslim contexts. Only as we practice hospitality and generosity can we experience the joy of giving and receiving.

Finally, at some times and in some places we may be called to work together with Muslims to alleviate suffering when the help we can offer by ourselves is not sufficient. As we engage with Muslims, we must also remember that the way we care is distinctively impacted by our relationship with the Triune God and how God cares for human beings. More specifically, as we announce good news to the poor, we cannot ignore the One who announced it two thousand years ago, standing before needy people in Nazareth.

For Discussion

1. Identify Bible verses and missional models of human caregiving. How do they shape your witness among Muslims?
2. Why and how do Muslims show compassion and care for others?
3. What are ways Christians can engage in joyful witness when caring for the needy in Muslim societies?

7

Meeting Muslim Urbanites

The urban fabric of the world is rapidly changing. Recently, a prominent Christian leader stated: "The world has moved to the cities!"[1] He is right. Over half of the world population today lives in urban areas, with migrations toward cities taking place in staggering numbers. Another Christian leader believes that by 2050, 70 percent of the world population will be urban.[2] I have visited many Muslim-majority cities and experienced how diverse they can be. I enjoyed wandering through the bustling *souks* in Istanbul, Turkey, or Xi'an, China, where traditional craftspeople mingle with high-tech Muslim urbanites living in modern buildings close by. I have met Muslim hipsters on the streets of Tunis and toured the panoply of sacred places in Delhi ranging from the seventeenth-century Jama Masjid mosque to the Sufi shrine of Nizamuddin Auliya. I have visited some poor neighborhoods in Cairo and places of lavish luxury in Dubai. I have observed how Muslims live in pluralistic contexts such as in Beirut and Singapore. In some European cities, such as Brussels or London, I have seen how people from various faiths seek to address giant challenges that face both Muslims and non-Muslims with respect to the public sphere.

1. Tim Svoboda, "The Urban Challenge," YWAM SF [Youth With A Mission San Francisco], 2013, http://www.ywamsanfrancisco.org/wp-content/uploads/2013/01/Theurbanchallenge.pdf, 1. Svoboda is international urban missions director for Youth With A Mission.
2. Mac Pier, "Global City Influence: A Personal Reflection," *Lausanne Global Analysis* 2, no. 3 (June 2013), http://www.lausanne.org/content/lga/2013-06/global-city-influence-a-personal-reflection.

Cities have taught me much about Muslim peoples. I encourage everyone not just to read about Islam but also to walk in the streets of Muslim cities, to feel the pulse of its communities and understand its desires and needs.

I personally noticed a difference when I moved from my hometown, with only a few Muslim families, to the city of Paris, with hundreds of thousands of Muslims. The opportunity to engage with them increased exponentially. It was natural to make Muslim friends, since we were sharing the same urban space: the same restaurants, laundromats, and parks. Urban contexts afford their own distinctive opportunities for joyful witness. Since theologians and missiologists are increasingly interested in urban mission, their reflections can help us understand how to engage with Muslims in urban contexts.

Cities matter in Islam. Cities have played a key role in the history of Muslim societies, and they continue to influence relationships between Muslims and Christians today. They can be places of positive influence, transformation, and encounter. But cities can also present economic and social problems, challenge traditions in ways that produce irreparable ruptures within religious communities, and generate conflicts between Muslims and Christians when they compete for urban space, positions, and power.

When we understand relations between Muslims and Christians and cities, we will have greater confidence to engage with Muslim urbanites, who have often been neglected or misunderstood by Christians. We may actually learn to look at Muslim-majority cities not only for their beauty or for their needs but because God loves cities and invites us to love them as well.

Cities in Muslim Societies

Like the rest of the world, Muslims increasingly live in cities. The Greater Cairo Region is a megacity currently with close to twenty million inhabitants.[3] With an estimated population of eighty-five million people in Egypt, this means that nearly one in four Egyptians live in this vast agglomeration. Mohammad Qadeer, a professor of urban planning, shows that, similarly, "Pakistan has become an urban society," instead of the rural country it used to be a few decades ago.[4] With globalization, Muslim societies have undergone tremendous changes that missiologists have not yet fully explored.

3. Patrick Kingsley, "A new New Cairo: Egypt plans £30bn purpose-built capital in desert," The Guardian online, March 16, 2015, http://www.theguardian.com/cities/2015/mar/16/new-cairo-egypt-plans-capital-city-desert.
4. Mohammad Qadeer, *Pakistan: Social and Cultural Transformations in a Muslim Nation* (New York: Routledge, 2006), 81.

Before considering contemporary cities, let us consider the role of cities in early Islam. The capitals of several caliphates, such as Damascus, Baghdad, Fustat/Cairo, and Constantinople, to name a few, became influential places that attracted people from all corners of the Muslim world and beyond. The concept of "world city networks," developed by Peter J. Taylor, helps us understand the scope of these cities. These networks are "groupings of leading cities," each with a population of eighty thousand or more[5] and with at least ten cities in the network. Taylor claims that the Muslim world city network of the tenth and eleventh centuries was the most impressive "to have been developed outside East Asia before modern industrialization."[6] He lists sixteen cities in this network,[7] "spread from Iberia to central Asia."[8] Thus, as confirmed by historian Albert Hourani, the rise of Islam produced "a chain of great cities running from one end of the world of Islam to the other."[9] For a long time, one of the most important cities was Baghdad. According to historian Ira M. Lapidus, at one time Baghdad "was the largest city in the world outside China."[10] It was cosmopolitan and multiethnic and accommodated communities from various faith traditions. It became a major place of trade. During medieval times Baghdad may have had over a million people.[11] But besides its economic, religious, cultural, and social influence, Baghdad, as we will soon see, became a significant center for Muslim-Christian relations.

Contemporary Muslim cities have also gained status in the world. Several have joined the ranks of megacities, meaning that they have over ten million people.[12] In 2014, Delhi, India; Cairo, Egypt; Karachi, Pakistan; and Dhaka, Bangladesh, each had populations of over fifteen million. Other cities with a large Muslim population such as Istanbul, Turkey; Lagos, Nigeria; and Jakarta, Indonesia, had over ten million inhabitants.[13] Delhi, India, and Lagos,

---

5. Peter J. Taylor, "Historical World City Networks," in *International Handbook of Globalization and World Cities*, ed. Ben Derudder et al. (Cheltenham, UK: Edward Elgar, 2012), 12.

6. Ibid., 17.

7. The sixteen, with their populations, are as follows: Baghdad (1,200,000), Cordova (450,000), Fustat/Cairo (200,000), Samarkand (200,000), Alexandria (175,000), Nishapur (130,000), Basrah (100,000), Samarra (100,000), Kairouan (100,000), Bokhara (100,000), Mopsuestia (100,000), Al Ahsa (100,000), Seville (100,000), Isfahan (100,000), Tinnis (100,000), Ravi (100,000). Ibid., 18.

8. Ibid., 17.

9. Albert Hourani, *A History of the Arab Peoples* (New York: Warner Books, 1991), 110.

10. Ira M. Lapidus, *A History of Islamic Societies*, 3rd ed. (New York: Cambridge University Press, 2014), 74.

11. Tertius Chandler, *Four Thousand Years of Urban Growth: An Historical Census*, rev. ed. (Lewiston, NY: Edwin Mellen, 1987), 527.

12. Andre Sorensen and Junichiro Okata, eds., *Megacities: Urban Form, Governance, and Sustainability* (New York: Springer, 2011), 1.

13. World Urbanization Prospects: The 2014 Revision, United Nations, 2014, table 2, http://esa.un.org/unpd/wup/highlights/wup2014-highlights.pdf.

Nigeria, have over sixteen million inhabitants. As we think of these megacities, we have to understand that their makeup is so complex, rich, and multilayered that Christians must conduct a meticulous exegesis of the city if they want to understand its population. Christians must also be sensitive to the voice of the Holy Spirit and listen carefully to the manifold rhythms of each city in order to understand its spiritual needs. Those who wish to meet urban Muslims must first let go of their assumptions about Islam, since cities may provide surprising expressions of it. In any case, today, Christians who want to engage with Muslims cannot ignore the cities. I would even dare to say that cities should become a top priority.

What Are Islamic Cities?

Christians have long reflected theologically and missiologically about the nature and roles of cities. The famous fifth-century work by church father Augustine that he titled *The City of God* illustrates the fact that Christians have long been interested in understanding how religion shapes the social and political rules governing urban spaces.[14] Likewise, the Protestant Reformer John Calvin spent considerable time reflecting on how his city of Geneva, Switzerland, could incarnate the principles of the kingdom of God.[15] Likewise, modern Christian authors continue to reflect missiologically on how Christians should understand cities.[16]

Muslims, likewise, explore the meaning of cities. Although the Qur'an does not refer to cities as often as the Bible, they still occupy an important place in Islam. For example, Muslims worldwide turn five times daily toward the city of Mecca as they pray to God. Several qur'anic passages mention that God sent messengers to cities to alert them to their unrighteous conduct and call them to repent, as described in 16:112: "Allah sets forth a Parable: a city enjoying security and quiet, abundantly supplied with sustenance from every place: yet was it ungrateful for the favours of Allah: so Allah made it taste of hunger and terror (in extremes) (closing in on it) like a garment (from every side), because of the (evil) which (its people) wrought."[17]

14. Augustine, *The City of God* (Peabody, MA: Hendrickson, 2009).

15. Herman J. Selderhuis, ed., *The Calvin Handbook* (Grand Rapids: Eerdmans, 2009).

16. See, e.g., Robert C. Linthicum, *City of God, City of Satan: A Biblical Theology of the Urban Church* (Grand Rapids: Zondervan, 2011) [Linthicum is director of the Office of Urban Advance, World Vision International]; Ray Bakke, *A Theology as Big as the City* (Downers Grove, IL: IVP Academic, 1997); Charles Van Engen and Jude Tiersma, eds., *God So Loves the City: Seeking a Theology for Urban Mission* (Eugene, OR: Wipf and Stock, 2009).

17. *The Holy Qur'ān*, trans. Abdullah Yusuf Ali (Ware, UK: Wordsworth Editions, 2000).

But Muslim-majority cities should not only be considered Islamic cities. Several scholars of Islam argue that the term "Islamic" is reductionist. Urban sociologist Janet Abu-Lughod posited that Orientalists gave this qualifier to differentiate Western cities from Oriental cities.[18] She did not think that urban spaces in Muslim-majority cities were shaped only by gender differences or the public/private dichotomy, as is often indicated in Western studies. She highlighted semiprivate spaces, where these norms are looser. I believe that her arguments help Christians understand that cities are more complex than we think, or than we would like. Cities don't have a monolithic population, with everyone looking alike. Abu-Lughod shows that cities have spaces that do not fit the traditional patterns. Christians should not see Muslim cities as uniform urban spaces with millions of Muslims reacting the same way when the gospel is presented to them. They are made of different groupings, neighborhoods, and networks whose receptivity to the gospel may greatly vary. In his study of Muslim-majority cities, Ira Lapidus confirms that cities were not "unified social bodies defined by characteristically Muslim qualities."[19] Rather, "Cities were nodules of population woven into the fabric of a larger society—places which concentrated persons and activities, facilitated the organization of populations which cut across their own space, and helped them to resolve their relations to one another."[20]

In cities people intermingle and are thereby transformed; urban people are culturally different from rural people. Cities are in constant movement. Even physical patterns of Muslim-majority cities are changing today. Traditionally they comprised the *suq*, or covered market; the mosque, with additional buildings offering various services; the city walls; private neighborhoods; and public spaces. But it has been shown that "not only have most urban centers grown exponentially in population and territory, they have already set aside, or are at the risk of forgetting their own past experiences with urban living. The area of historical fabric per city probably does, at best, not reach more than 10–15 percent of the built-up zone."[21] It is easy to imagine that architectural changes may also affect the religiosity of city populations. Architecture shapes culture even as cultures create architecture.

18. Janet L. Abu-Lughod, "The Islamic City—Historic Myth, Islamic Essence, and Contemporary Relevance," *International Journal of Middle-East Studies* 19, no. 2 (May 1987): 155–76.

19. Ira M. Lapidus, "Muslim Cities and Islamic Societies," in *Middle Eastern Cities: A Symposium on Ancient Islamic and Contemporary Middle Eastern Urbanism*, ed. Ira M. Lapidus (Berkeley: University of California Press, 1969), 73.

20. Ibid.

21. Renata Holod, Attilio Petruccioli, and André Raymond, introduction to vol. 2 of *The City in the Islamic World*, ed. Salma K. Jayyusi, Renata Holod, Attilio Petruccioli, and André Raymond (Leiden: Brill, 2008), xix–xx.

Despite these transformations, Muslim cities generally preserve religious symbols. Some have recently undertaken projects to construct gigantic mosques, such as the Hassan II mosque in Casablanca, Morocco, with the world's tallest minaret. Other religious symbols pepper the streets of cities in the Muslim world. Some are visual, like the Islamic calligraphy on buildings or buses. Others are auditory, like the call to prayer issued five times a day from many minarets simultaneously in Cairo.[22] There are also olfactory symbols during festivals, such as the delicious food aromas engulfing the streets each evening at the breaking of the Ramadan fast. Instead of intimidating Christians, the profusion of these symbols should remind them that to Muslims spiritual "things" matter. They invite God into the streets of their cities. They welcome the sacred into their physical spaces. Although Christians do not agree with all Islamic beliefs, and rightly so, the desire of Muslims to remember God in their cities is still very touching.

But these sacred symbols can sometimes become so omnipresent that Muslims forget they are there. Many Muslims go about their daily activities ignoring the call to prayer that gushes out of the mosque's minaret. They do not always pay attention to the Muslim confession of faith[23] displayed on sacred buildings. Perhaps they do not feel attracted to the teachings that those texts reflect. If they look for other perspectives on God, they often cannot find other symbols in their cities. Unfortunately, Muslim urban contexts contain few representations of Christ crucified and risen from the dead. Many neighborhoods also lack churches. How will Muslims hear the gospel if Christ is not visible or audible in the city? This presence does not have to be architectural; the presence of Christian believers whose communities form the body of Christ (1 Cor. 12:27) is even more important than stones. But such communities also are sometimes blatantly absent from Muslim neighborhoods.

Urban Witness

Growing up, the mission books I read on the Muslim world tended to focus on monocultural contexts. It seemed more urgent to share Christ in rural or tribal contexts where there was no church. Anthropologist Gabriele Marranci has noticed a similar phenomenon in anthropology and remarked that recent reviews of anthropological articles overlook Muslims "as actors within the

22. Cairo has been called the city of one thousand minarets because of its abundance of mosques.
23. "There is only one God and Muhammad is his Prophet."

'global village' instead of the *duar*."[24] When the unreached people group concept became popular in missionary circles, it was easier to find these groups in their traditional contexts, away from cosmopolitan centers.[25] I don't know how many books I read on rural contexts before I found a book on urban mission in Muslim contexts.[26] I suppose that a certain number of missionaries neglected the cities because they felt that Muslims had easier access to the gospel in an urban context. They did not realize that cities can be as challenging for Christian witness among Muslims as rural contexts. For a long time, it also seemed that urban and rural missionaries did not talk much to each other. But this changed. After numerous missiological debates, according to Harvie M. Conn, missiologists came to agree that "the global city and the unreached people concept belonged together."[27] Both concepts are now important in mission. But research on witness in global Muslim cities is still sparse.

Cities play an important role in mission, as evidenced by the many references to cities in the Bible, such as Jerusalem and Babylon. Many verses show God's delight in cities that follow his precepts. But God also sternly warns cities: "I [God] will make Jerusalem a heap of ruins, a haunt of jackals; and I will make the cities of Judah a desolation, without inhabitant" (Jer. 9:11 NASB). The book of Jonah focuses entirely on a city that needs God's salvation. God's heart for the city of Nineveh is clearly manifested when he says to Jonah, "Should I not have concern for the great city of Nineveh, in which there are more than a hundred and twenty thousand people. . . and also many animals?" (Jon. 4:10 NIV). Likewise, in the New Testament, Jesus reveals his love for Jerusalem when he weeps over it. I often wonder how many churches lovingly cry over Muslim cities and pray for God's blessing, peace, and salvation to come to them.

24. Gabriele Marranci, *The Anthropology of Islam* (New York: Berg, 2008), 53. *Duar* is an Arabic word that can mean "small group of dwellings," "village," or "rural area."

25. For a historical study of how the concept "unreached people group" came into existence after missiologist Ralph Winter used the concept "Hidden People Group" at the International Congress on World Evangelization in Lausanne, Switzerland, in 1974, read the following article: Alan Johnson, "Major Concepts of the Frontier Mission Movement, Part II," *International Journal of Frontier Missions* 18, no. 2 (2001): 89–97. Included in this article is the following definition for "unreached people group" as worded by the Lausanne Strategy Working Group in Chicago (March 25–26, 1982): "people or people group among which there is no indigenous community of believing Christians with adequate numbers and resources to evangelize the rest of its members without outside (cross-cultural) assistance" (92).

26. Greg Livingstone, *Planting Churches in Muslim Cities: A Team Approach* (Grand Rapids: Baker, 1993).

27. Harvie M. Conn, "Unreached Peoples and the City," *Urban Mission* 8, no. 5 (1991): 3–5.

Christians are becoming more and more interested in understanding how the gospel currently spreads in a city.[28] Reflecting on mission and the cities, Roger Greenway, professor of world missiology, and Timothy Monsma, director of Cities for Christ Worldwide, stated, "Missions during the twenty-first century must face the fact that the majority of the world's population increasingly will be living in cities."[29] Today the unreached people groups are not in the rural areas only. They can also be found in large cities where people grow up without exposure to the gospel and where the church often does not know how to relate to them. The 2010 Cape Town Commitment says, "Cities are crucially important for the human future and for world mission."[30] It outlines four types of people that churches must reach in the city: "(i) the next generation of young people; (ii) the most unreached peoples who have migrated; (iii) the culture shapers; (iv) the poorest of the poor."

If I had more space, I could develop each point in relation to the Muslim world, because I see churches in large cities moving toward reaching Muslims in each of these categories. The Commitment adds, "We must love our cities as God does, with holy discernment and Christ-like compassion, and obey his command to 'seek the welfare of the city,' wherever that may be."[31] This clear and strong call to love the city and care for urban realities should permeate our interactions with Muslims. As I write these lines, cities like Baghdad and Damascus are in the center of devastating armed conflicts; many other Muslim-majority cities are facing enormous challenges of all sorts. As we pray and reflect on how to address them, our actions should be motivated by the remembrance of the love and care that God demonstrated toward cities like Jerusalem, Nineveh, and Ephesus.

I have not mentioned the great suffering of cities yet. Cities suffer. As Christians we need to bring hope to places of deep hurt. Crime is often higher in cities than in rural places. Ghettos exist in many cities. Inequalities between rich and poor; interfaith conflicts; pollution; an absence of churches in inner cities or in suburbs, depending on the country—all these need to be addressed and prayed for. At Fuller Theological Seminary, we offer a popular course titled "Exegeting the City." It is helpful to walk in a city with a sound theology, led by the Holy Spirit and using solid anthropological and sociological methods

28. See, e.g., Stephen T. Um and Justin Buzzard, *Why Cities Matter: To God, the Culture, and the Church* (Wheaton, IL: Crossway, 2013).

29. Roger S. Greenway and Timothy M. Monsma, *Cities: Missions' New Frontier*, 2nd ed. (Grand Rapids: Baker Academic, 2000), 20.

30. *The Cape Town Commitment: A Confession of Faith and a Call to Action*, Lausanne Movement, 2011, http://www.lausanne.org/content/ctc/ctcommitment, section IID.

31. Ibid.

to understand the makeup of cities and how to participate in their shalom as Christians. Jeremiah reminds us to "seek the peace and prosperity of the city . . . because if it prospers, you too will prosper" (Jer. 29:7 NIV). We should pray this prayer for all Muslim-majority cities. In our interconnected world, it is easy to see how if one city does not prosper, it will affect many others that are connected to it.

Influential Places

Cities are influential places. It is not surprising that the apostle Paul visited so many cities, whose ruins, for example in Turkey, are still visited by tourists today. He knew that novel ideas travel well in cities. He did not hesitate to pick prominent platforms for preaching his message, such as the Areopagus in Athens (Acts 17:22). Then, despite anticipated dangers, he did not hesitate to go to Rome, the influential capital of the Roman Empire, for the sake of the gospel (Acts 27–28). Cities have also played an influential role in Muslim-Christian relations since the earliest days of Islam. One of the first known Christian apologists to interact with Islam in his apologetic writings, John of Damascus, born in the seventh century, spent significant time at the court of the Muslim caliph Abd al-Malik in the city of Damascus, where he learned much regarding Muslim-Christian interactions. His work is still read today. Several decades later, the Eastern Orthodox patriarch Timothy I debated the Abbasid caliph al-Mahdi in another important city, Baghdad, which for centuries was one of the most influential cities in the world, as we have seen earlier. Since these times, cities have not stopped being places where meetings between Christians and Muslims received major attention. They often become the hub of Muslim-Christian encounters. For example, evangelical leaders choose London or major cities in Australia and the United States to debate Muslim polemicist Ahmed Deedat on controversial issues between Islam and Christianity.[32]

Cities also influence the larger society because they are knowledge hubs. Muslim cities have historically been centers of intellectual life. Sam Gellens, a history professor who specializes in Islamic history and the Middle East, reports that in AD 941 a Muslim leader from Cordova spent two years traveling to various learning centers in the Muslim world, including "Mecca, Medina, Jidda, Yemen (Sana'a, Zabid, Aden), Fustat, Jerusalem, Gaza, Ashkelon,

---

32. The Muslim organization Mojadala produced a video of one of these London debates featuring Ahmed Deedat debating with Anish Shorrosh. The video is titled "Full Debate: Is Jesus God?" July 7, 1985, https://www.youtube.com/watch?v=kXIBBCcJfRc.

Tiberias, Damascus, Tripoli, Beirut, Caesaria, Ramla, Farama, Alexandria, and Qulzum."[33] What an amazing academic program at a time when jets, trains, and cars did not exist![34] Imagine adopting the same format for one's studies. I know by experience how important it is for my students to travel abroad when they study Islam. Many return from their practicum in Lebanon with a deeper understanding of Islamic realities and a renewed vision to share Christ with Muslims. But imagine if they could hop from one global Muslim city to another in two years to gather knowledge about the needs and desires of their population! And imagine, conversely, if Muslim students could hop from one global city to another to engage with evangelical leaders and students to better understand biblical faith. I can report that these visits actually happen from time to time, as they did at Fuller Theological Seminary during a research project on conflict transformation.[35] Hopefully, Muslims will feel increasingly attracted to investigate our faith as we open more spaces of encounter in our cities.

Today, cities seem to exert more influence than countries. "The great global cities of the world (New York City, London, Tokyo, Hong Kong) have more influence over the world than do many nation states."[36] A recent article stated, "The 21st century is the era of cities, the metropolises where more than half the earth's people live, where its business is done, where some of its most complex services are developed and ideas generated."[37] Likewise, Muslim-majority cities, although they have not reached the top ranks of the A. T. Kearney global city index,[38] continue to shape religious thinking. Cities greatly influence the spread of religions. They have "always functioned as the locus of religious practice for Muslims. . . . Any congregational mosque had to be situated in an agglomeration of contiguous buildings designated as *madina*."[39]

---

33. Sam I. Gellens, "The Search for Knowledge in Medieval Muslim Societies: A Comparative Approach," in *Muslim Travellers: Pilgrimage, Migration, and the Religious Imagination*, ed. Dale F. Eickelman and James Piscatori (Berkeley: University of California Press, 1990), 55.

34. Today, new Muslim-majority cities are also contributing to the pursuit of knowledge. The Bibliotheca Alexandrina in Egypt, which opened in 2002, is a landmark building that continues to manifest the thirst for knowledge of Islamic societies. The state-of-the-art King Abdullah University of Science and Technology opened in 2009 in Saudi Arabia, seeking excellence in scientific studies and research. See the university's website: http://www.kaust.edu.sa/index.html.

35. See, e.g., Mohammed Abu-Nimer and David Augsburger, eds., *Peace-Building by, between and beyond Muslims and Evangelical Christians* (Lanham, MD: Lexington Books, 2010).

36. Pier, "Global City Influence."

37. *The Urban Elite: The A. T. Kearney Global Cities Index 2010*, A. T. Kearney, 2010, https://www.atkearney.com/documents/10192/efd4176a-09dd-4ed4-b030-9d94ecc17e8b.

38. *Global Cities 2015: The Race Accelerates*, A. T. Kearney, 2015, https://www.atkearney.com/research-studies/global-cities-index/2015.

39. Holod, Petruccioli, and Raymond, introduction to *City in the Islamic World*, xviii.

Urbanite Muslim Case in China

Enoch Jinsik Kim, Fuller Theological Seminary

Miss Arett* is a Muslim woman who grew up as part of an ethnic minority in Xinjiang, a northwest province in China. She moved to a major city in China for her college education when she was a teenager.

One day, she began to teach Chinese to a foreign couple to earn money on the side. She was quite defensive toward these foreigners at first, but as time went on she began to trust them, little by little. As she observed their way of life she began to respect it. She saw how the foreigner husband, Terry, loved his wife, and how the wife submitted to and loved her husband. Moreover, she saw how parents should teach and discipline their children.

About three years later, Miss Arett received Jesus in the presence of Terry's wife. That night, in tears, she shared her struggle for the first time: "When I think about the fiancé chosen by my parents, I do not want to get married. However, I still want to have a beautiful family like yours." Her parents had chosen a fiancé for her when she was young, and recently the young couple-to-be had had to register their marriage. As Terry's wife heard Miss Arett's honest sharing, Terry explained to Miss Arett that Jesus was the one who could give her the answer to her problem. Eventually our prayers for Miss Arett were answered. We rejoiced that our prayers were answered and that we had been able to share about Jesus, who can give answers to our problems. It was truly a joyful witness.

A Chinese city provided a stepping-stone for Miss Arett to walk across to Jesus one step at a time. Growing up, she had learned that her ethnic culture was correct and other ethnic cultures were dangerous. However, as she lived in a city during her college years, she was surprised to see many good sides to other ethnicities in China.

A city in China also enabled Miss Arett to meet foreigners for the first time. A city can also be a blessing to foreign Christians, enabling them to meet Muslims, because there was almost no way to get government permission to live in rural areas without a special reason. On that day, Terry and his wife reaped the fruit sown by the city. To share the joyful news with Chinese Muslim, God uses cities in China. This news gives joy both to the one receiving the news and to the one bringing it.

*For security reasons, "Miss Arett" and "Terry" have been substituted for their real names.

The religious influence of cities is sometimes symbolized by gigantic architectural structures. As someone who lived for several years only five miles away from the Eiffel Tower and the same approximate distance from Notre Dame Cathedral in Paris, I am interested in landmarks like these, which attract millions of visitors to Paris. Unfortunately, today Notre Dame has lost some of the religious influence and fame it had in the Middle Ages, and the Eiffel Tower (301 meters) seems very small compared to new structures in the Muslim world such as the Burj Kahlifa (828 meters) in Dubai.[40] In 2018, the Kingdom Tower in Jeddah, Saudi Arabia, should become the tallest tower, at 1,000 meters. These examples show the vitality of Muslim cities, symbolized by great architectural achievements. One can easily deduce from the desire and energy Muslims have to witness and influence that they are animated by the same zeal as Christians to share their faith. While some Christians worry about such vitality and attempt to stop it by all means, others (and I prefer this approach) spend time and energy finding creative ways to witness to Muslim urbanites even in places where they are most devoted.

Transformational Places

Cities foster transformation. First, they affect faith. Muslims who move from villages to cities may alter their religious practices. They also may become secular or radical in their beliefs. Christian witness must be aware of these various transformations of Islamic expressions. For example, to witness to secularized Muslims, one may not need to become an expert on Islam, but when talking to Muslims who deeply respect the Qur'an and the Hadith, one must master these texts.

Second, Islam in cities is more diverse than in rural areas. In a local newspaper of a Muslim city one can often find contradicting religious legal opinions regarding a particular family or societal issue. This is not a new phenomenon. Ira M. Lapidus explains that even in the early centuries of Islam "the Muslim urban communities embodied not one but a number of conflicting orientations. Some Muslims emphasized the authority of the scholarly tradition, others the teaching of the imams or the charismatic presence of the saints."[41] As Muslims encountered other religious groups in early Islamic cities such as Damascus, Baghdad, or Aleppo, they also incorporated some of the ideas of

40. The Skyscraper Center: The Global Tall Building Database of the Council on Tall Buildings and Urban Habitat, http://skyscrapercenter.com/buildings.
41. Lapidus, *History of Islamic Societies*, 170.

those other groups into their religious thinking and practices.[42] Today, religious forms continue to morph due to their exposure to diverse religious practices in urban contexts. Christian witness must be aware of this diversity in order to offer a message that is relevant to individual Muslims. A "one size fits all" presentation of the gospel does not exist. Jesus did not use the same words with every person he encountered. Since religious practices and beliefs may change from one neighborhood to the next, Christians must be attentive and adapt their interaction accordingly, even within the same city.

Third, and conversely, Islam can also unify across the lines of various communities or families in large cities. It can act as a catalyst, drawing people of the same faith together in common neighborhoods. Although cities tend to create distance in family networks, Muslims still maintain certain ties. I have noticed that my Muslim friends in Paris try to communicate more often with their families than non-Muslims do. It might be that although many are secular, their social behaviors are still very much impacted by the qur'anic prescription of honoring parents and caring for their relatives (Qur'an 2:83). When Muslims form their own networks in large cities, Christians feel sometimes intimidated and thus afraid to reach out to them. I have seen whole Muslim areas in Europe with no Christian witness. It sometimes feels as if churches have completely abandoned these places, with no prospect of return. This is very unfortunate.

Fourth, cities can transform Muslim communities in such a way that those communities retain their close ties with the rural areas. Many scholars reject the dichotomy between city and village that has so often been used by anthropologists and has also impacted mission strategists, who have thought in urban-versus-rural terms when they trained their workers. Today's scholarship seems to reveal that the boundary between the two is not as clear as originally imagined. In many places in the Muslim world, one cannot think of the urban without the rural context, with which Muslims often maintain certain links. I have seen North African migrants in France return to the village of their parents to share the gospel; I have also seen parents travel from North African villages to share the gospel with their children in France. But I have also noticed that the so-called anonymity that a large city can create does not always apply to Muslims. I have several friends who decided to follow Christ anonymously but still worried that their Muslim uncle or aunt living in their Parisian neighborhood might report their conversion to their family in their home country. Cosmopolitan cities do not necessarily destroy traditional networks. Extended family connections continue to matter and may weigh heavily on religious decisions.

42. Ibid., 260.

I have also met many Muslim youth who have had to navigate between the traditional customs of their migrant parents at home and the secular culture at school. It was important for the church to know that, especially when they were trying to understand why Muslims who became followers of Christ struggled with identity issues. But the opposite can be true. I have met Muslim families who are secular at home and whose children have become more devoted through Muslim friends at schools. There is not one single model. When one reaches out to Muslims in cities today, one must face the great diversity of faith expressions, customs, and movements. It is more and more difficult to find homogeneous groups in large cities, because of the wide spectrum of influences that affect extended families. Nevertheless, it is still possible to find pockets of monocultural spaces where Muslims, for example, marry only people from their own group or tribe. These monocultural communities, when they come to Christ, usually prefer to attend Christian fellowships that speak their mother tongue or eat the same food as they do. Nothing is straightforward in cities, and especially not in megacities. Even witness is in constant movement and transformation, requiring attentiveness and humility.

Fifth, cities cannot be conceived without their connections to a larger global network. No city is an island. Sociology professors Paul M. Lubeck and Bryana Britts used the city of Cairo as a case study to identify the factors that led to Islamic revival. They write, "While diversity and locality remain paramount features of Muslim cities, globalization has inadvertently nurtured transnational Muslim networks from the homeland of Islam and extended them into the web of interconnected world cities."[43] This influence of global networks is manifest in the current rise of radical Islamic groups, but it can also have other effects, since all sorts of ideas and beliefs travel through transnational networks. It is not uncommon for young urbanites to connect globally without traveling. Muslim glocals are a new kind of young people who grow up thinking not just about their own context but about the world. I was recently in New York and met a Parisian Muslim in her teens. She had traveled to this city from Europe for a few days of leisure to meet friends from college who were scattered around the world, in universities or jobs. They picked New York for their reunion because any city in the world would have been geographically close to at least one of them.

I believe that glocals are unique people whom we have not encountered enough in mission. It sometimes seems easier for them to connect with their

43. Paul M. Lubeck and Bryana Britts, "Muslim Civil Society in Urban Public Spaces: Globalization, Discursive Shifts, and Social Movements," in *Understanding the City: Contemporary and Future Perspectives*, ed. John Eade and Christopher Mele (Oxford, UK: Wiley-Blackwell, 2002), 305.

peers globally than with someone of another generation in their own culture.[44] The research of Enoch J. Kim, a mission professor, highlights that "this modernized Muslim class is theoretically influential among its own people, open to new information, specific in its media consumption of similar applications, and similar in many ways to young adults within similar demographics from foreign populations."[45] These young people, Muslims included, "are connected to each other in terms of how they relate to information, how they relate to new technologies, and how they relate to one another."[46] If we follow this argumentation, it may be possible to imagine witness from Christian to Muslim glocals through these networks, because they share a common global language and worldview.

Sixth, cities are places toward which people, including many Muslims, migrate to find a better life and new job opportunities. William Wager Cooper, professor of finance and management, and Piyu Yue, an economist, report that "the urbanization in Muslim countries has proceeded with great speed and has and is occurring on a large scale due to the rapid expansion of Muslim populations and the accelerating growth of young Muslim males."[47] Muslims migrate not only toward Muslim-majority cities but also toward cities in which they will be in the minority. A recent survey from the Pew Research Center shows that Muslims can be found virtually everywhere on the planet.[48] Whereas in the past Christian missionaries to Muslims often had to move to a Muslim-majority country, today many are witnessing in their own urban context among large Muslim populations.

God has often revealed himself in multicultural societies. At Pentecost, the Holy Spirit descended on people gathered from many places around the world in the city of Jerusalem (Acts 2:1–41). Earlier, foreigners who had dwelt with the Israelites during their migration out of Egypt had witnessed the mighty works of God (Num. 9:14). What do churches think of the Muslims in their cities? Do they see in the presence of Muslims an opportunity to include them in the church's journey with Christ so that Muslims can see the mighty works of the Triune God? I have met many North African migrants in France who now follow Christ because they met Christians who cared for them. The

---

44. See Enoch J. Kim, "A New Entrance Gate in Urban Minorities: Chinese Muslim Minority, the Hui People Case," *Missiology: An International Review* 39, no. 3 (July 2011): 353–71.

45. Ibid., 353.

46. John Palfrey and Urs Gasser, *Born Digital: Understanding the First Generation of Digital Natives* (New York: Basic Books, 2008), 13.

47. William Wager Cooper and Piyu Yue, *Challenges of the Muslim World: Present, Future, and Past* (Boston: Elsevier, 2008), 161.

48. "The Future of the Global Muslim Population," Pew Research Center, January 27, 2011, http://www.pewforum.org/2011/01/27/the-future-of-the-global-muslim-population/.

megacities, despite all the challenges they generate, also become a place where Muslims can be exposed to the gospel, in ways never experienced before.[49]

Finally, cities are not only places of transformation but also places of innovation. They can become places were Islamic expressions are morphing. There are today unique changes taking place in cities, which come from the fact that in cities, there are many cultural interactions that can influence religion. Urban public spaces in pluralistic cities also offer new spaces for Muslims to investigate their faith or the faith of others. Peter Mandaville, professor of public and international affairs, described "cosmopolitan, transnational spaces of cities such as London and Paris," where a new kind of religious reflection takes place. He describes young urbanites who reflect on their personal faith, a faith "that addresses the social predicaments and daily experience of life in the modern West." He then explains, "The myriad range of cultures, ideas and people that flow through these spaces produce rich sites of hybridized intellectual activity. The syncretisms and interminglings which inhabit these cities also constitute the cutting edge of critical Islam."[50]

I myself have observed several expressions of this rethinking of Islam in the United States. The Interfaith Youth Core initiative, started by Muslim author Eboo Patel, explores how young Muslims in America may contribute positively to their society through interfaith activities.[51] Then there is the movement related to the film *Unmosqued*, which encourages a conversation on the role of the mosque and alternative spaces of worship in contemporary America.[52] The *Hijabistas* are rethinking Islamic modesty in postmodern times.[53] They are young Muslim women who launched a new fashion of wearing the hijab in trendy styles and colors and with pride. There are the Muslim taggers, like Mohammed Ali (not related in any way to the famous boxer), "who sprays large graffiti with a short message in Latin and Arab script, such as *dhikr* (Remembrance of God) or *iqra* (Read). His graffiti are legal and sought after by cities around the globe."[54] There are many kinds of "Mipsterz"[55] (or Mus-

49. See Jean-Marie Gaudeul, *Called from Islam to Christ: Why Muslims Become Christians* (Oxford, UK: Monarch, 1999).

50. Peter Mandaville, "Towards a Critical Islam: European Muslims and the Changing Boundaries of Transnational Religious Discourse," in *Muslim Networks and Transnational Communities in and across Europe*, ed. Stefano Allievi and Jorgen S. Nielsen (Leiden: Brill, 2003), 138.

51. See the About page of Interfaith Youth Core, http://www.ifyc.org/about-us/eboo-patel.

52. See the website of the film *Unmosqued*, http://www.unmosquedfilm.com.

53. For examples of Hijabista fashion, see the website http://www.hijabistas.net/home/.

54. Maruta Herding, *Inventing the Muslim Cool: Islamic Youth Culture in Western Europe* (Bielefeld, Germany: Transcript Verlag, 2013), 107.

55. Farhan Shaikh and Dinesh Sharma, "Islam and Consumption: Religion Interpretations and Changing Consumerism," in *Islamic Perspectives on Marketing and Consumer Behavior:*

lim hipsters) today "at the forefront of the latest music, fashion, art, critical thought, food, imagination, creativity, and all forms of obscure everything."[56] These young urbanites may rethink Islam without rejecting its major tenets, as observed in the following statement: "Where a couple of decades ago teenage and young adult Muslims might be religious but downplay their Muslim identity in public, today's young Muslims are almost defiant in proudly proclaiming their Muslimness."[57]

Thus, when Muslims encounter urban forces that make it difficult to maintain a Muslim identity, Islam does not disappear from the city; instead, it is transformed. Therefore, among young people one now hears expressions such as "pop Islam," "Islamic chic,"[58] and the "Muslim Cool."[59] The reason I have added this long list of new forms of Islam is to help those who want to engage in Christian witness to evaluate contemporary descriptions of Islam. I still meet church members who rely on very traditional interpretations of Islam and would not be able to connect with these Mipsterz or with the vast numbers of young people who were born Muslims but do not believe anymore and prefer not to mention religion. An example of good rethinking about mission in urban contexts is provided by Kim, who writes of "a newly emerging young, urban, Chinese Muslim class that is evolving during a time of significant modernization."[60] This well-researched study leads its author to suggest that these urban communities of Muslims may be more receptive to the gospel because of their openness to receive new information. The young urban Muslims Kim describes are less interested in arguing about faith tenets than their forebears, and therefore Christian workers need not be as sophisticated in learning these young people's religious beliefs. We need more engagement and research like this to understand young urbanites.

Places of Encounter

Cities offer amazing opportunities for Muslims and Christians to meet. This is not new. An exhibition at the Oriental Institute of Chicago described the

Planning, Implementation, and Control, ed. Bikramjit Rishi (Hershey, PA: Business Science Reference, 2015), 110.

56. Ibid.

57. Syed Ali and Douglas Hartmann, *Migration, Incorporation, and Change in an Interconnected World* (New York: Routledge, 2015), 137–38.

58. Ariel Heryanto, "Upgraded Piety and Pleasure: The New Middle Class and Islam in Indonesian Popular Culture," in *Islam and Popular Culture in Indonesia and Malaysia*, ed. Andrew N. Weintraub (New York: Routledge, 2013), 60.

59. Herding, *Inventing the Muslim Cool.*

60. Kim, "New Entrance Gate," 353.

life in medieval Fustat/Cairo (seventh to twelfth centuries) and how Muslims, Christians, and Jews interacted in this urban context: "These three communities practiced their own beliefs and enacted communal self-government, but they also intermingled on a daily basis and practiced shared traditions of life."[61]

Today, one does not have to travel far away to meet Muslims. They are in all major cities of the world. According to Ray Bakke, teacher and leader in the area of urban studies, "Yesterday the cities were in the nations. Today the nations are in the cities."[62] When I first envisioned helping churches in Muslim contexts, I never thought I would join a Christian ministry in my home country. To me, witnessing among Muslims meant moving in a Muslim-majority country. When I realized that several million Muslims lived in France, I changed my mind and stayed in Paris for several years while traveling regularly on short-term trips to Muslim-majority countries. In the early 1980s only a few churches were reaching out to Muslims in Paris. But God had touched the hearts of several Muslims, who became followers of Christ and started to pray and invite Muslim urbanites to their meetings. They invited me to join their newly formed group, called *L'Ami*. Through their witness and the ministry of similar groups afterwards, they have seen thousands of urbanites follow Jesus. But there are still many Muslims living in big cities who have never heard the gospel in a language that is accessible to them.

Social interactions are rich and complex in urban contexts. They involve people from many cultures. Because urbanites pass by hundreds of unfamiliar people daily in buses, subways, at work, or at college, it is impossible to pay attention to all of them. However, when one has a heart to reach out to Muslims, it is possible to intentionally focus on Muslims during daily activities. I like to remember how Jesus met people as he traveled from town to town. Who would have noticed a man who had climbed a sycamore-fig tree to have a better view of Jesus passing by (Luke 19:4)? Or who would have noticed when one's garment was touched by a sick and needy woman in a crowded area (Mark 5:28)? Jesus did, because he was sensitive to the needs of people. If I had their permission, I could tell the countless stories I have heard from Christians living in large cities and deliberately making connections with Muslims in daily and ordinary encounters, whether at the shopping mall, in a taxi, at work, at a hospital, in a park, during a concert—and the list goes on and on because the opportunities for encounter are endless.

61. From the details of the companion volume to the exhibit, *A Cosmopolitan City: Muslims, Christians, and Jews in Old Cairo*, ed. Tasha Vorderstrasse and Tanya Treptow (Chicago: Oriental Institute of the University of Chicago, 2015). For a description of the book, see the website of Casemate Academic, http://www.oxbowbooks.com/dbbc/a-cosmopolitan-city.html.
62. Quoted by Svoboda in "The Urban Challenge," 4.

When Witness Flows Naturally

Farida Saïdi, PhD, L'Ami, France and North Africa

People often ask me why the church in North Africa is growing so rapidly, especially in places where Christian witness is often restricted. I believe that the strength of the North African church lies in its members' belief in ordinary witness. Brothers and sisters just love to share the love of God through Jesus Christ with others, and they do it naturally as they go about their daily activities. They don't need training on how to witness. To them, it flows naturally. To them keeping silent about their faith would be equal to spiritual death.

I remember what a Christian woman said to me during the civil war in Algeria in the 1980s when I asked her if she was not afraid to talk about Jesus in such dire circumstances. She responded that because of street bombings, one could die any time while walking in the city. When she left the house in the morning, she was not sure she would come back in the evening. She left her house every morning with the thought that it was perhaps the last day of her life during which she could share the joy of knowing God with people she met. North African believers naturally share Christ with their family and friends, young and old.

Evangelism in the Bible is very relational. Jesus gives us examples of a life committed to love others. 1 Corinthians 9:16–22 gives us a perfect image of evangelism through human friendship. Paul writes, "To the weak I became weak" (v. 22 NIV). Loving others includes listening to them, having pure motivations (John 14:15), accepting people as they are, spending time with them, having dinner with them, and being a servant.

If God is the most important person in our life, don't we want to introduce him to others? If we don't joyfully share our faith, what will happen to Muslim people like Ali, Mohammed, Karim, Fatima, Fadila, Nora—all Muslims we may meet during our day? This has been my journey over the last fifty years: witnessing, and being overjoyed to see others grow in faith in God. It is not always easy, but as the Bible says, if we don't speak about Jesus, the stones will cry out (Luke 19:40).

Christian witness in urban contexts requires flexibility in one's perception of Islam, because in a single city, one can encounter a plethora of diverse theological, legal, ethnic, cultural, and individual expressions of Islam. It is impossible to be fluent in all, unless one becomes an expert on Islam. But an awareness of these differences will help one better appreciate Muslims one encounters and avoid conflicts that can arise when Muslims feel stereotyped. Although I use the term "Muslim" throughout the book, for the sake of simplicity and quick identification, I want to remind my reader that there are many expressions of Islamic faith.

Urban contexts provide more diverse spaces of encounter. In large cities, Muslims create a multiplicity of social groupings ranging from mosque congregations, to affinity groups, to whole societies. It is not difficult to find places where one can meet Muslims, as long as one is bold enough to connect. But not all these groupings need to be called Islamic to include Muslims. For many Muslims, faith is not a primary category of identification. Thus, an activity organized by a mosque may not be the most natural context in which to meet a Muslim neighbor who never attends worship and calls himself or herself a cultural or secular Muslim. In this case, the relationship may instead be established in a nonreligious setting.

Finally, cities offer Muslims and Christians the opportunity to partner in common projects for the good of the city. Some urban problems are beyond the capacity of any one faith tradition to fix. Many interfaith initiatives around the world are bringing Muslims and Christians together to address issues of injustice in the city, which could not be solved unilaterally. For example, A. Christian van Gorder, a professor of religion, explains how in Ghana, "Muslims and Christians are working together for social justice. . . . Multi-faith social justice partnerships can build trust and inclusion in countries such as Ghana or Nigeria, in which religious tensions are increasing among the various faith communities. Shared projects not only can result in tangible outcomes, but can also provide a social context where people can respectfully support and affirm each other."[63] Churches in the Central African Republic protected thousands of Muslims attacked by a pro-Christian militia.[64] In Mindanao-Sulu, Philippines, social action programs for the good of the city allowed Christians and Muslims to partner together. "This working together of ordinary Muslims and Christians strengthened their relationship of mutual respect and of mutual belonging to one community."[65] In fact, interfaith initiatives for social action are held in many places around the world.

63. A. Christian van Gorder, *Islam, Peace and Social Justice: A Christian Perspective* (Cambridge: James Clarke & Co, 2014), Kindle edition, location 4880.

64. Fredrick Nzwili, "War-Torn Churches Shelter Muslims in Central African Republic," *Sojourners*, February 20, 2014, http://sojo.net/blogs/2014/02/20/war-torn-churches-shelter -muslims-central-african-republic.

65. William Larousse, *A Local Church Living for Dialogue: Muslim-Christian Relations in Mindanao-Sulu (Philippines)* (Rome: Editrice Pontifica Università Gregoriana Roma, 2001), 452.

Joyful Witness in Cities

This book is about joyful witness. I cannot end this chapter without describing this joy in the cities. Have you experienced joy in the city? The joy I am talking about here, as in other chapters, is the joy flowing from a healthy relationship with God, people, and the earth. This joy can also be experienced in relationship with cities. People have rejoiced and wept over cities in the Bible. When Jerusalem was destroyed, Nehemiah wept. When Jerusalem was rebuilt, its people "offered great sacrifices and rejoiced because God had given them great joy, even the women and children rejoiced, so that the joy of Jerusalem was heard from afar" (Neh. 12:43 NASB). Imagine the sound of joyful celebration that people could hear from miles and miles away. God showed many times in the Old Testament how cities can experience restoration and joy, as when he said, "Whereas you have been forsaken and hated, with no one passing through, I will make you majestic forever, a joy from age to age" (Isa. 60:15 RSV). Jesus also rejoiced and wept over cities. He wept over Jerusalem but foresaw the new Jerusalem, in which there will be no tears, no mourning, no crying, and no pain (Rev. 21:4). Already on this earth there was great joy in the city of Samaria when the gospel was preached and demonstrated through healings and deliverance (Acts 8:8). Whenever the gospel of salvation, reconciliation, and transformation is preached and accepted, one can experience the rejoicing of a city.

Urban mission does include joy. Jude Tiersma, who teaches urban missiology, has expressed well how joy and tears are part of life in the city: "As we become neighbors in a neighborhood and begin to share our lives, we discover the joys and treasures of life hidden in neighborhoods forgotten by most of the world."[66] But joy is not the only emotion experienced in the city: "As we become immersed in life and open our hearts, we discover not only the treasures, but also the tremendous suffering, inhumanity, and evil that seem to surround us. . . . Sometimes we can even become overwhelmed, and the despair around us begins to take over within us."[67] Thus, joy, as in the other contexts we have seen, can be understood in witness only if we can also hold the painful emotions felt in the contexts in which we serve. Commenting on Psalm 55, which talks about the violence and destructive forces the psalmist sees in the city, Robert C. Linthicum writes, "Here is the beginning of the rhythm of the Christian life: to go into the city, with its

66. Jude Tiersma, "What Does It Mean to Be Incarnational When We Are Not the Messiah?," in *God So Loves the City: Seeking a Theology for Urban Mission*, ed. Charles Van Engen and Jude Tiersma (Eugene, OR: Wipf and Stock, 2000), 11.
67. Ibid.

violence and its joys, its malice and its compassion. Such ministry demands all that a person can give."[68]

But as we engage in urban mission, we must remember that God delights in cities. He wants his name to be known and claimed in cities. Linthicum writes, "We do not often think of our city as the City of Joy—but this name is to be more than simply the title of a book. God wants to delight over the city and wants God's people to find joy in the city, as well."[69] Thus, Linthicum invites us to celebrate over cities and discover good things in them. In other words, he says, churches should celebrate and be cheerleaders of cities. This is good advice. May I suggest that we also include Muslim-majority cities or neighborhoods in these cheerful expressions? Could we imagine by faith that the oppression, injustice, and intractable Muslim-Christian conflicts we see in some cities can turn into joy when Christ touches the hearts of their populations? What if we could delight in cities again, and if, with the same energy as Nehemiah when he rebuilt the walls of Jerusalem, we could rebuild broken relationships in cities (Neh. 1–5)? There is much to do, for in many places around the world Muslims and Christians don't always succeed in peacefully sharing the city. Sharing may start humbly, with small places of celebration and joy, like the ones I have seen in several cities of the world when churches were open to reaching out to their Muslim neighbors. There is much pain in urban contexts, but when a city welcomes the presence of the Triune God, it may soon discover what it means for a city to be "the joy of all the earth" (Ps. 48:2 RSV).

Conclusion

Many Muslims live in cities, but Muslim cities and urbanites are often misunderstood in Christian ministries. Given the paucity of research on urban contexts, Christians need to continue reflecting on the questions covered here and expand my field of investigation.

Focusing on cities does not mean that I neglect rural areas. In some parts of the Muslim world most people do not live in cities. For example, a UNICEF study on Bangladesh reports that almost three-quarters of that country's population live in rural areas.[70] There are many Christian ministries serving

---

68. Linthicum, *City of God, City of Satan*, 237. The author has just referred to Isa. 65:18–19, which talks about Jerusalem as a delight created by God and its people a joy. God is rejoicing over Jerusalem and takes delight in its inhabitant. Jerusalem is the City of Joy in this biblical passage.

69. Ibid., 165.

70. "Bangladesh Today," UNICEF, http://www.unicef.org/bangladesh/overview_4840.htm.

in rural areas that would have been worth discussing. But because of the trend toward urbanization and the few resources helping us understand Christian witness in Muslim urban contexts, I preferred to emphasize cities.

We have much to learn about Islam from observing the cities where Muslims live. Urban contexts have their own unique characteristics. They reflect religious beliefs but are also constantly moving and transforming their populations in unique ways. Those with an important message to share do it in cities, which are known for the influence they exert on the world, especially today, as over half of the world's population lives in cities; and this trend is only increasing.

As cities bring together people from various cultures and faiths, they also offer numerous possibilities of encounter that Christians, unfortunately, do not always seize. I hope that this chapter will encourage others to draw nearer to Muslim urbanites. They may discover that Muslims' identities do not always correspond to the traditional image Christians have of them. Young Muslims living in megacities are not very different from other contemporary young people around the world. The Mipsterz, Muslim glocals, and other young urbanites often have more in common with other young people globally than they may have with the older generation at home.

Urban contexts are complex. Those who engage in them will experience both pain and joy. Such contexts should be explored carefully. Some urban problems are so challenging that they can be addressed only in partnership with Muslims. Christians will need to draw resources from research conducted on Christian-Muslim peacemaking and interfaith social action, since some problems involve both communities. I could have discussed at length the urban public sphere, which is sometimes shared in chaotic ways by Muslims and Christians. This also can change if we trust that God can restore cities just as he did in biblical times. Thus, I invite you to think globally—because all major cities are now connected—but also locally: seek out Muslims who may live in your neighborhood; find those who take the same bus daily and ride to work with them; or maybe a Muslim babysits your children, or you meet Muslims at the food court. Let's bless Muslims we encounter daily in our city, and pray for the welfare and peace of the city in which we live together with them.

For Discussion

1. What are some characteristics of Muslim-majority cities?
2. How can your church engage with Muslims in an urban context?
3. Discuss God's intentions toward Muslim-majority cities, and share this with others in your church.

8

Theological Conversations

When I moved to Paris, I regularly met with a group of students from a Christian organization called InterVarsity.[1] We used to pray and read the Bible together. Once a week, on Wednesdays, I would set up a table with Bibles in several languages at a university campus. Most students would pass by my book table without stopping. Most students were not interested in religious discussions, and certainly not in the Bible. However, even during the first weeks, some students noticed that I had books in Arabic. They first thought I was offering Qur'ans, but as they approached the table, they saw Bibles in Arabic. From that time on, many Muslim students would stop by regularly and chat with me about spiritual things. We enjoyed these conversations. Some topics were more pleasant than others, but what I learned during the two years I visited this campus weekly and met with students was that Muslims love to talk about faith and religion. They are not shy about it. One does not have to apologize to start a religious conversation. After a few weeks, I began looking forward to Wednesdays with pleasant anticipation. I knew my friends would be there, and we would continue a conversation started the week before. I learned a lot about Islam and Muslim communities through these conversations. These were my first theological encounters with Muslims. I did not know much about their doctrines, but I learned on the go and found myself increasingly conversant about Islam as the weeks went by. Thirty-five years

1. For information on InterVarsity, see http://www.intervarsity.org.

What Kind of Gospel Are They Going to Hear?

Ida Glaser

It is no longer only specialist missionaries who are witnessing to Muslims—all Christians who have Muslims living nearby are signs to them of what Christianity is about. It is not only those who you or I would identify as "Christian" that provide Muslims' understanding of Christianity: it is those whom the Muslims identify as "Christian" that determine their views. And, since to be Muslim is to be part of a community, that means that all those who are identified as being part of a Christian community may be considered Christian. Many Muslims assume that all white people are Christian. Witnessing to Muslims in Britain is therefore not an option. Muslims see people they consider to be Christian, and draw their own conclusions. This is also true of those who realize that there is a big difference between being Christian in name and being Christian in practice: they see all those in their area who attend church, and, again, draw their own conclusions. A little reflection on the inner-city areas in which the majority of Muslims live, and on media images of British life and church, will indicate that the question is not *whether* we share the Gospel with Muslims, but *what kind* of Gospel they are going to hear. This is a challenge for the whole church.

Quoted from Ida Glaser, "Millennial Reverie: Muslims
in Britain" *Anvil* 17, no. 3 (2000): 179.

---

later, I am still learning, while savoring the memory of many conversations that have made an eternal difference in the lives of people.

In the previous chapters, I have discussed diverse types of Muslim-Christian interactions. I offered examples of what scholars call the dialogue of life,[2] or ordinary encounters between Muslims and Christians. The primary focus of

---

2. Muslim professor Riffat Hassan says that the dialogue of life "arises 'naturally' as it were from the interaction, positive and negative, obvious and subtle, verbal and nonverbal, between various peoples or persons." "The Basis for a Hindu-Muslim Dialogue and Steps in That Direction," in *Muslims in Dialogue: The Evolution of a Dialogue*, ed. Leonard Swidler (Lewiston, NY: Edwin Mellen, 1992), 405. Christian scholar Johannes Verkuyl says the dialogue of life consists of "interreligious encounters founded in deep, personal and lasting friendships . . . where heart meets heart." "The Biblical Notion of the Kingdom: Tests of Validity for Theology of Religion," in *The Good News of the Kingdom: Mission Theology for the Third Millennium*, ed. Charles Van Engen, Dean S. Gilliland, and Paul Pierson (Eugene, OR: Wipf and Stock, 1993), 79.

those encounters is not theological. They do not center uniquely on conversations about God, although joyful witness can still occur. When Christians encounter Muslims, whether or not they discuss the nature of God in detail, there can be many occasions of sharing the gospel in words or deeds. In this chapter we look specifically at theological conversations, which have been one of the favorite forms of Muslim-Christian interactions recorded by historians.

Why did I wait until the last chapter of this book to talk about theology? Because, I believe, Muslim-Christian encounters do not consist primarily in discussions regarding doctrines. Instead, Muslims are first encountered as neighbors. Religion should not be the only marker of their identity that motivates us to reach out to them (or avoid their presence). Christians meet Muslims first and foremost because they have felt the joy of God radiating toward themselves and now feel that the same joy is leading them toward others. If we don't look at Muslims first as people deserving the joy of God, we run the danger of never learning to trust and care for them. Life together will be miserable. We will even miss opportunities to share the gospel, since the insecurity of our bond will prevent any kind of robust conversations about God. In today's global context, riddled in places by wars and conflicts, a discussion on the Trinity may not even be possible, since political and social preoccupations have severed the relationships between Muslims and Christians. Nevertheless, theological conversations are and always will be important and can enhance Christian witness, especially if they are joyful.

What Are Muslims Asking?

I once asked a Muslim-born woman, whom I will here call Aisha, who is now a follower of Christ: "What is your favorite book in the Bible?" She answered, "The book of Leviticus." I was surprised, since she was a fairly new believer and I remembered my reaction when I studied Leviticus in my first theological course. I found it challenging and did not always know how to relate its family and social laws to my own cultural context. Aisha did not think like me. She found the book fascinating because it framed religious questions in a familiar manner to her. While being raised in her Muslim family, she would often observe the anxiety of adults when they did not know the divine instructions for every aspect of their lives.

Thus, to her, Leviticus seemed very practical and down to earth. It provided guidelines for everyday life and not just abstract thinking about God or the afterlife. To her, as well as many other Muslims I met afterwards, right conduct was as important as right beliefs. After that conversation I realized that the intellectual framework that people use when they embrace a new faith is usually the same as the one they used in their former faith. This woman was raised in a Muslim context, in which the legal aspect of faith was as important as the theological one. The nitty-gritty of divine laws mattered a lot to her. She reminded me of religious teachers at the time of Jesus who were more interested in discussing why his disciples ate with unwashed hands (Mark 7:5) or why Jesus healed people on the Sabbath than in hearing the doctrine of salvation (Matt. 12:10).

I was ill-prepared for a theological conversation with Aisha. My early training in Muslim-Christian relations was limited to Muslim-awareness seminars in churches that traditionally covered the five pillars of Islam (confession of faith, prayer, fasting, almsgiving, and pilgrimage), the doctrines (God, angels, revealed books, prophets and messengers, judgment day, and the hereafter),[3] and, if time permitted, the theological schools of Islam. At the end of such training, I would go home clueless about how to integrate this information in my conversations with Muslims during ordinary encounters. So when Aisha wanted to discuss social issues similar to the ones in Leviticus rather than liturgical requirements, I was at a loss as to how to respond. I now know that it is far more important to understand how Muslims frame their spiritual quest than to inundate them with answers to questions they never raise and with forms of theological queries that they don't understand. When I spoke with Aisha, my witness was heavily influenced by a Western worldview, and I was unable to completely grasp other dynamics, such as the early Christian-Muslim encounter that was shaped by Eastern Christian realities, which were sometimes different from the Western ones.

I have met many Christians who wander around the Muslim world with prepackaged arguments, similar to the ones I had when I spoke with Aisha. They answer questions Muslims don't raise. You can quiz them on all the Muslim-Christian theological controversies, such as those concerning the Trinity, the incarnation of Christ, salvation, or sin. They will answer right away with a litany that they have painstakingly learned by heart; they always use the same arguments and believe they are right. They may even learn this argumentation before having ever personally met a Muslim. I find this rather dehumanizing. A conversation with such a person almost feels like a conversation with a robot. But theological encounters are not as simple as pushing a button for the correct answers; theological encounters are a form of human relation.

---

3. For a quick but robust overview of rituals and beliefs, I recommend Andrew Rippin, *Muslims: Their Religious Beliefs and Practices*, 3rd ed. (New York: Routledge, 2005), and Kenneth Cragg, *The Call of the Minaret* (Oxford: Oneworld Publications, 2000).

What I like about Jesus is that he did not respond mechanically to people who came to him with questions. He aligned his discourse with the interrogations of his audience. He could speak using different approaches. He spoke to the Samaritan woman differently than to Nicodemus or to the disciples. The apostle Paul was also very flexible in his approach. He did not use the exact same words when he spoke to the lame man in Lystra (Acts 14:10) or to Lydia (Acts 16:14). How can we follow their example today, especially those of us who are not born in a Muslim context and don't understand the spiritual interrogations of Muslims? The best way is to have many conversations with Muslims and not limit these conversations to controversial doctrines but rather share the gospel in ordinary conversations in the midst of ordinary joys and sorrows. I, for example, encourage my students to read novels, watch popular movies, and read the daily newspapers of the Muslim world so that they understand what matters to ordinary Muslims. Jesus was able to have theological conversations—in other words, discuss God—in real-world situations, such as weddings, walking through fields, traveling through villages and towns, or around meals. His message about God was not detached from the daily affairs of people. Likewise, we don't have to disincarnate witness and make it unintelligible as we would if we presented it as so far removed from the daily realities of Muslims.[4]

Yet theological conversations will be complicated by the fact that ordinary Muslims are not very different from ordinary Christians in their approach. Their reflection on Christianity, like our reflection on Islam, is shaped by fourteen centuries of conversations and debates that have produced in their communities one-paragraph rebuttals that they conveniently use when Christians present the gospel to them. They state that Jesus did not die, that the Bible is corrupt, or that they don't need Jesus as Savior since good works and God's mercy, as attested in the Qur'an, are sufficient to lead them to paradise. They don't even listen carefully to Christians, because they think that Christians will merely repeat the same discourse as their predecessors. Muslims are trapped, like us, in the consequences of a doctrinal status quo that is the product of centuries of Muslim-Christian theological conversations.

In order to break this cycle of automatic speech, one must learn to listen more carefully to the religious other. Doing so helps Muslims and Christians be attentive to specific and individual discourses that may challenge the traditional argumentation of their communities. Christian scholars and practitioners have recently developed approaches that help people practice this type of listening.

4. See, e.g., Paul-Gordon Chandler, "Mazhar Mallouhi: Gandhi's Living Christian Legacy in the Muslim World," *International Bulletin of Missionary Research* 27, no. 2 (April 2003): 54–59.

In a book on Anabaptist-Muslim relations, the authors show how a "ministry of presence in the way of Christ" is important.[5] The practice of hospitality is also important in theological encounters, fostering a listening attitude.[6] I have often adopted the approach of Miroslav Volf that he calls the "Inverted Perspective," which allows me to examine from the Muslims' vantage point my discourse and theirs.[7] These models and many others can help Christians listen to Muslims and identify what questions Muslims are actually asking. Such models may be very different from the scholar-framed discourse.

I have experienced this inverted perspective many times in my encounters with Muslims. One vivid memory comes from my theological conversations during a dialogue with Muslim leaders in the Middle East. I was asked to talk about God and politics. After my presentation and a panel discussion, several young people in the audience asked me to explain how I can state that the biblical God loves justice when they were seeing so much injustice perpetrated in his name by people who come from countries with solid Christian legacies. This question, which I heard reiterated several times in my conversations with Muslims, helped me understand one primary concern of Muslims: the love for justice. It then became easier to start talking about the incarnation of Jesus from this vantage point.

Listening Is Not Enough

Listening, however, is not sufficient in witness. Christians have to understand the spiritual quest of Muslims and how the Bible relates to their questions. I like to give my students a piece of advice from scholar Kenneth Cragg. He once introduced his series of Bible studies at a conference in Asmara, Eritrea, with these words: "The world of Islam is looking over our shoulder as we meet here. In our study of the Bible, we should be conscious of the Muslim sitting beside us."[8] To him it was important to read the Bible with Muslims looking over our shoulders. By this statement he also is inviting those who are serious about witnessing to Muslims to read the Bible with questions raised

5. James R. Krabill, David W. Shenk, and Linford Stutzman, *Anabaptists Meeting Muslims: A Calling for Presence in the Way of Christ* (Harrisonburg, VA: Herald Press, 2004).

6. Paul-Gordon Chandler, "Sacred Hospitality 'Middle Eastern Style,'" *Inland Episcopalian*, December 2005.

7. Miroslav Volf, "Living with the 'Other,'" in *Muslim and Christian Reflections on Peace: Divine and Human Dimensions*, ed. John Dudley Woodberry, Osman Zümrüt, and Mustafa Köylü (Lanham, MD: University Press of America, 2005), 3–22.

8. Quoted in R. Park Johnson, "Renewal of the Christian Mission to Islam: Reflections on the Asmara Conference," *International Review of Mission* 48, no. 4 (October 1959): 438–44.

by Muslims in mind. When we share the gospel with Muslims, they may not be attracted to or puzzled by the same words or passages as we are.

I remember reading the Bible in my apartment in Paris with Sabrina, a North African woman. I can't remember now exactly what passage we were reading, but in one of them Sabrina saw the word "grace," and she got very annoyed because she could not grasp the meaning of it. I knew that I could not explain this word in a few minutes. She had no theological background to which she could relate God's grace in Christ. She could understand the words "compassion" and "mercy" from the first chapter of the Qur'an, but the word "grace" as explained in Romans 3:24, "and [you] are justified freely by his grace through the redemption that came by Christ Jesus," did not ring the same bell for her. Of course, just by looking at the words "justification," "grace," and "redemption" we can understand why this was an extremely challenging verse for someone unfamiliar with the Bible. Sabrina had encountered the word "grace" before in a qur'anic verse, which says "And whatever you have of favor [grace]—it is from Allah. Then when adversity touches you, to Him you cry for help" (16:53). I built on what she knew. Since she was a mother of three girls, I had an idea. She would know what it meant for a mother to be able to care freely and generously for her daughter. Once I used this image to explain the concept of grace, she started smiling and we continued reading. Of course it took her much longer to comprehend the meaning of God's grace in Christ, and how it is larger than the grace explained in the qur'anic verse above. But during our conversation, in which I used a concept that she knew to point her toward realities that she did not know, I allowed her to catch a glimpse of God's unique grace revealed in Christ.

We often think the controversial issues that have divided Muslims and Christians for centuries are what will prevent Muslims from coming to Christ. We therefore try hard to refute their arguments, hoping that they will eventually be convinced. These controversies prevent Christians from engaging more deeply in the journey of discovery with Muslims. I have met too many Christians who focused all their energy on trying to convince Muslims that they are wrong. If they don't succeed, they give up any kind of theological conversation and even relationship. Unfortunately, since these arguments have been discussed for centuries, I don't see how, unless one is extremely well-versed in the theology of Islam, one could win these core arguments that divide Muslims and Christians.

I remember trying once to win one of these controversies with a few Muslims I had met during a trip to the Middle East. When I offered some evidence showing that the Bible was not corrupted, instead of listening with attention to my arguments, they sent for an imam who lived in the neighborhood, because they felt he could better argue with me since he was more knowledgeable in the Qur'an and the Bible. Did I have a fruitful conversation with these people? Not the one I anticipated. My passionate debate quickly alienated me from this group, because our encounter was about who was right and who was wrong. Since then, I have learned to always leave a door open for future conversation.

I don't mean to diminish the value of apologetics, which the Bible endorses in many places,[9] or even some forms of polemics (though I rarely use polemics myself, because in hostile environments such as one observes today in many places, Muslim-Christian polemics can rapidly turn to horrific violence). But I also want to emphasize that the goal of our witness is to prepare the way for Christ to reach the hearts of Muslims—not to block the way. I have personally observed that for some Muslims it may take years to trust the biblical message, essentially because they have been told for centuries that Islam is God's final revelation to humankind that Christians had earlier received but have then misread.

If I had foreseen the reaction of these Middle Eastern Muslims I argued with, I would have spent less time debating doctrines and instead focused on the biblical narrative, which most did not know at all. The only passages they knew from the Bible were the controversial texts that they had learned in the Muslim community. When Muslims are not familiar with the Bible, why start with doctrinal debates that necessitate a theological expertise that many believers don't master? I am encouraged in this endeavor by the example of Jesus, who, when engaging people, did not discuss only theological points, but spoke of God as he performed healings or fed the crowds. I like to pray the Psalms with Muslims; this is a way to discuss the nature of God. And I now like to walk Muslims through the Old Testament and underline the patience and love of God for his people and the nations.

Theological conversations with Muslims take time. We are not talking to people who have no beliefs, but to people whose beliefs have challenged ours for centuries. Daniel A. Madigan, a Jesuit scholar of Islam, believes that many Christians in the West "have engaged more often with lack of belief than with different belief."[10] This may be true also of missionaries who have tried to evangelize other parts of the world, where major faith traditions have been so resistant to the gospel that churches in these contexts have lost their interest

9. This verse, e.g., shows that apologetics (in other words, the defense of one's faith) is supported by the Bible: "Always be prepared to give an answer [*apologia*] to everyone who asks you to give the reason for the hope that you have. But do this with gentleness and respect" (1 Pet. 3:15 NIV).

10. See "Daniel A. Madigan," website of Georgetown University, http://explore.georgetown .edu/people/dam76/?action=viewresearch&PageTemplateID=360: "Since the Enlightenment— and there has been a contemporary push as well—theology has focused substantially on engaging lack of belief rather than different belief."

in reaching out to them. I like to remember that the disciples lived with Jesus for three years before they understood what he meant when he talked about certain realities, which have now become major biblical doctrines. The disciples originated from a religious context very similar to the Muslim one. They were strong monotheists who recited the *Shema*: "Hear, O Israel! The LORD is our God, the LORD is one!" (Deut. 6:4). Muslims are strong monotheists too. *Tawḥīd*, the qur'anic term for the oneness of God, is one of the central tenets of Islam (Qur'an 112). Their confession of faith states that there is no god but God. Muslims must experience the same drastic paradigm shift as Jesus's disciples did to make sense of the divine sonship of Jesus. And remember how the disciples struggled, argued, debated, and doubted until they came to this understanding. Like Muslims, they resisted vehemently, at first, the idea that Jesus could die for them. We must let Muslims walk with Jesus for as long as is necessary for them to understand who he is. It took, for example, Mazhar Mallouhi, a Muslim-born novelist, one year of reading the Scriptures before he could say, "This Christ is my Lord."[11]

Despite these controversies, and despite the beliefs of many Muslims that the Bible currently used by Christians is made up of texts that have been falsified, an increasing number of Muslims and Christians read the Bible and the Qur'an together in order to discuss their commonalities and differences.[12] It would be difficult to argue that there are no commonalities.[13] The Qur'an's many references to biblical characters, as well as legal and liturgical requirements of the Qur'an that resemble requirements found in the Torah and the Talmud, make it easy for a Christian to build conversational bridges. For example, Chawkat Moucarry, a Christian scholar of Islam, has compared the *Fatiha*—the first chapter of the Qur'an, which Muslims recite in their daily prayers—and the Lord's Prayer in the Bible, so as to discuss the concepts of mercy, judgment, love, and fatherhood of God.[14] He found both similarities that could be used as bridges to relate to Muslims and differences that explained

---

11. Chandler, "Mazhar Mallouhi."

12. I am not discussing here the question of whether or not Christians should read the Qur'an. Some Christians refuse to read it even to better understand the religious worldview of Muslims. Three evangelicals recently discussed the topic: Nabeel Qureshi, Roy Oksnevad, and Mark Pfeiffer, "Should Christians Read the Qur'an?," *Christianity Today*, October 22, 2013, http://www.christianitytoday.com/ct/2013/november/should-christians-read-quran.html?start=3.

13. See, e.g., Rick Brown, "Who was 'Allah' before Islam? Evidence That the Term 'Allah' Originated with Jewish and Christian Arabs," chapter 8 in *Toward Respectful Understanding and Witness among Muslims: Essays in Honor of J. Dudley Woodberry*, ed. Evelyne A. Reisacher (Pasadena, CA: William Carey Library, 2012), Kindle edition, locations 4354–5553.

14. Chawkat Moucarry, *Two Prayers for Today: The Lord's Prayer and the Fatiha* (Tiruvalla, India: Christava Sahitya Samithi, 2007).

Conversation with a Muslim Sheikh

Henri Aoun, LifeAgape International

During a big world event that took place in a European city, a group of Christian disciples came to our mission organization from several Arab countries to share their faith with Muslims in that city. One of the disciples did not really enjoy the training in how to share our faith with Muslims in a friendly and biblically based discussion. One evening, I saw him sitting with a Muslim sheikh from North Africa; they were arguing using verses from the Qur'an and the Bible. I sat by them and watched them for more than thirty minutes. At the end I asked if I could share something with the respected sheikh. Only because they were tired, they said yes. I opened my Bible to Genesis 3:13–15 and asked the sheikh if I could read this to him. He said yes. I read it, making sure he saw the words I was reading. I then asked him if he had any idea who is the only person in the world born from only a woman, not a woman and a man? He responded correctly: "Jesus, born of Mary." Then: "I didn't know that the Bible said that!" I read him several other verses, and he responded the same way: "I didn't know that the Bible said that."

Finally, the sheikh asked politely, "Do you have another copy of the Bible I can take home to read?" "Of course," I responded, and gave him one. He was delighted to get his own copy of the Bible, and he promised to read it carefully. It was another joyful occasion on which a Muslim, once he had seen and heard the Word of God, changed his reaction and desired to read it. No, it is not magical, but rather it is the living and powerful Word of God, which can affect a Muslim in such a way that he or she desires to follow Christ.

the unique characteristics of the biblical God, especially characteristics pertaining to his triune nature and to salvation through Christ. Similarly, Barbara J. Hampton, a Christian leader and author, has prepared a study guide to help Muslim and Christian students explore their sacred texts together calmly, in a way that enables them to respect their differences.[15] And many other initiatives combine theological conversations with pleasant togetherness, such as faith clubs[16] or the blog of Michal and Sondos discussed in chapter 3.[17]

15. Barbara J. Hampton, *Reading Scripture Together: A Comparative Qur'an and Bible Study Guide* (n.p.: Dialogue of Witness Press, 2014).
16. See the website of Circles of Faith, http://www.circlesoffaith.org/#about.
17. See website of Miss Understanding, http://www.missunderstanding.co/.

Some Christians have raised the level of these common readings to academic encounters. The Centre for Muslim-Christian Studies at Oxford, United Kingdom, has brought Muslims and Christians together for research and teaching. Its vision is "to see Muslim-Christian relationships transformed through shared academic study and by following the example of Jesus Christ."[18] Ida Glaser, the Center's director, shows how important it is for Christians to study Islam and hear Muslim voices if they want to enhance their engagement with Muslims.[19] It is important to practice "Christian theologizing in relation to Islam."[20] Numerous seminaries around the world now include courses on Islam. In teaching at Fuller Theological Seminary in the Islamic Studies program, I have personally observed how beneficial it is for students to study Islam not just from an anthropological or sociological perspective— to cover areas discussed in previous chapters of this book—but also from a theological perspective, to deepen their biblical hermeneutics in the Muslim context. It is not sufficient to deepen one's understanding of the Bible on one side, and to better understand the Qur'an on the other. What is most useful for Christians who engage with Islam is to read the Bible with Muslims in mind.[21] And to this end, they need to know the texts that shape the current religiosity of Muslims.

Monologue or Dialogue?

We have noticed that in theological encounters between Muslims and Christians the participants do not always understand each other's interrogations, because they do not listen to each other. But a discourse in which a person speaks but does not listen is called a monologue. A conversation, or dialogue, involves at least two parties, and a true conversation, religious or otherwise, allows both parties to feel heard and to express their views. One cannot simply preach a message without wrestling with the difficulties the other encounters in trying to comprehend it. This is particularly true with Muslims, who

18. "Our Vision and Ethos," Centre for Muslim-Christian Studies, http://cmcsoxford.org .uk/about-us/ethos/.

19. Ida Glaser, "'Get Wisdom, Get Understanding': How Study Contributes to Muslim-Christian Engagement," *Anvil* 23, no. 2 (2006): 113–23.

20. Daniel A. Madigan, SJ, "Some Aspects of Christian Theologizing in Relation to Islam," *Asian Christian Review* 2, no. 2–3 (Summer/Winter 2008): 24–30.

21. See, e.g., Ida Glaser, "Reading the Bible with Islam in Mind," *Anvil* 31, no. 1 (March 2015): 18–31. See also Glaser, "'Get Wisdom, Get Understanding,'" 122. Her latest book written with Hannah Kay, *Thinking Biblically about Islam: Genesis, Transfiguration, Transformation* (Carlisle, UK: Langham Global Library, 2016), is providing rich resources for Christians who want to reflect biblically on Islam.

developed their beliefs and practices while living near Christian and Jewish communities at the time of Muhammad. I agree with Christian scholar of Islam Lamin Sanneh when he says with respect to Muslim-Christian relations, "Few things divide people more than what they have in common."[22]

But dialogue sometimes gets bad press in evangelical circles. It seems that evangelicals have been afraid of this term for three reasons. First, they have believed dialogue could be conducted only by people of faith who are not exclusivists—in other words, who do not believe that one has to accept Jesus Christ as personal Savior to be saved. Second, they have not known how to reconcile respectful theological conversations with their passion for sharing the good news. They have thought that dialogue meant giving up evangelism, because this type of engagement usually includes a rule that participants won't try to convert each other. This measure, I suppose, was taken to curb hostility, since theological exchange can often lead to polemical encounters, where both parties only quarrel without listening to each other. Since evangelical Christians and Muslims are both mission minded, I suspect that despite these rules, many secretly hope that they can persuade the other to join their community.

Third, evangelicals have often refused to engage in dialogue because they have felt that Islam and Christianity have nothing in common, and therefore evangelicals could not abide by the rules of interfaith dialogue that invite both parties to talk about issues on the basis of something that they share. Such a dialogue is often easier to conduct through the forms we explored earlier, such as art, humanitarian aid, and creation care, than through theological discussions centered on divisive doctrines.

But today, evangelicals engage increasingly in theological dialogue, confident that this will not affect their commitment to Christ and that they don't have to water down the gospel in order to adopt this form of conversation. New definitions arise as Christians feel more confident. Christian theologian John Stott, for example, reports that a National Evangelical Anglican Congress held at Keele, United Kingdom, in 1967 defined "dialogue" as "a conversation in which each party is serious in his approach both to the subject and to the other person, and desires to listen and learn as well as speak and instruct."[23]

Some even transform the rules, stating spontaneously that they wish the other party would join their community. Others are convinced that without

22. Lamin Sanneh, "Secular Values in the Midst of Faith: A Critical Discourse on Dialogue and Difference," in *Theology and the Religions: A Dialogue*, ed. Viggo Mortensen (Grand Rapids: Eerdmans, 2003), 137.

23. John Stott, *Christian Mission in the Modern World*, with a foreword by Ajith Fernando (Downers Grove, IL: InterVarsity, 2009), 43.

dialogue there will be no peace, since in many places quarrels turn into fierce conflicts between Muslims and Christians. They believe that dialogue can lead Muslims and Christians to live peacefully with each other, despite their theological differences.[24] Others believe that we have not yet explored the dialogue between evangelical Christians and Muslims enough to break new ground.[25] These dialogues can be held in many formats, ranging from formal conferences to books that circulate in the hands of thousands of people.[26] Others, besides committing themselves to interfaith dialogue, are developing promising new models, such as the "kerygmatic approach" by Martin Accad, scholar of Islam. Without negating the other models of interaction, Accad contends that the kerygmatic approach is "devoid of polemical aggressiveness, apologetic defensiveness, existential adaptiveness, or syncretistic elusiveness."[27] It focuses on the biblical *kerygma*, the joyful proclamation of God's good news, in which Christ, not religious systems, is at the center.[28] Accad contends that the kerygmatic approach allows us to "think the most Christlike about Islam and Muslims."[29] In our contemporary world, innovative ideas are popping up at a rate never seen before. Theological innovations are affecting Muslim-Christian encounters. Joseph Cumming, for example, offers new insight on passages in Muslim commentaries that address the question of Jesus's death on the cross. His research shows that Muslim theologians offered a much wider range of interpretations throughout history on this issue. Cumming even posits that there cannot be an Islamic correct response to that question

24. See Evelyne Reisacher, "Peacemaking between Muslims and Christians: Drinking Lots of Cups of Tea," *Theological News and Notes* (Fuller Theological Seminary), Spring 2009. See also the book edited during several years of dialogue led by Fuller Theological Seminary and the Salam Institute for Peace and Justice (Washington, DC): Abu-Nimer and Augsburger, eds., *Peace-Building by, between, and beyond Muslims and Evangelical Christians* (Lanham, MD: Rowman & Littlefield, 2009). Fuller hosts a journal titled *Evangelical Interfaith Dialogue*, edited by Cory Willson and Matthew Krabill. According to the journal's website, its vision is to "seek to create space for evangelical scholars and practitioners to dialogue about the dynamics, challenges, practices, and theology surrounding interfaith work, while remaining faithful to the gospel of Jesus and the mission for his church." "About EIFD," http://cms.fuller.edu/EIFD/About_EIFD.aspx. See also the blog by Rick Love on the website of Peace-Catalyst International at http://www.peace-catalyst.net.

25. See, e.g., *Evangelical Interfaith Dialogue*. See also Martin Accad, "Mission at the Intersection of Religion and Empire," *International Journal of Frontier Missiology* 28, no. 4 (Winter 2011): 179–89.

26. See, e.g., Badru D. Kateregga and David W. Shenk, *A Muslim and a Christian in Dialogue*, 2nd ed. (Harrisonville, VA: Herald Press, 2011).

27. For a more detailed description of the kerygmatic approach, read Martin Accad, "Christian Attitudes toward Islam and Muslims: A Kerygmatic Approach," in Reisacher, *Toward Respectful Understanding*, Kindle edition, location 870.

28. Ibid.

29. Ibid., location 847.

since the commentaries leave room for debates and even fruitful discussion with Christians.[30]

These new models offer fresh ways to look at witness with increasing joy in Muslim-Christian encounters. I regularly visit the blog on the Miss Understanding website, where Michal and her friend Sondos continue to explore each other's faith by sharing friendship. On their blog they write: "Join Sondos and Michal as they study lessons learned from side-by-side readings of the Qur'an and the Bible, laugh and cry at life's twists and turns, and foster a deeper understanding of God's purpose for them."[31]

When, in July 2008, I attended a dialogue titled the Yale University Workshop and Conference on *A Common Word*, I was pleasantly surprised to see how much the extended coffee breaks and meals during which the participants gathered in a relaxed atmosphere contributed to joyful witness. Participants had come together to discuss the applications of a document called *A Common Word between Us and You*, which Muslim scholars and religious leaders drafted as evidence of common ground between Muslims and Christians.[32] When the group I was with debriefed about this conference, we all felt that the theological discussions were fruitful not only for their academic rigor but also because joyful encounters between participants contributed significantly to an honest and robust theological exchange.[33] Richard McCallum, a scholar of Islam, has also observed the positive impact of joyful moments during dialogue in his evaluation of Interfaith Summer School.[34] He described the feelings of the participants and then concluded, "Finally, perhaps the most significant part of the programme was the free time when participants could interact informally over a meal, a walk in the gardens or a game of croquet. Several reported profound conversations that would not have taken place in another context. As trust built difficult questions surrounding identity, belief and politics were discussed with openness and respect."[35]

---

30. Joseph Cumming, "Did Jesus Die on the Cross? Reflections in Muslim Commentaries," in Woodberry, Zümrüt, and Köyluü, *Muslim and Christian Reflections*, 32–50.

31. "Our Friendship," Miss Understanding website, http://www.missunderstanding.co /?page_id=190.

32. *A Common Word between Us and You*, A Common Word, http://www.acommonword .com/the-acw-document/.

33. "Major 'A Common Word' Events," A Common Word, http://www.acommonword.com /category/new-fruits/major-a-common-word-events/.

34. Interfaith Summer School is run by the Cambridge Interfaith Programme. See their website at http://www.interfaith.cam.ac.uk/en/education/summerschool.

35. Richard McCallum, "An Evaluation of the Cambridge Interfaith Programme Summer Schools, 2011–13," November 2013, http://www.academia.edu/9516572/Evaluation_of_the_Cam bridge_Interfaith_Programme_Summer_School.

I have talked a lot about joy in Christian witness, but it would be unfair to not mention in this book the joy experienced by Muslims. Ranya Tabari Idliby insists, "Muslims need to remember that there is an Islam other than the joyless, angry Islam that has metastasized as the recognized Islam. I want to remind Muslims that God is not a punitive God of fear, concerned with what you cannot do, but rather a forgiving God, inspiring what you can do. I am a Muslim to remind Muslims that you can be a Muslim and fly a kite. . . . For the sake of us all, let there be joy![36] Certain Islamic rituals amplify this joy. Anthropologist Maria F. Curtis observed, "Ramadan is a sacred and joyful period, bringing quiet days of fasting from sun-up to sun-down when one tries to remain 'clean' in one's thoughts, speech, and action."[37] Kenneth Cragg also noticed a similar positive emotional mood: "Ramadan often brings an uplifting sense of joy."[38] The list could go on and on. Joy is part of the religious experience of many faiths. Christians don't have to negate the joy of other faiths to share the one they experience as followers of Christ. However, both human and spiritual joys have unique characteristics shaped by their source and the contexts in which they emanate. Christian witness includes sharing with Muslims the joy that they and their communities experience in the Triune God, as described in chapter 1.

Ordinary Encounters

Usually theological encounters are run by experts who are conversant with the sacred texts of both faiths that are in dialogue. But today, the environment of Muslim-Christian interactions is rapidly changing. Experts are not the only ones shaping Muslim-Christian dialogue. Muslims and Christians are interacting on a much larger scale today, and Christians feel a greater need to understand Muslim societies, since they are more likely to meet Muslims than in past years. Islam and Christianity are the two largest faith traditions in the world. According to the latest research from the Pew Research Center, there are approximately 2.17 billion Christians and 1.6 billion Muslims in the world today. If another Pew prediction is accurate, the number of adherents of the two faith traditions should be

36. Ranya Tabari Idliby, *Burqas, Baseball, and Apple Pie: Being Muslim in America* (New York: St. Martin's Press, 2014), 215.

37. Maria F. Curtis, "On Fasting in Fes: Learning about Food, Family, and Friendship during Fieldwork in Morocco," in *Studying Islam in Practice*, ed. Gabriele Marranci (New York: Routledge, 2013), 10.

38. Kenneth B. Cragg, *Christians and Muslims: From History to Healing* (Bloomington, IN: iUniverse, 2011), 23.

nearly equal in 2050.[39] Muslim and Christians will increasingly rub shoulders with each other. Given this proximity, Christians may be required, in their daily routines, to engage in theological conversations with Muslims without the help of experts.

Therefore, it would be wise for Christians to become conversant about Islam. As I said at an event marking the fortieth anniversary of the Lausanne Movement, every Christian should feel at ease sharing the gospel with Muslims, and every church leader should be able to lead his or her congregation to love and respect their Muslim neighbors.[40] John Azumah, professor of Islam and senior associate for Islam for the Lausanne Movement, declared during the 2013 Lausanne Leadership Forum in Bangalore, India, that ordinary Christians are the ones who will take the gospel to all Muslims.[41] Professionals or specialists are not sufficient for the task. Putting the number of Christians on this planet at 2 billion, Azumah insisted that evangelism to Muslims is the job of every Christian who is able to confidently share God's good news with Muslims.

Azumah further proposed that this task requires education. Without delay, church leaders must take measures to deparalyze their churches from their fears of Islam and free them from their current divisions regarding models of Muslim ministry.[42] But do ordinary Christians also need to become theologically savvy to engage with Muslims? At first sight, it may not appear so. Many Muslims come to Jesus through dreams, visions, healings, and miracles that are not attended by sophisticated theological conversations or doctrinal debates. According to research by J. Dudley Woodberry, the second reason why Muslims follow Jesus is that they experience the *"power of God* in *answered prayers* and *healing."*[43] Since the supernatural work of God touches their hearts without a theological boost, is it necessary to really study hard to understand Islam?

Although I have witnessed the miraculous work of God in the lives of Muslim-born followers of Christ, I have good reasons to advocate for better

39. *The Future of World Religions: Population Growth Projections, 2010–2050,* Pew Research Center, April 2, 2015, http://www.pewforum.org/2015/04/02/religious-projections-2010-2050/.

40. "Uniqueness of Christ in Islam and Europe - Evelyne Reisacher," YouTube video, 21:52, from a presentation given at the Lausanne European Leaders Meeting, Vevey, Switzerland, May 6–9, 2014, posted by Lausanne Movement, June 23, 2014, https://www.youtube.com/watch?v=pMYqGuwFBRk.

41. John Azumah, in "Islam Steering Committee," video of a speech given at the Global Leadership Forum, Bangalore, India, June 2013, http://www.lausanne.org/library?_sft_post_format=post-format-video&_sfm_wpcf-select-gathering=2013+Bangalore.

42. Ibid.

43. J. Dudley Woodberry, Russell G. Shubin, and G. Marks, "Why Muslims Follow Jesus," *Christianity Today,* October 24, 2007, http://www.christianitytoday.com/ct/2007/october/42.80.html (italics original).

knowledge of Islam. We notice today that theological ignorance can lead to social conflicts. Why should Christians (or Muslims) continue to misquote or misrepresent each other's religions when knowledge and information have never been as accessible as they are now? Too many Christians are still illiterate when it comes to reading Muslim realities. The more accurately and honestly we can represent the religious other, the better for world peace. Ordinary Christians sometimes cannot have fruitful conversations with well-informed Muslims because they, the Christians, did not do their homework well and have not been curious about the faith of the other. In a chapter titled "Portraying Muslim Women," I underline the many myths still believed by Christians concerning gender issues in Islam.[44] These myths would not be so problematic if they did not fuel wars and conflicts. The status and role of Muslim women have sometimes been at the heart of armed conflicts.[45]

With Islam in the news so often nowadays, Christians must acquire a clearer understanding of Muslim tenets than they have had till now. Christians contact me almost every week for help understanding the rise of Islamism in the world. If they try to understand this current phenomenon only from a theological perspective, they will not succeed. Learning to identify the various factors that shape political changes in the Middle East and analyzing how anthropological, psychological, sociological, and theological perspectives intersect with each other are also essential to the education that is required today for fruitful engagement with Muslims.

How much should Christians know about Islam? Instead of answering this question with numbers, sizes, or degrees, I would rather locate Christians on a path of lifelong learning. Christians should never think that they are done with learning about Islam. The greatest scholars of Islam continue to learn until their death. Samuel Zwemer, one of the fathers of modern mission in the Muslim world, was not ashamed to wrestle with theological issues and models of mission and change his mind. John Hubers, a former pastor in Oman and Bahrain, wrote an article whose title expresses well this trajectory of never ceasing to learn: "Samuel Zwemer and the Challenge of Islam: From Polemic to a Hint of Dialogue." Hubers highlights how Zwemer wrestles with questions as diverse as the prophethood of Muhammad and the doctrine of God. Although first resistant to dialogue, Zwemer learned the value of respectful interactions. Hubers shows how Zwemer modified his views: "Nurtured on nineteenth-century triumphalist polemic, the mature

44. Evelyne A. Reisacher, "Portraying Muslim Women," in Reisacher, *Toward Respectful Understanding*, Kindle edition, locations 1783–2341.

45. See Lila Abu-Lughod, *Do Muslim Women Need Saving?* (Cambridge, MA: Harvard University Press, 2013).

Zwemer evolved into a more thoughtful critic, exhibiting a greater respect for people he had always loved and an increased admiration for the faith that shaped their lives."[46] I am always troubled when I hear Christians say that they know Islam. What do they mean by "know"? How can one "know" a faith of fourteen centuries with so many writers, interpreters, and critics—not to mention the many self-identifications of Islam by ordinary Muslims? Knowledge of Islam is important for witness, but we will only ever know incompletely.

If we can never reach perfection in our knowledge, should we give up? Not at all! Today, Christians have amazing opportunities to learn so much more about Islam than in the past. Most of the early apologists who engaged in theological conversations with Muslims did not have access to the entire Qur'an. One of the first Christian apologists to address Islam, John of Damascus, whom I mentioned earlier, knew only a few passages. Even the German reformer Martin Luther, when he wrote about Islam, said that he was acquainted with only part of its sacred text. How would you respect someone who questions the authenticity of the Bible but knows only parts of it or even misquotes it? You would probably not take such questioning seriously. Today, however, many important resources for the study of Islam are easy to access. One can find online copies of the Qur'an[47] and the Hadith[48] and even major commentaries online.[49] One can take classes and access the works of authoritative scholars of Islam in one's mother tongue. A plethora of works written by Muslims are now accessible to non-Muslims. It is inconceivable today to study Islam without the voices of Muslims who practice this faith. Ignoring their voices would be the same as if Muslims would learn about Christian faith without ever reading a book by a Christian author. Unfortunately, a few centuries ago, this was common practice. Most students of Islam would never read a book by a Muslim author. Today, it would be unwise to only read about Islam through Christian authors if one wants to understand Muslim realities.

We are also privileged, in our time, to have links with churches worldwide that provide diverse perspectives on Muslim societies. What a delight to be able to learn a great deal about Islam from Christians in other parts of the world. These global perspectives are precious for identifying how cultures and societies are shaping Muslim-Christian encounters. For example, today

---

46. John Hubers, "Samuel Zwemer and the Challenge of Islam: From Polemic to a Hint of Dialogue," *International Bulletin of Missionary Research* 28, no. 3 (July 2004): 121.

47. See The Noble Qur'an website, www.Quran.com.

48. See *The Hadith of the Prophet Muhammad at Your Fingertips*, www.Sunnah.com.

49. Altafsir.com is a website offering a collection of online qur'anic commentaries found at http://www.altafsir.com.

Korean Christians reflect on Islam together with Kenyan Christians,[50] or Ghanaian Christians with Indian Christians.[51] These global conversations are indispensable in our world, where information shapes worldview. Churches in different parts of the world have been heatedly debating questions such as the use of dialogue and the value of models of mission followed by churches in the Muslim-majority world.

While Christians may have different opinions on how to engage with Islam, these controversies should not jeopardize Christian witness. This is why it is important to grow the bonds between churches worldwide that engage with Muslims. I recommend that while Christians have theological conversations with Muslims, they also have worldwide conversations on Islam with fellow Christians who may greatly differ with them, because Muslim-Christian relations are different in the two contexts. As we joyfully engage with churches in other parts of the world, we will soon discover that environments can be extremely diverse. Western churches and Muslim-majority churches sometimes disagree over what models of witness or churches are more appropriate. Although sometimes painful, we should not give up these conversations, which help us gain a global perspective on theological conversation with Muslims.

Inviting Muslims to Follow Jesus

Theological conversations can sometimes become meaningless chatter that masks the real spiritual needs of the participants. Christians must remember that they have a precious story to share. They should never be ashamed of it. This entire book is about inviting Muslims to know the story of God as revealed in the Bible and in Christ. As Christians interact with Muslims, whether through personal relationships, social media, the arts, earth care, caring for the needy, urban encounters, or theological conversations, the story does not change. God invites Muslims to know him through Christ. Thus Christians should always be open to being God's agents, extending this invitation to Muslims. If Christ is real to them, Muslims will certainly see it and want to know the reason why.

50. See, e.g., the work of Caleb Chul-Soo Kim, Professor of Islam at the African International University in Nairobi, Kenya. One example would be Caleb Chul-Soo Kim, "Afflictions by Jinn among the Swahili and an Appropriate Christian Response, in *Toward Respectful Understanding & Witness among Muslims: Essays in Honor of J. Dudley Woodberry*, ed. Evelyne A. Reisacher, (Pasadena, CA: William Carey), Kindle edition, locations 7326–718.

51. See, e.g., the video presentation of the Global Consultation on Islam convened in Ghana in 2014 where forty leaders from twenty countries gathered to reflect on ministry to Muslims (https://www.lausanne.org/networks/issues/islam).

A friend of mine was so enthusiastic about his relationship with Christ that he wanted his Muslim colleague to know about Jesus as well. One day, he left a Bible on the colleague's desk. This was his invitation to Muslims. His colleague read the Bible and was fascinated by the life of Jesus, which he had never read about except for the passages in the Qur'an that talk about Jesus's birth, prophethood, and return to God. Weeks later, the colleague decided to follow Jesus. Other Christians invite Muslims with more sophisticated theological questions of the sort that appear in published conversations between Muslims and Christians, such as the dialogue between Badru Kateregga and David Shenk.[52]

One day, I watched a film that narrated the life, death, and resurrection of Jesus with a Muslim woman.[53] I knew that the part about the death and resurrection would be one of the most challenging parts to watch for this woman, who was told in her faith community that Jesus did not die or rise from the dead. She watched, cried, sobbed, and at the end of the movie told me that she wanted to follow Christ. Invitations to know God can take many, many forms, from the simplest to the most sophisticated.

The joy that one experiences when encountering the Triune God cannot be restricted. Joy expands, explores, and amplifies as it infects other people. More and more books are being published today that show joyful encounters between God and Muslims as they follow Jesus.[54] When I first started my journey in the Muslim world forty years ago, there were very few stories of this kind of encounter. The only one I found was related in a book containing the testimony of a Pakistani woman, named Bilquis Sheikh, who had suffered much rejection when she became a follower of Jesus.[55] Times have changed. Lots of stories are being told of individuals, families, and entire people groups turning to Jesus.

Inviting (not forcing) others to follow Jesus is a characteristic of Christian witness. One of the greatest joys in my ministry is seeing people come to Jesus. Since the conversion of the friend whose story I told earlier, I have

52. Christian scholar of Islam Ida Glaser confirms my concerns when she writes, "It is easy to talk to Muslims about God, about creation and judgment and sin and godly living. It is even easy to talk about Jesus' birth, life and teachings. But, when it comes to His death, even young children will say, 'He did not die.' This bare denial means that, as far as the Muslim is concerned, there is nothing to talk about." "Cross-Reference Theology: Speaking, Thinking and Living the Cross in the Context of Islam," in *Jesus and the Cross: Reflections of Christians from Islamic Contexts*, ed. David Emmanuel Singh (Oxford: Regnum Books International, 2008), 139.

53. Information about this film and a preview can be seen at "The Jesus Film," http://jesus filmhd.com/.

54. See, e.g., V. David Garrison, *A Wind in the House of Islam: How God Is Drawing Muslims around the World to Faith in Jesus Christ* (Monument, CO: WIGTake Resources, 2014).

55. Bilquis Sheikh with Richard H. Schneider, *I Dared to Call Him Father: The Miraculous Story of a Muslim Woman's Encounter with God* (Grand Rapids: Chosen Books, 2003).

seen scores of Muslims come near Jesus in all kinds of contexts. Today, many who once followed Islam follow Christ. Scores of authors write about conversion, explaining the reasons why Muslims come to Jesus.[56] I have never tried to compare and contrast Islam and Christianity in terms of conversion rates. This is not my business; it is God's. I do not think that we must run a competition about who has more members or whose community is more attractive. But if joy is found in the Triune God and if he radiates joy to the world, his followers will radiate this joy in the world.

An invitation is not a method. I never present a method of witness. There are certainly very good books presenting models of ministry among Muslims, and from these books one can learn a lot. But the word "method," when we're talking about relationships, is dehumanizing. Last week, I had a conversation with a Christian friend who was leaving for a visit in a Muslim-majority country. He asked if I could give him some advice about witnessimg to Muslims, since he was going to be in a Muslim-majority country for a few weeks. I gave him the advice that Ida Glaser published in an article and with which I wholeheartedly agree: "People often ask me, 'How do I share the Gospel with Muslims?' Some want just a booklet that will tell them how to do it. I tell them that there is no such booklet, and that I do not know how they should share the Gospel with Muslims. It all depends on the particular Muslims with whom they want to share."[57] I also agree with her when she says, "One cannot give any 'method' by which all can hear the Gospel effectively." This position is characteristic of joyful witness. Real joy is spontaneous. It is not fabricated. One never knows when Jesus is going to show up. God is the host, he is the one who invites; we just distribute his invitations in the Muslim world.

Conclusion

Theological encounter is one of many types of human encounters. Although the interactions studied in previous chapters are important modes of witness, theological conversations cannot be ignored. They are important for challenging one's assumptions about Islam and causing one to revisit some models of witness that may not be fruitful. There is no method for sharing the gospel in the Muslim world; there are only encounters with individual Muslims, who hold diverse perspectives and practices and will uniquely engage with the message of Christ.

56. See, e.g., the chapter by David Greenlee, "How Is the Gospel Good News for Muslims?," in Reisacher, *Toward Respectful Understanding*, locations 6184–705.

57. Glaser, "Millennial Reverie," 184.

Christians who want to engage in theological encounters must adopt a listening attitude and learn to understand how Muslims interpret the Bible. Often Muslims ask challenging questions about the Bible because they have never heard the entire biblical narrative; they have been prevented from reading further by doctrinal hurdles that they could not peacefully discuss. To address this need, Christians must be open to a lifelong educational journey. Illiteracy concerning Islam is not an option in our world. Religion is the pretext of too many conflicts. And many conversations between Muslims and Christians remain unfinished. Thankfully, today more Christians than ever before are enthusiastically involved in conversing about the Triune God with Muslims. They learn to read the Bible with Muslims in mind and develop innovative models of theological encounters. They converse globally with other Christians to better grasp the variety of contexts that shape Muslim-Christian encounters.

We should not think that encounters with Muslims take place only for the purpose of convincing them of our views about God. An interfaith dialogue of life involves the kind of human relationships that we discussed in chapter 2. Jesus did not refuse to eat with people who were not interested in the gospel, but was always ready to invite them into a closer relationship with God. Thus, whether or not we encounter Muslims for theological reasons, we can always be the joyful carrier of God's invitation.

I have been part of many theological conversations with Muslims—whether in the Middle East, in Europe, or in the United States. Some were held in formal settings such as academic institutions. At other times, these same questions came up in informal settings such as in restaurants over a meal. I never considered such conversations awkward or threatening. On the contrary, worshiping the Triune God entails joyful sharing with others what is written in 1 Peter 3:15: "But in your hearts revere Christ as Lord. Always be prepared to give an answer to everyone who asks you to give the reason for the hope that you have" (NIV). But what I also like about this verse is what I learn about the style with which these conversations with anyone, including Muslims, should be held: "But do this with gentleness and respect."

For Discussion

1. How do theological encounters contribute to Christian witness in the Muslim world?
2. Give examples of theological encounters that you want to have.
3. How would you invite Muslims to follow Jesus?

Conclusion

This entire book has been about joy in Christian witness among Muslims. Chapter after chapter, I have searched for joy in fresh encounters between young contemporary Muslims and Christians: through social media, the arts, earth care, care for the needy, urban relations, and theological conversations. I hope that I have instilled in my readers the desire for engaging in new kinds of encounters with Muslims. There are many more circumstances of joyful encounters that I wish I could have included. I trust that readers will discover more as they continue on this journey of witness.

Circumstances have not always been joyful during my writing. There were depressing days, such as when I visited a dear Muslim friend who is battling brain cancer, or watched a television splashing horrific pictures of beheadings or bombings in Muslim-majority countries. On other days, work stress, family problems, or personal sickness prevented me from fully feeling the joy that I was writing about. I continued to write despite ups and downs in my emotional life and without feeling that I was dishonest in my enterprise. I consider those emotional variations part of the normal way of life in Christ. Long before contemporary affect regulation theory, the Teacher in Ecclesiastes 3:4 stated that there is "a time to weep and a time to laugh, a time to mourn and a time to dance." Joy is not a continuous feeling. It comes and goes. Actually, high-energy states like extreme joy can be exhausting when they last too long. Humans are not created to be in a continual joy-state. There is therefore no need to pretend to be happy for the sake of witness when one is not.

Conversely, one should not be in a continual state of fear or shame. If one is scared to meet Muslims, one should not deny it. It is important to be true to one's feelings. Fear is a useful emotion that protects in hostile environments. But fear that is ungrounded may unfortunately prevent us from enjoying others. The fact that the world comprises dreadful events and people does not mean that there are no delightful people and events to enjoy. It is even possible that God's joy arises in the direst of circumstances: as when the jailer of the prison of Philippi in which Paul and Silas were imprisoned "was filled with joy because he had come to believe in God—he and his whole household" (Acts 16:34). Even the supremely great joy of incarnation did not take place in a world without pain. Joy may appear at unexpected times. Through its energy-expanding nature, it helps us explore new spaces and communities. Thus, this book should remind us that Muslim-Christian relations are not all about fear or violence. They can also be about savoring lots of moments of joy.

Working one's way through this book may feel at times disturbing, since "joy" seems to appear on almost every page. I could not do otherwise, since one of the reasons why I wrote this book is that joy is so neglected in Christian witness among Muslims. This explains why joy holds here pride of place. On the other side, I must admit that talking too much about joy can have the reverse effect. An excess of joy sometimes makes people immune to it. I have noticed that recently more and more Christian and non-Christian books refer to joy. Scholars are currently integrating in their respective academic disciplines the wealth of findings from scientific research on the neurological underpinnings of joy. Though useful, this trend can become tiresome. Even I sometimes am a little annoyed when the word "joy" shows up in too many conversations, because I think that it is best communicated not by words alone but by a joyful tone that reflects joy in the heart.

Reading about the importance of joyful witness may not automatically produce joy. Of course, self-induced joy is possible, as in the practice of meditation or laughter yoga. The results may be astonishing. But the joy produced is not the same as the joy that flows from the Father, Jesus, and the Holy Spirit, as described in chapter 1. It may also be different from the joy that binds people together, as described in chapter 2. Relational joy is best felt when it is spontaneous and not prescribed. It happens in the presence of God or people we connect with and can be recalled in their absence. One can claim to enjoy Muslims only if one has actually experienced joyful encounters with them. Some readers may talk about enjoying Muslims without ever having encountered a Muslim. This is not real joy. This book will not help unless they meet Muslims and feel joy in their presence. The various social contexts explored in this book offer a host of possibilities to have these forms of encounters.

Some readers now may want to see joy in every encounter as a remedy for conflict, a way to overturn it. This may not be possible. While joy is critical for fostering relations and exploring a new environment, it is not the only emotion that nurtures bonds. After the joy of connecting, or of reconnecting after the rupture of a bond, relationships are best maintained when there is tranquility and peace. This absence of stress that characterizes meaningful moments is well described by the Psalmist, talking about his stilled and quieted soul (Ps. 131:2), and by Jesus, promising his peace to his disciples (John 14:27) and to those near and far away (Eph. 2:17). This trust, security, and safety in a relational bond should hold the relationship together between times of joy, or after joy repairs any of the various relational ruptures described in chapter 2. Joy also widens the spaces of witness, letting those who hear the gospel feel secure, free of the relational stress that would hinder them from attending to the words of Christians sharing the gospel.

Someone asked me the other day if people can acquire relational joy like they acquire a language in order to communicate. Yes, joy can be acquired, but through a different learning method than language acquisition. This is what I explained in chapters 3 through 8. In all the encounters described in this book (social media, the arts, earth care, care for the needy, urban relations, and theological conversations) joy must be felt in the actual presence of others and of God. Learning through books is not sufficient.

The second purpose of this book was to move from the extraordinary in Christian witness among Muslims to the ordinary. Although experts and professionals have certainly benefited from new information, I kept the ordinary witnesses in mind in my writing. I trust that the various contexts of encounters presented here will offer new ways to meet Muslims. They are not meant to be a method or a strategy for sharing the gospel. I fervently believe that witness happens in places where one naturally encounters people. To use these exchanges only as a pretext for sharing the gospel would be to misunderstand my intentions. Encounters generated in this manner could not be called "ordinary" anymore, since they would conceal a hidden agenda. Furthermore, readers could easily fail to commit their heart to what they are involved in with Muslims, as described in chapters 3–8, because the shared interests, tasks, or activities are only an excuse for engaging with Muslims. I state this in the conclusion to this book because I hope that others will continue to research the topics that I addressed here and to develop even broader findings and theories based on their proficiency in these fields. Many research questions remain to be addressed. I hope that a future book will include myriad stories from around the world, illustrating the concepts presented here.

I have looked at only six spaces of ordinary encounters between Muslims and Christians that can be infused with joy. I don't pretend I am an expert in all. My expertise lies in the study of Islam, Muslim societies, and interpersonal relations across cultures. What I wrote in chapters 3 through 8 I learned from my observations in ministry, my readings, and my travels throughout the Muslim world. I have also benefited much from the research conducted by my colleagues at Fuller Theological Seminary and at other academic institutions. They know better than I do some of the disciplines that I covered in this book. But they have not all made the link with the Muslim world. This was my job here. I hope others will continue to explore other areas for the benefit of our world. For example, I could have included health, education, business, leisure, and so on. My purpose was not to cover all the topics of inquiry, but rather, by discussing a few, to invite my reader to think more creatively about how to meet Muslims. Let's be perpetual learners. We will never exhaust all the possibilities and options for encounter. As Christians now step into new environments, I trust that they will confidently share their faith and write their own story of encounter with Muslims.

In ordinary encounters we have chosen to be with Muslims not because of their religion but because of common social interests. We may soon discover their religious beliefs, but many Muslim-born people are not always interested in the religion of their parents, and an increasing number do not practice their faith. Often, we will not even know they are Muslims unless an explicit symbol reveals their faith. This is another strength of encountering Muslims in ordinary life. We discover that they are not all the same, and that their personal questions (not the ones dictated by their religious clerics) regarding the Christian faith can vary greatly.

An ordinary encounter also presumes that sophisticated apologetics or polemics may not always be center stage. They should certainly not characterize the opening remarks in a new relationship. Instead, ordinary witness will often take the form of sharing personal stories. The various events and circumstances shared illustrate the gospel, just as when Jesus, walking through fields with his disciples, pointed toward various things they saw to explain divine realities. Muslims may additionally be touched by attitudes or behaviors they observe during daily exchanges with Christians. One must learn to relate the gospel to the activities that bring Muslims and Christians together. Thus, for example, someone meeting Muslims through the arts will probably share their faith in a way that directly addresses the preoccupations of artists, in a language and form they can easily understand. New forms of apologetics will probably evolve in these new contexts.

Ordinary encounters with Muslims will, hopefully, remove some of the prejudice and negativity that Christians may harbor against them. I hope that I have convinced my audience that relating with Muslims can be fun. If I have one wish for the twenty-first century, it is that it may be characterized by joyful Muslim-Christian encounters. I know that current conflicts and wars have discouraged many Christians from reaching out to Muslims. They are afraid, like Muslims are, that "the other" cannot be trusted, or may be dangerous. In some cases, they are right. Both Muslims and Christians can be dangerous when they have hostile intentions. But generalizing will hinder us from discovering who is truly dangerous and who is not, and will prevent us from experiencing delightful encounters.

Finally, this book is all about witness. Not just witness, but joyful witness! I have talked about challenging situations, shameful encounters, and painful witness. This is all part of our walk with Christ. Not all witness will be joyful. Some people are persecuted for their faith, some suffer from the consequences of their choice to follow Christ, and others will be killed because they do not want to deny Christ. Muslims still face many challenges when they decide to follow Christ. Some arise from Muslim texts talking about harsh consequences for those who reject Islam. Others arise within Muslim family and society, which feel the burden of preventing their own from betraying their Muslim community by joining a community whose head is Christ. Thus, joyful witness in this context means taking all these difficulties into account. I did not expand on these aspects, because many other Christian books do. But I still want to encourage my readers to become more familiar with the consequences of following Christ in the Muslim world. In the context of these struggles and pain they will also discover manifestations of the joy of the Triune God. They will find what joyful witness truly means. It is not the absence of pain; it is not the joyful clapping of Christians when a Muslim converts because now they feel they have won the battle over conversion rates; it is not self-happiness in the midst of a world that is self-centered. No, joyful witness is joining in Jesus's joy and sharing it with the world.

Thus, the upshot of my message concerning joyful witness in ordinary encounter is the following. Joy arises from connections. First, Christians who want to engage with Muslims need to be connected with the Triune God: one cannot know God's joy without encountering him and remembering how at various times God's joy entered this world, from Genesis through Revelation, through Christ and the Holy Spirit and through the witness of the church. We want to invite Muslims to experience this joy. Second, we must connect with Muslims: one cannot say one loves or enjoys Muslims without experiencing joy in their presence. We have a great example in Christ, who enjoyed people when he was on earth and brought good news—in other words, news that would bring joy to all people, including Muslims. We have a message of joy to bring to the Muslim world. In daily encounters with Muslims, the human joy we experience can help us connect in ways never imagined before. As negative emotions can rupture relations between Muslims and Christians, joy can repair the bond and allow for spiritual conversations through which

God's joy can touch the lives of Muslims. Finally, our connection with the world is also transformed through joyful witness. As Muslims and Christians interact, through all the types of enterprises described in this book, which seek the good of God's earth and humanity, this joyful witness will resonate throughout the Muslim world.

Index